GATHERING *to* NAUVOO

GATHERING to NAUVOO

FRED E. WOODS

Covenant Communications, Inc.

Cover image *The Saints Embark from Liverpool, England* by Ken Baxter ©IRI, Courtesy Museum of
Church History and Art

Cover design copyrighted 2002 by Covenant Communications, Inc.

Published by Covenant Communications, Inc.
American Fork, Utah

Printed in Canada
First Printing: May 2002

09 08 07 06 05 04 03 02   10 9 8 7 6 5 4 3 2 1

ISBN 1-59156-032-2

Library of Congress Cataloging-in-Publication Data

Dedication

To JoAnna,

who has made every situation beautiful.

Acknowledgments

I appreciate the help I have received from the staff and holdings at the following repositories: Mercantile Library, a special library at the University of Missouri-St. Louis; Missouri Historical Society (St. Louis, MO); Henry E. Huntington Library (San Marino, CA); Southern Illinois University (Edwardsville, IL); and particularly the L. Tom Perry Special Collections, Harold B. Lee Library, Brigham Young University (Provo, UT); as well as The Church Of Jesus Christ of Latter-day Saints Church Historical Department Library and Archives (Salt Lake City, UT).

I am grateful for the excellent editorial assistance provided by Lisa McMullin (contract editor for Covenant), the staff of Don E. Norton at BYU, Lynn Merrill, and especially my wife, JoAnna. I appreciate Whitney Thompson's commendable work as my research assistant. I thank Donald Q. Cannon, Richard E. Bennett, and Larry C. Porter, colleagues in the department of Church History and Doctrine at BYU, for reading my manuscript and offering helpful suggestions. I thank the kind and competent staff of Covenant Communications, especially Shauna Nelson, for their support in bringing this manuscript to publication. Finally, I express my gratitude to my family for their patience, encouragement, and love.

*Author's Notes:
1. The original spelling, grammar, and punctuation have been kept intact in quotations found throughout this book.
2. In citing works in the notes, *short titles* are generally used after the first full citation.
3. Two *abbreviations* have been used after the first full citation:
   –HC History of the Church of Jesus Christ of Latter-day Saints
   –HDA Historical Department Archives, The Church of Jesus Christ of Latter-day Saints

Table of Contents

PROLOGUE

The year 2002 marks the reconstruction of the Nauvoo Temple, which lay in ruins for over 150 years. The remains—a few white foundation stones nestled in the earth—cry out as remnants of the glorious days of the Nauvoo gathering (1839–1846). The unprecedented rebuilding of this new temple rising from the ashes of its predecessor is nothing short of remarkable. How fitting that the dedication day is scheduled for 27 June 2002, which marks the anniversary of the martyrdom of Joseph Smith the Prophet and Hyrum Smith the Patriarch, who sealed their lives' work and testimonies with their innocent blood. "The testators are now dead, and their testament is in force" (D&C 135:5).

This work catalogues the inspiring conversion and migration of faithful people caught up in the magnetic pull of the gathering to erect a temple. This is especially true of the British immigrants, who represented at least one-fourth of the Latter-day Saint population in Nauvoo before the exodus. Laced with many captivating eyewitness narratives, this book provides vivid detail of the intimate experiences encountered by hundreds of British converts as they traveled thousands of miles to gather to the city Beautiful.

These accounts include the anticipation of embarkation, the mixed feelings of leaving loved ones and native country, and the thrill of traveling down the Mersey River and first capturing a view of the sails harnessing the magnificent ocean winds. Testimonies abound of miraculous preservation of life through the use of priesthood power, which rebuked not only disease, but the winds and waves. Seagoing Saints also relate the joys and sorrows of the ocean crossing, ranging from dancing and singing to wretched seasickness and sober sea burials. Maritime pioneers describe the stark contrast between raging Atlantic storms and the sea of glass, which allowed the children to play a game or enjoy the company of the captain. Shouts from a sailor range from "Land in sight," to the cry of "The ship is in a state of mutiny." River narratives provide realistic descriptions of the vile runners at the Crescent City, slave auctions, the constant toil of "wooding up," picturesque river towns, and the natural beauty of Old Man River. They also warn of the influence of St. Louis apostates, "like spider webs set to catch flies." Derogatory cries of "Joe's rats" are shouted from the shore as the Saints make their way up the Mississippi on the *Maid of Iowa,* a Church-owned steamboat recognized by the inhabitants of river towns.

Vexations of the long journey are soothed by the affectionate welcome bestowed by the Nauvoo Saints. Church leaders, including the Prophet Joseph Smith himself, often greet foreign converts as they approach the shore. Some recognize him as they discern his radiant countenance. Although occasionally challenged by prejudice, most British Saints accept the invitation to assimilate and to be "no more strangers and foreigners, but fellowcitizens with the saints" (Eph. 2:19). Their early trying years bespeak marshes, mosquitoes, and malaria, but also of the conquering of these maladies through priesthood power which raised the sick and the dead.

The triumphant synergism of British immigrants and Mormon proselytes gleaned from various pockets of North America resulted in the building of a grand city and a glorious temple. In the midst of dire poverty, theirs was the daunting task of feeding and clothing themselves, building appropriate shelter for winter, and protecting the city from threatening enemies who lay in wait to destroy. The dream of a glorious temple was kept in mortal check by the reality of aching backs and bloody knuckles from a day's tithe at the temple quarry. As they toiled to build Zion, the Zion within them emerged. These faithful Saints discovered they had acquired the faith necessary to surrender the city and temple they had built with sweat and tears when the compulsory call came that required yet another migration and another challenge to raise Zion in the western wilderness. Before their departure, thousands entered the Nauvoo Temple and individually made sacred covenants, each to "use all his influence and property to remove this [covenant] people to the place where the Lord [would] locate a stake of Zion" (D&C 136:10). *Gathering to Nauvoo* was inspired by these valiant Saints who heeded the call to gather; and intertwined themselves with strangers and foreigners of uncommon faith. Together they matured in integrity and strength which enabled them to build Zion in Nauvoo and later in the West.

CHAPTER ONE

Nauvoo Beginnings

"The loveliest place and the best people under the heavens"
—JOSEPH SMITH

Three days prior to their martyrdom, Joseph and his brother Hyrum left for Carthage with members of the Nauvoo City Council and a few supportive friends to answer charges stemming from the destruction of a printing press.[1] On the way out of town, the Prophet passed by the Nauvoo Temple and lingered as he gazed upon the sacred edifice. "This is the loveliest place and the best people under the heavens,"[2] he remarked. Who were these noble people? How did they end up in the state of Illinois? Where had they all come from? By what means did they migrate? Why did most Saints choose to gather in Nauvoo? What made Nauvoo such a lovely place—the location or the people?

A CALL TO GATHER

A decade after Joseph Smith's first vision, the true Church of Jesus Christ was once again established, and a call to gather the elect of God sounded among all the inhabitants of the earth. The Prophet received this revelation for a universal gathering during the second conference of the restored Church, less than six months after its organization in 1830.[3]

JOSEPH SMITH JR.

And ye are called to bring to pass the gathering of mine elect; for mine elect hear my voice and harden not their hearts; Wherefore the decree hath gone forth from the Father that they shall be gathered in unto one place upon the face of this land, to prepare their hearts and be prepared in all things against the day when tribulation and desolation are sent forth upon the wicked (D&C 29:7–8).

The call to gather was not a new concept to a covenant people. "The gathering of the people of God has been a subject of great importance in all ages of the world," proclaimed the Latter-day Saints British periodical, the *Latter-day Saints' Millennial Star,* in 1841.[4] Just two months later, the *Millennial Star* also noted, "The spirit of emigration has actuated the children of men from the time our first parents were expelled from the garden until now."[5]

The latter-day emigration came largely as a result of the doctrine of the gathering of Israel preached by Joseph Smith, the prophet of the Restoration, who ingrained in the Saints a desire to gather with the people of the Most High God. The prophet Joseph Smith once asked rhetorically, "What was the object of gathering the Jews, or the people of God in any age of the world?" He continued, "The main object was to build unto the Lord a house whereby He could reveal unto His people the ordinances of His house and the glories of His kingdom, and teach the people the way of salvation."[6]

DRIVEN FROM MISSOURI

During the first decade of the reestablishment of the Church, those who heard the beckoning voice of the Lord learned firsthand what He meant when He said, "And ye shall be hated of all *the world* for my name's sake. . . . But when they persecute you in one city, flee ye into another" (JST–Matt. 10: 19–20). And from city to city, from state to state, the Latter-day Saints certainly fled. They were a people on the move. From upstate New York they clustered first in the Kirtland, Ohio, region and then a portion of them moved to Jackson County, Missouri. Due to persecution in both regions, they migrated to Far West in northern Missouri, but were eventually forced to leave the state completely and to cross the Mississippi into Illinois during the winter of 1838–1839.

The infamous extermination order issued 27 October 1838 by Missouri governor Lilburn W. Boggs was the devastating blow that forced thousands of Latter-day Saints to flee Missouri. While most of the Saints remained refugees in Far West for several months, some Church members with means soon traveled down the Missouri River from Richmond in search of winter lodging and employment in the only two solid options they had, Quincy, Illinois, or St. Louis, Missouri.[7]

Although St. Louis lay within the borders of the state of Missouri, because of its multicultural diversity and vast size it was considered at that time an oasis for the fleeing Saints.[8] A cosmopolitan city with a large influx of European immigrants, St. Louis was tolerant of the diverse people who infiltrated her city

GOVERNOR
LILBURN W. BOGGS

limits. Because of this tolerance, many Saints fled to this eastern Missouri city. A minority of Mormon migrants traveled by steamboat, while the majority fled western Missouri to its eastern border (some 150 miles) by carts, wagons, or on foot.

Most of that first group to leave Far West, however, simply crossed the Mississippi by ferry, where they found a welcome haven in the Quincy region. Others soon followed.[9] And by 20 April 1839, nearly all of the Saints who had been left in Far West had joined the main cluster of the Church at Quincy or other locations in Illinois.[10]

ILLINOIS REFUGE

Mormon historian Richard E. Bennett asked the question, "Why Quincy?" He points out that not only was Quincy the closest and safest city, but it also provided an oasis for Saints who sought redress from the Missouri persecutions. Also advantageous to the Latter-day Saint refugees was that Mormon missionaries had visited the city in the early 1830s, and by 1838 several Latter-day Saint families were established there. Finally, Quincy provided employment opportunities, tolerated German immigrants and incoming New England migrants, and had proven itself a small Mecca for "intellectual inquiry, equality, and humanitarian care and relief."[11]

Not only Quincy, but the entire state of Illinois (established in 1817), had high hopes for its future. Like the rest of America, Illinois had been smitten with the economic depression of 1837. In such a needy condition, the people of Illinois welcomed the Mormons for three central reasons. Financially motivated, the state viewed the Latter-day Saint influx as an opportunity to raise its population to boost the economy through tax collection. Politically driven, the Whigs and the Democrats sought to secure the Mormon block vote. Lastly, and perhaps more philanthropically, there was a genuine humanitarian concern. The good citizens of Quincy simply desired to relieve the Mormon exiles of their wretched conditions of homelessness and hunger in the winter of 1839.[12]

CARE FOR THE DRIVEN POOR

On 27 February 1839, the Democratic Association of Quincy appointed a committee to relieve, so far as in its power, the wants of the destitute and homeless and to strive diligently to find employment for those willing to labor. The association recommended that Quincy citizens' interactions with the Latter-day Saints be proper, and counseled them to "be particularly careful not to indulge in any conversation or expression calculated to wound their [the Latter-day Saints'] feelings, or in any way to reflect upon those who, by every law of humanity, are entitled to our sympathy and commiseration."[13]

Quincy citizens were not alone in their readiness to help the beleaguered Saints. At Far West in January 1839, a Latter-day Saint committee of seven had been formed to aid the evacuation of the poor fleeing Missouri. This charge to take care of the poor is a scriptural theme central to covenant people in all ages. For example, Enoch's people had been translated "because they were of one heart and one mind, and dwelt in righteousness; and there was no poor among them." (Moses 7:18). In contrast, we see that one reason Sodom was destroyed was because she did not "strengthen the hand of the poor and needy" (Ezek. 16:49).

The doctrine of caring for the poor was renewed in the last dispensation when the Lord declared, "Look to the poor and the needy, and administer to their relief that they shall not suffer" (D&C 38:35), and again, "Thou wilt remember the poor, and consecrate of thy properties for their support that which thou hast to impart unto them" (D&C 42:30). This charge was taken seriously by the Lord's covenant people.

The minutes of a Church meeting held at Far West 29 January 1839 state, "On motion of President Brigham Young, it was resolved that we this day enter into a covenant to stand by and assist each other to the utmost of our abilities in removing from this state, and that we will never desert the poor who are worthy."[14]

The members of the relocation committee, chaired by William Huntington, covenanted to do all in their power to aid their struggling brothers and sisters. Two hundred and fourteen Saints signed their names in a covenant to help evacuate the poor.[15] They were aided by an additional four hundred Missouri Saints who voluntarily gave their means to assist these poverty-stricken winter wanderers, some of whom traveled with "few clothes or blankets and no household goods . . . barefoot. Eating roasted corn, elm bark, and herbs, and sleeping in the open."[16]

WHERE SHALL ZION AGAIN BE BUILT?

Having successfully evacuated the poor from Far West, the question of where the Saints would choose to build another Zion remained. The best option presented itself when one group of a few dozen Mormon evacuees under the leadership of Israel Barlow fled Missouri and inadvertently got lost on their way to Quincy, wandering northeast to the area of what is now Montrose, Iowa. There at the Des Moines River they noticed an abandoned army post known as Fort Des Moines. They were told that Isaac Galland held claim to this area known as the Half-Breed Tract. Barlow's group contacted Galland and after hearing of their

ISRAEL BARLOW

forced evacuation from Missouri, he offered them (via Barlow) not only the Half-Breed Tract in Iowa, but also adjacent land on the other side of the river in Commerce, Illinois.

Barlow was not authorized to act officially on the Church's behalf so arrangements were made to meet with Church leaders in Quincy.

After a scouting party inspected the lands for sale, the Prophet Joseph
and other Church leaders accepted Galland's generous offer by
purchasing thousands of acres of land in the areas of Lee County,
Iowa, and Commerce, Illinois, in the year 1839.[17] The minutes of a
Church conference in Quincy stated that "a liberal offer had been
made by a gentleman, of about twenty thousand acres, lying between
the Mississippi and Des Moines rivers, at two dollars per acre, to be
paid in twenty annual installments, without interest."[18]

Although much of the land was a muddy swamp, the Prophet and
his trusted associates believed the area could be drained and eventually become a prosperous city. Less than seven years later, the city
which came to be known as Nauvoo, meaning "beautiful situation,"
rivaled Chicago in population. In this short span of years, the industrious Saints left their imprint by creating a city that was not only
bustling and beautiful, but more importantly a mecca to the Saints.
The city was recognized by its magnificent temple, which stood as a
beacon on the highest hill, inviting converts to come and partake of
the highest of all blessings. And come they did, eager to enter into
covenants binding them with God and each other. In the eyes of
Joseph Smith the Prophet, theirs is the story of the "best people under
the heavens" who transformed an uninhabitable swampland into "the
loveliest place." The stories of the journeys of these remarkable people
who recognized the call to gather with God's elect beg to be told in
their own words.

NOTES TO CHAPTER ONE

1. James B. Allen and Glen M. Leonard, *The Story of the Latter-day Saints,* 2d
ed. (Salt Lake City: Deseret Book Co., 1992), 206. Note that the destruction of the
printing press was ordered by Nauvoo mayor Joseph Smith, who also instructed the
city marshal to scatter the type and burn the offensive anti-Mormon newspaper, the
Nauvoo Expositor. This libelous newspaper was created by a group of apostates who
charged Joseph as a fallen prophet and an immoral scoundrel. The Nauvoo City
Council had not legally erred in destroying the newspaper, but it probably went too
far in destroying the printing press and thus was charged with riot.

2. Joseph Smith, Jr., *History of the Church of Jesus Christ of Latter-day Saints,* ed.

B. H. Roberts, 7 vols., 2d ed. (Salt Lake City: Deseret Book Co., 1965), 6:554 (hereafter cited as *HC*).

3. The date of this conference was 26 September 1830; the date of the organization of the restored Church was 6 April 1830. Although it was known as the Church of Christ at the time of its organization, the official name of the Church was given on 26 April 1838 as The Church of Jesus Christ of Latter-day Saints, by which it has been known ever since. See D&C 20:1; 115:4.

4. "Important From America," *Latter-day Saints' Millennial Star* 1, no. 10 (February 1841): 252 (hereafter cited as *Millennial Star*).

5. "Epistle of the Twelve," *Millennial Star* 1, no. 12 (April 1841): 310.

6. Joseph Smith, Jr., *Teachings of the Prophet Joseph Smith,* selected and arranged by Joseph Fielding Smith (Salt Lake City: Deseret Book Co., 1976), 307–308.

7. William G. Hartley, "Missouri's 1838 Extermination Order and the Mormons' Forced Removal to Illinois," in *A City of Refuge: Quincy, Illinois,* ed. Susan Easton Black and Richard E. Bennett (Salt Lake City: Millennial Press, 2000), 8.

8. For further information regarding the story of the Latter-day Saints in St. Louis during the mid-nineteenth century, see Stanley B. Kimball, "The Saints and St. Louis, 1831–1857: An Oasis of Tolerance and Security," *BYU Studies* 13, no. 4 (Summer 1973): 489–519.

9. Allen and Leonard, *Story of the Latter-day Saints,* 153.

10. *HC* 3:326. Larry C. Porter, "Brigham Young and the Twelve in Quincy: A Return to the Eye of the Missouri Storm, 26 April 1839," in *A City of Refuge: Quincy, Illinois,* ed. Susan Easton Black and Richard E. Bennett (Salt Lake City: Millennial Press, 2000), 142–148, notes that there were some refugees in Far West and vicinity by 20 April 1839.

11. Richard E. Bennett, "'Quincy the Home of Our Adoption': A Study of the Mormons in Quincy, Illinois, 1838–1840," in *A City of Refuge: Quincy, Illinois,* ed. Susan Easton Black and Richard E. Bennett (Salt Lake City: Millennial Press, 2000), 86–87.

12. *Church History in the Fullness of Times,* 2d ed. (Salt Lake City: The Church of Jesus Christ of Latter-day Saints, 1993), 213–214.

13. Quincy Branch Manuscript History and Historical Report, Feb. 27, 1839, Historical Department Archives, The Church of Jesus Christ of Latter-day Saints, hereafter cited as HDA. Henry Ashbury, *Reminiscences of Quincy, Illinois* (Quincy, Ohio: D. Wilcox and Sons, Printers, 1882), 164, notes that he was a member of a mediating committee sent from Quincy to prevent further problems during the

Battle of Nauvoo. Reverend Landry C. Genosky, "The Story of Quincy, Illinois, 1819–1860" (master's thesis, Catholic University, 1949), 52, cited in Fred E. Woods, "Two Sides of a River: Mormon Transmigration through Quincy, Illinois, and Hannibal, Missouri," *Mormon Historical Studies* 2, no. 1 (Spring 2001): 139, note no. 2, explains that seven years later (1846) when the Mormons were forced from Nauvoo, some of the remaining Latter-day Saints who had witnessed the Battle of Nauvoo "had escaped to Quincy and asked the town to mediate."

14. *HC* 3:250.

15. *HC* 3:251–254. This list included the names of at least eight women who signed the covenant. The binding promise to assist the poor and downtrodden provided the underlying strength of God's peculiar people. This Missouri covenant to assist the poor breathed the same spirit of the baptismal covenant that inspired Alma at the waters of Mormon. It required that the people of God be "willing to bear one another's burdens, that they may be light"; to be "willing to mourn with those that mourn; yea, and comfort those that stand in need of comfort, and to stand as witnesses of God at all times and in all things, and in all places" (Mosiah 18:8–9).

The Missouri covenant to assist the poor was renewed in the Nauvoo Temple before the Saints were again forced to leave their beautiful city. Later, when they were headed west, Brigham Young received what may be called an "emigration revelation." Among other things, the revelation reemphasized, "Let every man use all his influence and property to remove this people to the place where the Lord shall locate a stake of Zion. And if ye do this. . .ye shall be blessed." (D&C 136:10–11). William G. Hartley, "How Shall I Gather," *Ensign,* October 1997, 7, notes that this covenant to assist the poor became an essential base for Latter-day Saint emigration procedures for the duration of the nineteenth century.

16. Allen and Leonard, *Story of the Latter-day Saints,* 153–154.

17. Lyndon W. Cook, "Isaac Galland—Mormon Benefactor," BYU Studies 19, no. 3 (Spring 1979): 267. See also Robert Bruce Flanders, *Nauvoo: Kingdom on the Mississippi* (Urbana: University of Illinois Press, 1965), 35. The land between the Mississippi and Des Moines Rivers, south of the northern boundary of Missouri and in the southeast corner of Iowa, had been set aside by a naive Congress in 1824 as a reservation for half-breed Sac and Fox Indians. Anyone who could prove mixed ancestry was a beneficiary. However, most were not interested in acquiring the land for farming purposes, but rather chose to hang around the trading posts and take odd jobs. After the Blackhawk War, Iowa was opened up for white settlement, but no provision had been made for converting the Sac and Fox Indians' interests until

a decade later. In 1834, Congress authorized issuance of land titles to individual Sac and Fox Indians, but left to the territorial government the mechanism for distributing the land. Into this opportune situation stepped Galland, persuading about thirty Sac and Fox Indians to put their "X" on quitclaim deeds, though they had no conception of what the document really meant. Other whites competed with Galland to acquire the land for sale, but he accumulated more claims than anyone else. Due to the questionable land titles, the 1840 census notes that fewer than one thousand whites settled in this area, nearly half of which were Mormons.

18. *HC* 3:260.

THE KIRTLAND TEMPLE, 1907

CHAPTER TWO

The Latter-day Saint Gathering at Home and Abroad

"Yea, verily I say unto you again, the time has come when the voice of the Lord is unto you: Go ye out of Babylon; gather ye out from among the nations, from the four winds, from one end of heaven to the other. Send forth the elders of my church unto the nations which are afar off; unto the islands of the sea; send forth unto foreign lands; call upon all nations."
—D&C 133:7–8

THE DOCTRINE AND KEYS OF THE GATHERING

The doctrine of the gathering and the preaching of the restored gospel went hand in hand. Missionary work was launched from New York and Kirtland in the 1830s, and missionaries were sent to various places in the United States and Canada.[1] The missionaries served for indefinite periods of time, often for only a matter of weeks or months before returning to their labors at home or in their fields.[2] Often they did not wait to be called but volunteered to labor in areas where they had previously lived. They taught the doctrine of the gathering and the necessity for new converts to assemble with the main body of the Church where they could receive instruction, strengthen each other, and partake of greater blessings through the acceptance and compliance of higher laws and covenants.

Missionary work was confined to North America during much of the first decade of the restored Church of Jesus Christ, and Church members did not enter into temple covenants until the construction of the Kirtland Temple. Foreign proselyting did not commence until the necessary priesthood keys were restored to the earth. These priesthood keys were restored 3 April 1836, just one week after the dedication of the Kirtland Temple (D&C 110). In this holy temple, the ancient prophet Moses appeared and restored to Joseph Smith and Oliver Cowdery "the keys of the gathering of Israel from the four parts of the earth" (D&C 110:11).[3]

INTERIOR VIEW OF THE KIRTLAND TEMPLE.

Great spiritual manifestations made this a pentecostal season for the Saints in Kirtland as they rejoiced in the blessings received in their temple. Such blessings included the bestowal of necessary priesthood keys not the least of which was the sealing power (see D&C 110:11–16). Many thought the Millennium was nigh at hand and that Satan would no longer be able to tempt them. Alarmed, the Prophet Joseph Smith warned the Kirtland Saints that if they did not draw nearer to the Lord, they would apostatize.[4]

EVENTS PRECIPITATING FOREIGN PROSELYTING

The following year, the Prophet's warning became a sad reality when economic disaster swept over the United States (later referred to as the Panic of 1837) and hundreds of banks closed. The Saints were not immune to this financial depression. Because they had not been able to incorporate their own bank in Kirtland they had established a unique banking system. The Kirtland Safety Society Anti-Banking Company opened for business on 2 January 1837. Unfortunately, other banks had not accepted the notes and many hostile to the Church claimed the company's notes were not legal tender. Because the Kirtland Safety Society did not have enough specie to redeem large amounts of paper currency, the collapse of the new company was imminent. The Panic of 1837 hastened its arrival. With the culmination of these desperate economic conditions, the spirit of speculation crept into the Saints. Several began borrowing money from the Kirtland Safety Society to purchase land, only to quickly sell it to their fellow Church members for profit.[5] This combination of disturbing events led many Latter-day Saints to apostatize.[6] The members were left spiritually weak and ailing.

An infusion of fresh new converts, not yet soured on the rancid greed and human failings of straying members was needed to heal the ailing Church.[7] In the Kirtland Temple on 4 June 1837, Joseph Smith approached one of his trusted associates, Apostle Heber C. Kimball, and confided in him, "Brother Heber, the Spirit of the Lord has whispered to me: 'Let my servant Heber go to England and proclaim my Gospel, and open the door of salvation to that nation.'"[8] A short time later, Elder Kimball, with fellow Apostle Orson Hyde, prepared to lead a small group of missionaries across the Atlantic to England. The members of this group included Willard Richards, Joseph Fielding, Isaac Russell, John Snyder, and John Goodson. Prior to their departure, Joseph warned Heber to "remain silent concerning the gathering . . . until such time as the work was fully established, and it should be clearly made manifest by the Spirit to do otherwise."[9] Perhaps this warning was given so that the new converts, as tender plants, could receive proper nourishment and cultivate their faith before being transplanted to Nauvoo. Certainly deep roots

Heber C. Kimball

Orson Hyde

GARRICK; VESSEL WHICH BROUGHT THE FIRST
LATTER-DAY SAINT MISSIONARIES TO GREAT BRITAIN.

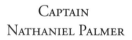

CAPTAIN
NATHANIEL PALMER

would be necessary for the sacrifices and challenges inherent to immigrating.

The missionaries gathered at New York in the summer of 1837 and embarked on a very fast-sailing vessel called the *Garrick.* The *Garrick* was guided by Captain Nathaniel Palmer, known for his explorations in the Antarctic as well as for the bets he made against other sailing vessels. On this voyage he wagered and won ten thousand dollars on a race to England. The *Garrick* arrived in Liverpool on 20 July 1837, after a mere nineteen-day voyage, which was about half the time it usually took to cross the Atlantic in a sailing vessel.[10]

MISSIONARY WORK IN GREAT BRITAIN
A GOOD OMEN

After disembarking, the missionaries journeyed about thirty miles north to the town of Preston where Joseph Fielding's brother, the

Reverend James Fielding, lived with his family. They arrived two days later on election day. Queen Victoria had just ascended the throne and thousands were in the streets parading for their candidates of choice. A banner carrying the motto, "Truth Will Prevail" caught the eye of the elders. The missionaries believed this a good omen for their success and, true to their suppositions, the Reverend Fielding allowed the missionaries to preach in his chapel, and conversions commenced.[11]

OPPOSITION

The light of the restored gospel penetrated honest hearts, and soon several people desired baptism. On Saturday night, plans were made for Elder Heber C. Kimball to baptize the proselytes in the River Ribble the following day. Kimball noted, "By this time the adversary of souls began to rage, and he felt determined to destroy us before we had fully established the kingdom of God in that land, and the next morning I witnessed a scene of satanic power and influence which I shall never forget." Among other things, Elder Kimball recounted the following:

> I was struck with great force by some invisible power, and fell senseless on the floor. The first thing I recollected was being supported by Elders Hyde and Richards, who were praying for me; Elder Richards having followed Russell up to my room. Elder Hyde and Richards then assisted me to get on the bed, but my agony was so great I could not endure it, and I arose, bowed my knees and prayed. I then arose and sat up on the bed, when a vision was opened to our minds, and we could distinctly see the evil spirits, who foamed and gnashed their teeth at us. We gazed upon them about an hour and a half (by Willard's watch). We were not looking towards the window, but towards the wall. Space appeared before us, and we saw the devils coming in legions, with their leaders, who came within a few feet of us. They came towards us like armies rushing to battle. They appeared to be men of full stature, possessing every form and feature of men in the flesh, who were angry and desperate; and I shall never forget the vindictive malignity depicted on their countenances as they looked me in the eye; and any attempt to paint the scene which then presented itself, or portrayed their malice and enmity, would be vain.[12]

SUCCESS

The missionaries were delivered, and performed the baptisms. During the space of just nine months they brought more than fifteen hundred converts into the fold and organized many branches. At the conclusion of this nine-month period, Apostles Kimball and Hyde returned to America while Elders Fielding and Richards and English convert William Clayton served in an interim British Mission presidency.[13] This initial success was bolstered less than two years later when eight members of the Twelve embarked on another mission to Great Britain (January 1840–April 1841). They went to expand the missionary work and to revive the lethargic spirit which had crept in among some of the British converts.[14]

The Twelve found great success and by the spring of 1840, the desired foothold had been obtained. On 14 April 1840, in a council meeting of the Twelve in England, the following decision was made: "Moved by Elder Brigham Young, seconded by Elder Heber C. Kimball, that the Saints receive a recommend to the Church in America to move in small or large bodies, inasmuch as they desire to emigrate to that new country."[15] Less than two months later, this motion was realized as convert migrations to America commenced.

TIDINGS OF FIRST BRITISH IMMIGRANTS ENCOURAGE ADDITIONAL BRITISH CONVERTS

The British Saints began their immigration to Nauvoo with the launching of the sailing vessel, *Britannia*, 6 June 1840.[16] English convert John Moon led a group of forty Saints from Liverpool.[17] At the time of embarkation, Hugh Moon, John's brother, recalled that members of the Twelve were present to lend their support: "We found Elders Brigham Young and Heber C. Kimball aboard. They had

BRITANNIA; VESSEL THAT BROUGHT THE FIRST COMPANY OF BRITISH SAINTS TO AMERICA.

stretched a curtain across our cabin and commenced blessing the company. They bid us walk in."[18] After arriving safely in Nauvoo, Francis Moon wrote back to his native homeland in England to describe the favorable temporal and spiritual conditions that now surrounded him at Nauvoo. The February 1841 edition of the *Millennial Star* published his letter wherein Moon referred to Nauvoo as a refuge in the troubled last days, and further noted that a purpose of gathering the people of God in any age was to "build a sanctuary to the name of the Most High."[19] After living among the Nauvoo Saints, Francis became infused with the temple-building fervor. Gathering with the Saints was synonymous with conversion and building the temple, the hallmark of one's "fellowcitizenship." Moon expressed the hope that

> What I might say on this subject might have the tendency of encouraging my fellow Englishmen in the point of gathering. Now I would hold out unto them every thing that is desirable, and would say if you can get to this land, you will be better off than in England, for in this place there is a prospect of receiving every good thing both of this world and that which is to come: then be faithful, for the Lord has said that his saints shall inherit the earth, and if the Lord has promised it, it is something that will do his people good. Then those who have the means delay no longer but come and unite with us in building the house of the Lord, and in bringing to pass the great things belonging to the kingdom of our God. My fellow-Englishmen and brethren, you may rely upon what I say, for it would be nothing to my profit for to deceive you, then believe me when I say this land is good—the things that have been taught you are true, and Joseph Smith is a prophet of the Most High.[20]

This initial voyage paved the way for many British Saints who soon followed. Moon's glad tidings to his homeland and the letters from other early Latter-day Saints immigrants encouraged the British Saints to gather.

An 1841 *Millennial Star* article entitled, "Emigration" commented, "The news from the emigrants who sailed from this country last season, is so very encouraging that it will give a new impulse to the spirit of emigration."[21] One passionate letter from Nauvoo by William Clayton to Edward Martin written 29 November 1840, stated: "It is impossible for pen to describe to you the difficulties you will have to endure you must come or suffer the vengeance of heaven and for my part I will say that if I was in England now and had experienced all the journey it would not in the least deter me from coming for I have often found that in the greatest seasons of suffering we have the greatest cause of rejoicing."[22]

WILLIAM CLAYTON

OUTSIDERS' OBSERVATIONS

Running concurrent to the *Millennial Star* were several non-Latter-day Saints newspapers in England that printed their observations of the emigrating Saints. For example, the *Liverpool Mercury* began to carry accounts of the British Saints and those who were leaving "Babylon" to come to Zion. One article entitled, "New Mormonite Colony," announced that 180 "Mormonite converts" were going to Illinois "with the view of forming a settlement of persons professing this new faith." The report also noted that most of the converts were farmers who had come "east of Scotland."[23]

About this same time, a London newspaper, the *Times*, gave a negative report of misguided Mormons who had created a bit of a stir in the Bristol region "by the departure of great numbers of deluded country people (Mormonites), old and young, for the 'New Jerusalem' in America. Some of the unfortunate dupes . . . have broken up comfortable establishments at home."[24] This pessimistic view was later countered by a more objective article in the *Liverpool Albion* concerning Latter-day Saint migrants which appeared in September 1842. The newspaper noted that "most of the [Mormon] emigrants were farmers and farmer's servants, with their wives and families. In appearance and worldly circumstances they were above the usual run of steerage passengers."[25]

EXTENDED EFFORTS TO PROSELYTE ETHNIC GROUPS AT HOME & ABROAD

Although Great Britain was the most active area for foreign proselyting throughout the early 1840s, missionaries were also traveling from Nauvoo to take the message of the restored gospel to other countries, including Germany, South America, Jamaica, India, and Australia. At that time, these foreign missions generated very limited success with only a sprinkling of converts.[26] Obviously, some ethnic groups had immigrated to America prior to having contact with the Latter-day Saints. Therefore, some Mormon missionaries did not have to travel too far to feel like they were among a foreign people. One Scandinavian group which clustered two hundred miles northeast of Nauvoo to a place they named Norway, Illinois, deserves special attention.

AMERICAN NORWAY

These Norwegians had crossed the Atlantic in the early nineteenth century and converted to Mormonism after arriving in America. They were largely influenced by Elder George P. Dykes, who journeyed to this area in 1842 from Nauvoo. While in Norway, Illinois, Dykes baptized five Norwegians and set up the Lacily Branch.[27] Later, other branches were established in that Illinois region. The Church recognized the legitimacy of the Lacily Branch, and in January 1846 a small group of these Norwegian Saints visited Nauvoo where they enjoyed communion with the Saints and the great blessing of receiving their endowments.[28]

GEORGE P. DYKES

ISLES OF THE SEA

Some missionaries traveled even farther to gain foreign converts. During the Nauvoo period (1839–1846) missionaries were even sent to the isles of the sea to reclaim scattered Israel. In the spring of 1843, Addison Pratt, Benjamin Grouard, Noah Rogers, and Knowlton Hanks were called from Nauvoo to take the good news of the restoration to the Pacific Islands. Much to their advantage, Pratt and Grouard had previous maritime experience as Pacific sailors. Unfortunately, Elder Hanks contracted tuberculosis on the voyage and died at sea. The three missionaries landed on the Island of Tubuai (three hundred miles south of Tahiti) in the spring of 1844. They had planned to sail

ADDISON PRATT

to the Sandwich Islands (Hawaii) but given the natives' desire to have a Christian minister on this island, Addison Pratt remained and the other two missionaries went on to Tahiti. By the end of Elder Pratt's first year, he had baptized one-third of the inhabitants of the island. In 1845, Elder Rogers returned to America, but Elder Grouard remained and found much success in a small portion of the Tuamotus Islands east of Tahiti. By the fall of 1846, Pratt and Grouard had converted 866 people and organized ten branches.[29] These converts included sailors and English residents, as well as Tahitians.[30] Rather than gathering to the mainland, the native converts generally remained in the Pacific due to the exodus from Nauvoo which had already commenced and because of their unique cultural circumstances. During this period their native lands were considered a permissible temporary gathering place.[31]

NATIVE AMERICANS

Latter-day Saints from Nauvoo also had contact with Native Americans, whom they likewise viewed as descendants of the scattered house of Israel. Some natives in the local region volunteered to visit Nauvoo without any coaxing. On 12 August 1841, a memorable experience presented itself as Chief Cacique and about one hundred Sac and Fox natives crossed from Montrose, Iowa, to Nauvoo by ferry. On arrival, they refused to allow the military band and members of the Nauvoo Legion to escort them to the grove, but insisted that the Prophet Joseph Smith come down and personally receive them. Joseph was happy to oblige them and cheerfully led them to the grove where he then preached concerning the promises given to their fathers in the Book of Mormon.

Cacique responded, "I believe . . . you are a great and good man; I look rough, but I also am a son of the Great Spirit. I have heard your advice—we intend to quit fighting, and follow the good talk you have given us." After sharing a meal together, the Indians entertained the Nauvoo Saints with a lively dance.[32]

Interaction with the Indians was not always so congenial. Elders actively proselyted outside the Nauvoo region among Native Americans

JOSEPH PREACHING TO THE INDIANS.

who were not as civilized as Cacique's braves. For example, John Butler vividly recalled, "In eighteen hundred and forty-two I started on a mission to the Sioux Indians, myself and Bro. Emmett. . . . We had but little success amongst the Indians this time; they did not like us at all; they stole our horses and shot our cattle and came very near shooting us. . . . We had to fly for our lives."[33]

A CALL TO BUILD THE TEMPLE HEIGHTENS DESIRE TO GATHER

The call to build the Nauvoo Temple and receive the blessings of sacred ordinances may have been the greatest stimulus for converts to gather to Nauvoo. In August 1840 the First Presidency issued an official call to erect the temple:

> Believing the time has now come, when it is necessary to erect a house of prayer, a house of order, a house for the worship of our God, where the ordinances can be attended to agreeably to His divine will, in this region of country—to accomplish which,

considerable exertion must be made, and means will be required—and as the work must be hastened in righteousness, it behooves the Saints to weigh the importance of these things, in their minds, in all their bearings, and then take such steps as are necessary to carry them into operation.[34]

Just a few months later, 19 January 1841, the Lord revealed to the Prophet Joseph a scriptural mandate that augmented the initial call to build the Nauvoo Temple:

And again, verily I say unto you, let all my saints come from afar. . . . Come ye, with all your gold, and your silver, and your precious stones, and with all your antiquities; and with all who have knowledge of antiquities, that will come, may come, and bring the box-tree, and the fir-tree, and the pine-tree, together with all the precious trees of the earth; And with iron, with copper, and with brass, and with zinc, and with all your precious things of the earth; and build a house to my name, for the Most High to dwell therein (D&C 124:25–27).

The Saints who heeded this call and gathered to Nauvoo usually settled in various pockets of Hancock County. Joseph once likened Nauvoo to the hub of a wheel, and the various settlements to its spokes.[35] Yet on 24 May 1841, the First Presidency issued an epistle, entitled "Letter of the Presidency to the Saints—Concentration at Nauvoo," in which they stated:

The First Presidency of the Church of Jesus Christ of Latter-day Saints, anxious to promote the prosperity of said Church, feel it their duty to call upon the Saints who reside out of this county [Hancock], to make preparations to come in without delay. This is important, and should be attended to by all who feel an interest in the prosperity of this corner-stone of Zion. Here the Temple must be raised, the University built, and other edifices erected which are necessary for the great work of the last days, and which can only be done by a concentration of energy and enterprise. Let it, therefore, be understood, that all the stakes, excepting those in this county, and in Lee county, Iowa, are discontinued, and the Saints instructed to settle in this county as soon as circumstances will permit.[36]

This meant that only the stakes of Nauvoo, Illinois (Hancock County), and Zarahemla (Montrose, Lee County, Iowa), would be authorized stakes. Not only did this affect settlements in those areas lying outside Hancock County, but as Nauvoo historian Robert Bruce Flanders noted, "Only the previous autumn new stakes had been approved for Springfield, for Morgan County near Geneva, and for Quincy, Lima, Columbus, Payson, and a place called 'Mt. Ephraim' in Adams County. . . . Futhermore, Smith's command would mean the abandonment of Kirtland."[37]

Keeping the Saints focused on moving forward and building the temple at Nauvoo was a priority to the First Presidency. They did not want the Saints to get sidetracked and linger too long in temporary settlements where they would be vulnerable to worldly influences and prey to unscrupulous leaders. Such was the occurrence at Kirtland. On 19 January 1841 Almon Babbitt received the following reprimand by the Lord: "And with my servant Almon Babbitt, there are many things with which I am not pleased; behold,

ALMON BABBITT

he aspireth to establish his counsel instead of the counsel which I have ordained, even that of the Presidency of my Church; and he setteth up a golden calf for the worship of my people" (D&C 124:84). Babbitt had previously been sent to preside over the Kirtland area to shepherd those Saints who did not have the means to continue on to Nauvoo. However, Almon was rebuked for his role in promoting Kirtland as the gathering place (where he owned a business) instead of encouraging the Saints to move on to Nauvoo, where the temple was being built.[38] Perhaps the "golden calf" imagery implies that Babbitt was torn between serving both God and mammon. The First Presidency felt that by gathering the Saints to Nauvoo, they would be strengthened by the community of faithful Saints, and their commitments deepened by temple covenants, making them less vulnerable to the temptations of mammon.

NORTH AMERICAN CONVERTS GATHER TO NAUVOO

The call to build a temple and partake of the blessings therein had a significant impact on Latter-day Saint migrants in the subsequent years of gathering to the Nauvoo region. Missionaries occasionally shepherded their new converts to Nauvoo from various sections of North America. One historian observes that with the commencement of the Nauvoo period, "There was a definite shift in area of concentration. Now it was into Illinois, and the cities of Boston, Philadelphia and New York, with thin lines of penetration into the Southern States; whereas formerly, centers had been in Ohio, New York, Canada and New England."[39] Notwithstanding this apparent emphasis, there was still a variety of missionary labors occurring in other areas.

ELIJAH FUNK SHEETS

One example of a missionary guiding his converts from the East comes from Elijah Funk Sheets, a convert from Chester County, Pennsylvania, who emigrated to Nauvoo in the fall of 1841. At age twenty-one, after volunteering to work on the temple for six months without pay, he left Nauvoo on 4 September 1842 with Joseph A. Stratton to serve a mission in his home state of Pennsylvania. Sixty people were converted in this area within twenty months. Sheets and Stratton then returned with a company of thirty of their converts, arriving in Nauvoo 4 May 1844.[40]

Although missionaries shepherding their converts would be an ideal pattern, many converts could not afford to travel with their missionaries immediately following conversion, or they stayed to continue proselytizing to local inhabitants before gathering to Zion.[41] Following his baptism in Tazewell County, Virginia, 20 November 1843, Henry Boyle was determined to earn money to journey to Nauvoo. However, in April 1844 at a regional conference held in Burk's Garden, Virginia, he was called to labor in his home state of Virginia, where he found success. After completing an honorable mission (about one year in length), he and all other missionaries in this Virginia region were released and told to gather to Nauvoo, where Boyle finally arrived 25 June 1845.[42]

Some missionaries also found success in other parts of North America but often their converts gathered to Nauvoo without them. Some proselytes migrated in groups from various branches of the Church. Benjamin Brown, a member of the Pomfret Branch (Chautauqua County, New York), wrote of his migration with his family and a portion of his fellow Saints after he was finally able to sell his farm:

> The Doctrine of Gathering had been taught the Saints at Pomphret, and, in common with the others, I felt a great desire to gather up and live with the body of the Church. . . .
>
> When the time arrived, with my wife and children, and part of the Branch . . . I started to find the Church, thinking it was still in Missouri, though we had heard that it had been mobbed and broken up. We journeyed until we came to Springfield, about a hundred miles from Nauvoo, where we met with some brethren, who had been driven out of Missouri, and who told us that the Church was collecting in Nauvoo, then called Commerce. We turned our course in that direction, and arrived there in June, the weather being very warm at the time.[43]

One member of this group, Jesse Crosby, noted that there were fifteen members from this branch who were bound for Missouri in the spring of 1839. He supports Brown's claim that on the way they met eastbound missionaries who redirected them to go to Commerce where this small company arrived 6 June 1839.[44]

In 1843, Jesse Crosby and Benjamin Brown journeyed east as missionary companions. Their proselyting labors took them through eastern Canada to Nova Scotia. As the first missionaries in some parts of the Quebec province and as early laborers in Nova Scotia, they met fierce resistance. After much persistence, they baptized fifty and organized two branches. Upon word of the martyrdom and concerned for their families, the missionaries returned to Nauvoo, but were not accompanied by their converts.[45]

While converts who gathered from diverse places usually strengthened the trunk of the Church in Nauvoo, it often weakened their branches of origin. For example, in May 1842 nearly half of the members of the Charity Branch in Benton County, Tennessee, emigrated to Nauvoo, leaving the few remaining members in a crippled condition.[46] The following year, other converts emigrated from the state of Tennessee, further dwindling Church membership there. John Workman and his family gathered with a company of thirty Tennessee Saints, arriving in Nauvoo 7 June 1843.[47]

SOME NORTH AMERICAN MIGRATION ROUTES TO NAUVOO

Those who gathered from the southern and central states often traveled by wagon, cart, or foot to reach the bustling city of Nauvoo, often under sorely trying circumstances. Due to severe persecution, one cluster of eighty to ninety Mississippi Saints journeyed in a company of forty wagons, arriving in Nauvoo in April 1842.[48] Many converts from eastern states made their way down the Ohio River to St. Louis before steaming up the Mississippi River to Nauvoo. Some traveled along the Erie Canal to Lake Erie and then steamed down the Illinois and Mississippi Rivers to their destination.

Benjamin Ashby and his family were converts from the Salem Massachusetts Branch. He described the route (which was largely by water) that their company took as they journeyed to Nauvoo in the fall of 1843.

> We left Salem the 14th of Oct. going to Boston where we stopped a few days with Mother's sister Elizabeth Stuart and with a large company from neighboring towns took passage by Rail Road for Albany only stopping one night a[t] Gloucester thence we traveled by the Erie canal to Buffalo there was no railroad at this time across the state of New York. From Buffalo we went by steamboat to Cleavland Ohio thence by canal across the state of Ohio to Wheeling near the head waters of the Ohio River thence by steamboat down the Ohio to Cincinatti where we changed Boats and continued down the Ohio and up the Mississippi to Nauvoo where we arrived on the 3 of Nov 1843.[49]

AN EVER-EXPANDING ZION

In America there was a new shift in the perception of the gathering which occurred just two months prior to the martyrdom. In April conference 1844, the Prophet Joseph broadened the concept of authorized gathering places in Zion. This expanded view soon impacted priesthood assignments and ecclesiastical units in the United States:

> You know there has been great discussion in relation to Zion— where it is, and where the gathering of the dispensation is, and which I am now going to tell you. The prophets have spoken and written upon it; but I will make a proclamation that will cover a broader ground. *The whole of America is Zion itself from north to south, and is described by the Prophets, who declare that it is the Zion where the mountain of the Lord should be. . . .*
>
> *I have received instructions from the Lord that from henceforth wherever the Elders of Israel shall build up churches and branches unto the Lord throughout the States, there shall be a stake of Zion. In the great cities, as Boston, New York, &c., there shall be stakes.*[50]

This same month, both the *Nauvoo Neighbor* and the *Times and Seasons* published a list of 337 missionaries who would be sent to various locales throughout America to preach and electioneer for Joseph Smith who was at this time running for president of the United States. This represented the most intense missionary effort initiated during the Prophet's lifetime.[51] However, due to the martyrdom which occurred just two months later, all missionaries throughout America were called home.[52]

Notwithstanding, as early as 15 August 1844, the *Times and Seasons* published "An Epistle of the Twelve," clearly denoting that they intended to carry out ecclesiastical programs which would echo the policies of their beloved, martyred prophet. Among other things, the epistle stated that, "The United States and adjoining provinces will be immediately organized by the Twelve into proper districts, in a similar manner as they have already done in England and Scotland, and high priests will be appointed over each district, to preside over the same."[53]

Less than two months later, at the October conference held in Nauvoo, Brigham Young appointed eighty-five high priests "to go abroad in all the congressional districts of the United States, to preside over the branches of the church." He also clarified their mission and instructed them "that it was not the design to go and tarry six months and then return, but to go and settle down, where they can take their families and tarry until the Temple is built, and then come and get their endowments, and return to their families and build up a stake as large as this."[54] During this post-martyrdom Nauvoo period, James Linforth explains that Church leaders still wanted Nauvoo to be built up. Nevertheless, he maintains that there was a policy for Saints emigrating from Britain during this interim period before the Nauvoo exodus. He notes that those "who were wholly dependent upon their labour for support, were advised to emigrate to New York, Philadelphia, Pittsburg, Salem, Boston, and other large towns in the eastern states, and where employment could be procured, which would give the emigrants the means to go west, when the way should open."[55] Although some may have clustered to these arteries, the vast majority of British Saints who crossed the Atlantic to immigrate to America during the Nauvoo period (1840–1846) gathered to Nauvoo, which was considered at this time to be the heart of Zion.

NOTES TO CHAPTER TWO

1. On the topic of missionary work being launched from Kirtland see Davis Bitton, "Kirtland as a Center of Missionary Activity, 1830–1833," *BYU Studies* 11, no. 4 (Summer 1971): 497–516.

2. Samuel George Ellsworth, "A History of Mormon Missions in the United States and Canada, 1830–1860," (Ph.D. diss., University of California, 1951), 302, notes that up until the time of the Nauvoo exodus, "the great bulk of missionary activity had been carried on by men taking care of their normal pursuits of life and taking voluntary missions in the time they could afford." However, Ellsworth also observes that the beginnings of a more regulated policy concerning missionary work occurred when the Nauvoo gathering commenced. In the spring of 1839, Church leaders gathered in Quincy, Illinois, and decided that the Presidents of the Seventies would be given the right to select and direct those sent out to proselyte. The decision was also made "that letters of recommendation were to be given to all elders

going out to preach and no elder was to preach without a recommendation" (223–224). When the Twelve returned from their mission to England (1840–1841), they selected "the individuals to go and preach in such places as they may judge expedient" (235).

3. In D&C 20:2–3, Joseph Smith and Oliver Cowdery were designated by revelation as the first and second elders of the restored Church.

4. Milton V. Backman Jr., *The Heavens Resound: A History of the Latter-day Saints in Ohio, 1830–1838* (Salt Lake City: Deseret Book Co., 1983), 308.

5. *Church History in the Fullness of Times,* 2d ed. (Salt Lake City: The Church of Jesus Christ of Latter-day Saints, 1993), 171–172.

6. Milton V. Backman Jr., "A Warning from Kirtland," *Ensign,* April 1989, 30, estimates that about 13 percent, or 50 out of 475 families left the Church at this time in the Kirtland region. However, he also notes that about 40 percent of this number later returned to the Church.

7. *HC* 2:489 notes that during this turbulent era, the Prophet Joseph Smith received revelation that "something new must be done for the salvation" of the Church.

8. Orson F. Whitney, *Life of Heber C. Kimball: An Apostle—The Father and Founder of the British Mission,* 8th ed. (Salt Lake City: Bookcraft, 1978), 103–104. The uneducated Kimball was initially overwhelmed by the thought of going to the learned country of England to preach the gospel. Nevertheless, he was determined to carry out what he knew to be the will of heaven.

9. *HC* 2:492. Apostles Kimball and Hyde left Kirtland for New York City with Willard Richards and Joseph Fielding. There they met Isaac Russell, John Snyder, and John Goodson who had journeyed from Toronto. See V. Ben Bloxham, James R. Moss, and Larry C. Porter, eds., *Truth Will Prevail: The Rise of the Church of Jesus Christ of Latter-day Saints in the British Isles, 1837–1987* (Salt Lake City: Deseret Book Co., 1987), 38–39.

10. Bloxham, Moss, and Porter, *Truth Will Prevail,* 37–43; Whitney, *Life of Heber C. Kimball,* 112–113. For more information on the Garrick, see Conway B. Sonne, *Ships, Saints, and Mariners: A Maritime Encyclopedia of Mormon Migration, 1830–1890* (Salt Lake City: University of Utah Press, 1987), 81–83.

11. James B. Allen, Ronald K. Esplin, and David J. Whittaker, *Men With A Mission, 1837–1841: The Quorum of the Twelve Apostles in the British Isles* (Salt Lake City: Deseret Book Co., 1992), 28–33.

12. Whitney, *Life of Heber C. Kimball,* 129–130.

13. Allen, Esplin, and Whittaker, *Men With A Mission,* 52–53. Apostles Kimball and Hyde left England on 20 April 1838.

14. For excellent reading on this subject see James B. Allen and Malcolm R. Thorp, "The Mission of the Twelve to England, 1840–41: Mormon Apostles and the Working Class," *BYU Studies* 15, no. 4 (Summer 1975): 499–526; Allen, Esplin, and Whittaker, *Men With A Mission.*

15. *HC* 4:119. Whitney, *Life of Heber C. Kimball,* 278, indicates that on the second day of this council meeting, the total membership of the Church in the British Isles was reported as 1,631, including 132 priesthood holders.

16. Sonne, *Ships, Saints, and Mariners,* 30–31. During this year (1840), both Britain and the United States were on the move. In the spring, Britain had published the world's first adhesive postage stamp to be used commercially. This invention benefitted the converts and their friends and families who corresponded frequently, amidst the vast Atlantic separation. It was at a time when the population of the United States had swelled to over seventeen million, increasing over four million in just a decade. Some 76,000 English and 207,000 Irish immigrants embarked for the United States. Immigrants were looking for a new life in America and were willing to risk their lives by crossing the perilous Atlantic. The timing for such an endeavor seemed to be right. See James Trager, *The Peoples' Chronology* (New York: Holt, Rhinehart and Winston, 1976); Neville Williams, 1776–1900: *The Changing World,* vol. 3 of *Chronology of World History* (Santa Barbara, ABC-CLIO, 1999), 220–222.

17. *HC* 4:134. This maiden voyage ended in New York. John Moon and his company then traveled by rail and steamboat through the cities of Philadelphia, Pittsburgh, Cincinnati, and St. Louis before arriving in Nauvoo.

18. Hugh Moon, *Autobiography of Hugh Moon,* HDA, 2. Such support was also provided on subsequent voyages destined for Nauvoo. See William Clayton, *Diary of William Clayton,* HDA, 73; Thomas Callister Collection HDA, 8. The Latter-day Saints were not the only religious group to bless the foreign converts prior to departing for America. In the London Illustrated News (10 May 1851), a Catholic priest is depicted with one hand on the head of a Irish emigrant departing for America, as his other hand is raised to a square while a blessing is apparently being given of spiritual and temporal safety.

19. "Important from America," *Millennial Star* 1, no. 10 (February 1841): 253.

20. Ibid., 254–255.

21. "Emigration," *Millennial Star* 1, no. 10 (February 1841): 263.

22. Paul E. Dahl, "William Clayton: Missionary, Pioneer, and Public Servant" (master's thesis, Brigham Young University, 1959), 22.

23. "New Mormonite Colony," the *Liverpool Mercury* 31, no. 1584 (17 September 1841): 5.

24. *The Times,* London (14 August 1841), cited in Wilbur S. Shepperson, "The Place of the Mormons in the Religious Emigration of Britain, 1840–1860," *Utah Historical Quarterly* 20, no. 3 (July 1952): 213.

25. M. Hamlin Cannon, "The 'Gathering' of British Mormons to Western America: A Study in Religious Migration," (Ph.D. diss., American University, 1950), 73–74.

26. Allen and Leonard, *Story of the Latter-day Saints,* 2d ed. (Salt Lake City: Deseret Book Co., 1992), 166.

27. Dykes would later be selected at the October 1849 general conference to go to Copenhagen, where he assisted Elder Erastus Snow and others in opening up missionary work in Scandinavia in 1850.

28. Keith A. Erekson and Lloyd D. Newell, "'A Gathering Place for the Scandinavian People': Conversion, Retention, and Gathering in Norway, Illinois (1842–1849)," *Mormon Historical Studies* 1, no. 1 (Spring 2000): 28. The authors also point out that these Scandinavian converts did not immediately go west with the larger body of Saints, but remained in their settlement. Due largely to the apostate influence of James J. Strang, who had proclaimed himself to be the true successor of the Prophet Joseph Smith, disillusionment settled in Norway, Illinois, concerning Mormon doctrine. However, after much patience, love, and labor by Reuben Miller, in the spring of 1849 twenty-two Norwegian converts left their Illinois settlement and finally arrived in the Great Salt Lake Valley at the year's end (30–31).

29. *Church History in the Fullness of Times,* 238–239. S. George Ellsworth, ed., *The Journals of Addison Pratt* (Salt Lake City: University of Utah Press, 1990), contains a wealth of information concerning the Pacific missions of Elder Pratt and other aspects of his life.

30. Allen and Leonard, *Story of the Latter-day Saints,* 166.

31. This policy of gathering converts locally from the Pacific Islands rather than having them immigrate to America was also largely continued in the latter half of the nineteenth century. One notable exception is that in the late nineteenth century, hundreds of Pacific converts (mostly Hawaiian) gathered to Salt Lake to receive their endowments. They then migrated to the desert west of Salt Lake to a place they called Iosepa in honor of one of the missionaries they dearly loved, Joseph F. Smith. They were aided by missionaries who could see their difficulties in adjusting to the Utah culture in the Salt Lake Valley. For more information on Iosepa, see Tracey E. Panek, "Life at Iosepa, Utah's Polynesian Colony," *Utah Historical Quarterly* 60, no. 1 (Winter 1992): 64–77. The challenge of islanders in assimilating into mainland Utah culture, may be the primary reason why others during the nineteenth century were

not strongly encouraged to gather to the Zion in the West, but were rather encouraged to build Zion in their native areas. As the twentieth century emerged, the Hawaii Temple (dedicated in 1919) became a gathering place for the Pacific Islanders.

32. *HC* 4:401–402.

33. John Butler, *Autobiography of John Lowe Butler,* 1808–1861, typescript, L. Tom Perry Special Collections Library, Harold B. Lee Library, Brigham Young University, Provo, Utah, p. 21–22.

34. *HC* 4:186.

35. Ibid., 5:296.

36. Ibid., 4:362.

37. Robert Bruce Flanders, *Nauvoo: Kingdom on the Mississippi* (Urbana: University of Chicago Press, 1975), 49.

38. It seems likely that the imagery of the golden calf was used to draw a comparison between Babbitt and Jeroboam (king of Israel), who was guilty of the same offense. In I Kings 12:26–33, Jeroboam discouraged the ten tribes of Israel from going up to Jerusalem to worship at the temple. Instead, he created golden calves, erected at Bethel and Dan, polluted the priesthood, and changed the feast days. For more information on the life of Almon Babbitt, see A. Gary Anderson, "Almon W. Babbitt and the Golden Calf," in *Regional Studies in Latter-day Saint Church History: Illinois,* ed. H. Dean Garrett (Provo, Utah: Department of Church History and Doctrine, Brigham Young University, 1995), 35–54.

39. Ellsworth, "History of Mormon Missions," 257–258.

40. *Latter-day Saint Biographical Encyclopedia: A Compilation of Biographical Sketches of Prominent Men and Women in the Church of Jesus Christ of Latter-day Saints,* s.v. "Sheets, Elijah Funk," 1:614.

41. Many elders volunteered to serve missions without being officially appointed to serve. Quite often they chose to proselyte in areas where they had once lived.

42. Henry Boyle, *Autobiography and Diary of Henry G. Boyle,* 1832–1855, typescript, L. Tom Perry Special Collections Library, Harold B. Lee Library, Brigham Young University, Provo, Utah, p. 3, 5, 10–11.

43. Benjamin Brown, *Testimonies for the Truth: A Record of the Manifestations of the Power of God, Miraculous and Providential, Witnessed in the Travels and Experience of Benjamin Brown, High Priest in the Church of Jesus Christ of Latter-day Saints, Pastor of the London, Reading, Kent, and Essex Conferences* (Liverpool: S.W. Richards, 1853), 18–19, Americana Collection, L. Tom Perry Special Collections Library, Harold B. Lee Library, Brigham Young University, Provo, Utah.

44. Jesse Crosby, *The History and Journal of Jesse W. Crosby, 1820–1869,* typescript,

L. Tom Perry Special Collections Library, Harold B. Lee Library, Brigham Young University, Provo, Utah, p. 5. Lorenzo Brown, *Journal of Lorenzo Brown,* 1823–1900, Volume One 1823–1862, typescript, L. Tom Perry Special Collections Library, Harold B. Lee Library, Brigham Young University, Provo, Utah, p. 6, notes, "April 21st [1839] Started on our westward journey to gather with the saints but where to go we hardly knew as this winter past the brethren were expelled from Missouri and there was now no particular location[.] Our company was composed of my Father with two teams Grandfather Mumford & Charles with one Enoch Crowel in one drawn by a single horse and John and Jesse Crosby who joined us two days after with a three hors team. We were altogether fifteen in number." Lorenzo was the son of Benjamin Brown. Benjamin later served a mission with Jesse Crosby to Nova Scotia.

45. Benjamin Brown, *Testimonies for the Truth,* 20–24.

46. LaMar C. Berrett, "History of the Southern States Mission, 1831–1861," (master's thesis, Brigham Young University, 1960), 192, notes that missionary George W. Brandon reported that he had created the Charity Branch in Benton County, Tennessee, in April 1842. The following month, eight of its eighteen members migrated to Nauvoo, while a few moved to other locations. The branch was thus left with four women (three of which had unbelieving husbands), and only one male, who was a young boy.

47. Ibid., "History of the Southern States Mission," 197.

48. Ibid., "History of the Southern States Mission," 208. Berrett points out that 1842–1843 were peak years for missionary work in the South and that 150 Saints emigrated during this period (217–218). In his appendix, he provides an annual summary of southern Latter-day Saints emigrants who gathered to Nauvoo 1839–1846. In addition, Berrett includes the names of the missionaries, states they served in, branches, and number of converts (296–299).

49. Benjamin Ashby, *Autobiography of Benjamin Ashby,* holograph, L. Tom Perry Special Collections Library, Harold B. Lee Library, Brigham Young University, Provo, Utah, p. 7.

50. *HC* 6:318–319.

51. Ellsworth, "History of Mormon Missions," 266–267.

52. Ibid., 273–274.

53. "An Epistle of the Twelve," *Times and Seasons* 5, no. 15 (August 1844): 619.

54. *HC* 7:305–307.

55. James Linforth, ed., *Route from Liverpool to Great Salt Lake Valley Illustrated with Steel Engravings and Wood Cuts from Sketches Made by Frederick Piercy* (Liverpool: Franklin D. Richards, 1855), 2.

THE DOCK AT PLYMOUTH, ENGLAND, 1863.

CHAPTER THREE

Embarkation and Crossing the Atlantic
Nauvoo Beginnings

The gallant ship is under way
To bear me off to sea
And yonder floats the streamer gay
That says she waits for me.
The seamen dip the ready oar,
As rippled waves oft tell,
They bear me swiftly from the shore;
My native land, farewell!
I go devoted to His cause,
And to His will resigned;
His presence will supply the loss
Of all I leave behind.
His promise cheers the sinking heart
And lights the darkest cell,
Exiled pilgrim's grace imparts;
My native land, farewell!
I go, it is my Master's call
He's made my duty plain;
No danger can the heart appall
When Jesus stoops to reign.
And now the vessel's side we've made,
The sails their bosoms swell,
Thy beauties in the distance fade,
My native land, farewell!

—W. W. Phelps[1]

Great Britain must have been rather subdued as she watched the voluntary emigration of nearly seventeen million of her countrymen within a century, commencing in 1815 and concluding with World War I (1914). The vast number of British citizens who left their homeland during this period is almost equal to the entire population of Great Britain in 1815. Factors contributing to emigration included not only social discontent and religious aspirations, but also the economic and political instability of the once-proud nation. Emigration in the nineteenth century for whatever reason (including religious) was largely a personal matter.[2] However, for early members of The Church of Jesus Christ of Latter-day Saints, it was a collective movement motivated primarily by divine decree—to establish a religious community where the Saints of God could dwell—and secondarily by economic opportunities. The Church, superior in its emigration organization and determined to move a covenant people to Zion, carefully orchestrated each step of the journey, with continual monitoring by dedicated Church leaders.

DIFFICULTY OF LEAVING HOME

The enthusiasm among those fortunate enough to gather to Zion was countered by the difficulty of leaving native lands and loved ones behind. Although voluntary, the anguish of embarkation wrenched heartstrings. Seventeen-year-old Mary Haskin Parker Richards remembered with pain the trial of leaving her family and friends before climbing aboard the *Alliance* in December 1840. "Nevver shall I forget the feeling that shriled through my Bosem this day. While parting with all my dear Brothers & Sisters. And all my kindred who were near & dear to me by the ties of nature."[3]

Such farewells often created heightened emotions. Twenty-one-year-old convert Thomas Callister left his homeland, the Isle of Man, 9 January 1842, to embark for Nauvoo. He wrote, "I left all my relatives and friends for the Gospel sake."[4] Although his parents were not alive to bid him farewell, one sibling decided he would

THOMAS CALLISTER

see him off. "His brother John went with him to the ship and there offered him half of all he owned if he would only give up going to America. When Thomas refused, his brother said he would be happier if he could lay him away on the hill with his parents."[5] (This familial episode would be only the initiation for Thomas and many others, of the many hardships and sacrifices that lay ahead.)

Two years later, Priscilla Staines voyaged on the *Fanny*. She recalled the difficulty of leaving her homeland two days after Christmas. While her journal entry presents a dismally somber scene, it also demonstrates the faith and commitment which made her sacrifice possible:

> I left the home of my birth to gather to Nauvoo. I was alone. It was a dreary winter day on which I went to Liverpool. The company with which I was to sail were all strangers to me. When I arrived at Liverpool and saw the ocean that would soon roll between me and all I loved, my heart almost failed me. But I had laid my idols all upon the altar. There was no turning back. I remembered the words of the Saviour: "He that leaveth not father and mother, brother and sister, for my sake, is not worthy of me," and I believed his promise to those who forsook all for his sake; so I thus alone set out for the reward of everlasting life, trusting in God.[6]

ECONOMICS DETERMINE THE DECISION TO EMBARK

For most of the British Saints, economics determined if and when one was able to gather to Zion. Sometimes families were temporarily divided. In the fall of 1841, Robert Pixton determined that notwithstanding being separated from his wife, he would lead the way to Zion. He wrote, "I spoke to my wife about it and she was willing that I should go and leave her behind until I could send for her as we had not sufficient means for both to go. . . . This was a sad parting but I was reconciled to go."[7]

ROBERT PIXTON

Many sincere Saints longed to set sail for the city Zion where they could consecrate their talents and labor towards the building of the temple, but the cold reality of procuring sufficient funds for the journey froze them to their present circumstances. George Cannon, voyaging on the *Sidney* in 1842, wrote, "Nothing caused me so much regret as leaving so many of the Saints behind, anxious to go but without the means to do so."[8] Some, such as Robert Crookston, a fellow passenger with Cannon, exercised considerable faith and sacrificed greatly. He recalled, "We had to sell everything at a great sacrifice. But we wanted to come to Zion and be taught by the Prophet of God. We had the spirit of gathering so strongly that Babylon had no claim on us."[9]

ROBERT CROOKSTON

LIVELY LIVERPOOL

The primary port of departure for these foreign converts fleeing Babylon was Liverpool.[10] It was not only the headquarters of the British Mission, but by 1840 Liverpool was the most active international port of emigration in the world. This was due to its prime location for rail connections and also for its excellent navigable channels in the Mersey River. And some two thousand pubs kept Liverpool the sailors dock of choice.[11] Though foreign converts found some degree of solace among their own society as they awaited embarkation, their arrival at Liverpool's railway stations left them exposed to the sheer size of Britain's second largest city and port. By 1840 over two hundred thousand people resided there alongside thousands of mariners, criminals, and migrants.

A decade later, Liverpool swelled to a population of 367,000, making it three-fourths the size of New York. By the mid-nineteenth century, two-thirds of the British emigrant trade belonged to Liverpool. In 1845, Albert the prince consort opened the Albert Dock, which was one of the largest and most splendid of the many docks there. The docks in general were marvellous, and the warehouses were adorned with Doric pillars. In his novel, *Redburn,* Melville described Liverpool's maritime splendour through the eyes of a sailor. He compared "the

THE SAINTS EMBARK FROM LIVERPOOL ENGLAND

miserable wooden wharves and slip-shod, shambling piers of New York" with the "mighty docks" of Liverpool. He wrote, "In Liverpool, I beheld long China walls of masonry; vast piers of stone; and a succession of granite-rimmed docks. . . . In magnitude, cost, and dura- bility, . . . surpass all others in the world."[12]

In stark contrast to Melville's description of near-deified docks, Nathaniel Hawthorne described the maritime city of Liverpool in appalling terms as a result of working there as an American consul for four years (1853–1857).[13] Historian Terry Coleman described Hawthorne's dismal view of the socioeconomic condition of Liverpool in the mid-nineteenth century:

> Almost every day Hawthorne walked about the city, preferring the darker and dingier streets inhabited by

NATHANIEL
HAWTHORNE

the poorer classes. Women nursed their babies at dirty breasts. The
men were haggard, drunken, care-worn, and hopeless, but patient as if
that were the rule of their lives. He never walked through these streets
without feeling he might catch some disease, but he took the walks all
the same because there was a sense of bustle, and of being in the midst
of life and of having got hold of something real, which he did not find
in the better streets of Liverpool. Tithebarn Street was thronged with
dreadful faces—women with young figures but with old and wrinkled
countenances, young girls without any maiden neatness, barefooted,
with dirty legs. Dirty, dirty children, and the grown people were the
flower of these buds, physically and morally. At every ten steps there
were spirit vaults. Placards advertised beds for the night. Often he saw
little children taking care of little children. . . . At the provision shops,
little bits of meat were ready for poor customers, little heaps and
selvages and corners stripped off from joints and steaks.[14]

Perhaps Hawthorne's most revolting portrayal of the wretched
conditions confronting the emigrants during this period is contained

Emigrant Ship Leaving Liverpool, 1853.

in his observation, "The people are as numerous as maggots in cheese; you behold them, disgusting, and all moving about, as when you raise a plank or log that has long lain on the ground, and find many vivacious bugs and insects beneath it."[15] Despite Hawthorne's grim opinion, sailors loved Liverpool where they could come into dock and get their fill of lewd living. On the other hand, naive emigrants had to be continually on their guard to avoid corrupt runners and rogues who lay in wait to take advantage of them at Liverpool:

> Before the emigrants even got on board ship they had to have dealings with ship brokers, otherwise known as emigration agents or recruiters; with runners, otherwise called crimps, touts, and man-catchers; with boarding-house keepers, who overcharged them and delayed them as long as they had money to pay for more lodgings; and the keepers of spirit vaults and provision stores, who sold them bad food and drink at high prices. Runners were almost always boarding-house keepers, and boarding-house keepers often ran spirit vaults or food shops on the side. It was all confused and disorderly, and almost always a racket. Each man took his cut, and the first and biggest cut went to the broker. As a policeman put it, there was a general impression that the emigrants were defrauded from the day they started from their houses. They had no remedy.[16]

LATTER-DAY SAINTS EMIGRATION AGENTS AT LIVERPOOL

While this may have been true for emigrants in general, the Latter-day Saints quickly concocted a remedy. Upon arrival in Liverpool, the Saints were directed to the British Mission office. There Church leaders advised the emigrants regarding provisions and lodgings and counselled them concerning the Atlantic crossing. Together they worked to obtain temporary lodgings while awaiting the departure of the sailing vessels that would carry them to America. When possible, the British Mission office made arrangements for the emigrants to sleep on the vessel prior to departure, as it was much safer and cheaper for them.

By the spring of 1841, the Quorum of the Twelve had appointed an agent in Liverpool to protect and direct the Saints through the emigration process. In an article appearing in the *Millennial Star*, April 1841, the Twelve provided several beneficial reasons why converts should follow the newly appointed Latter-day Saints emigration agent:

> We have found that there are so many "pick pockets," and so many that will take every possible advantage of strangers, in Liverpool, that we have appointed Elder Amos Fielding, as the agent of the church, to superintend the fitting out of the Saints from Liverpool to America. Whatever information the Saints may want about the preparations for a voyage, they are advised to call on Elder Fielding, at Liverpool, as their first movement, when they arrive there as emigrants. There are some brethren who have felt themselves competent to do their own business in these matters, and rather despising the counsel of their friends, have been robbed and cheated out of nearly all they had. A word of caution to the wise is sufficient. It is also a great saving to go in companies, instead of going individually. First, a company can charter a vessel, so as to make the passage much cheaper than otherwise. Secondly, provisions can be purchased at wholesale for a company much cheaper than otherwise. Thirdly, this will avoid bad company on the passage. Fourthly, when a company arrives in New Orleans they can charter a steam-boat so as to reduce the passage near one-half. This measure will save some hundreds of pounds on each ship load. Fifthly, a man of experience can go as leader of each company, who will know how to avoid rogues and knaves.[17]

Four months later, the *Star* reassured emigrating Saints that passage would "be obtained by Brother Fielding on the lowest terms, and provisions purchased to the best advantage, and divided to each passenger at the first cost; with a strict account of all these matters, and no other profit or charge on the part of Brother Fielding, except a reasonable renumeration for his time."[18]

Most of the emigrating Saints followed this sound counsel. Two years later (May 1843) the Saints were again cautioned to work only with the authorized Latter-day Saint emigration agents who were at that time Elders Amos Fielding and Hiram Clark.[19]

Less than three months passed before an unfortunate incident occurred which proved the warning invaluable to those who heeded counsel. A man by the name of Joseph Quail solicited the Saints' participation by sending announcements to the branches declaring that he had arranged passage to Nauvoo for his family and several other Latter-day Saints. A scathing editorial exposing Quail as an imposter without proper authority was published to warn the Saints of the deception:

> We at once denounce the projected scheme as utterly without authority from the Church, and shall consider the projectors, and all that may encourage them, as traitors to the order of the Church, and as rebelling against the authority of the priesthood. . . .
>
> And we are compelled, by every principle of righteousness, to consider the projectors and abettors of the plan as worthy (without a sincere repentance, ample restitution, and abandonment of the whole plot) of immediate excommunication from the Church of Jesus Christ.[20]

In addition to the threat of unauthorized agents, the British Mission also had plenty of other challenges to deal with. One article appearing in the *Millennial Star* provides a glimpse of some of the headaches the emigration agents had to endure:

> In consequence of not knowing the number of persons about to emigrate at the different periods of vessels sailing, those attending to the emigration department have been put to great inconvenience and expense; sometimes by numbers arriving of whom we had no previous intimation, so that preparation has not been made for them. . . .
>
> Again, many have given notice of their intentions to emigrate at a certain time who have failed and not come up at the time expected, which has either caused us to pay at the same rate for the ship as if they had gone, or in other cases has caused disappointment to ship owners and captains by not supplying the amount of passengers they had been led to expect.[21]

In order to deal with these difficulties, the British Mission office (which handled all aspects of emigration) requested that Latter-day Saints branches spread throughout Great Britain provide a detailed account of each Church member who was planning on emigrating. The request specifically required accurate information regarding the "names, ages, and occupations of all intending to emigrate (not by any means omitting the names of infants)."[22]

Besides the agents' demanding task of making arrangements for each voyage and keeping track of every departing emigrant, their job became even more hectic when faced with the migrants' immediate needs for lodging and provisions once they arrived at the British Mission office. In a letter to Brigham Young, Reuben Hedlock vividly describes his experience there as an agent in Liverpool: "There is much to do when a vessel is preparing to sail for some days; from ten to twenty emigrants coming to the office; one wants this and one that, and the third wants to know where he shall sleep all night, with a dozen or more women and children in the office to run over; one wants tin ware, another is short of cash and their children are hungry."[23]

ROLE OF THE MILLENNIAL STAR IN BRITISH EMBARKATION

The *Millennial Star* was an essential instrument for Church leaders and agents in providing continual information and direction to the passing migrants. Emigration agents chartered vessels each year, and departure times were published regularly in various editions of the *Star*. This Latter-day Saint periodical was established in April 1840, just two months before Mormon emigration was first launched from Liverpool. The first editor of the *Millennial Star* was Elder Parley P. Pratt. Among other things, Pratt indicated in his prospectus issued 27 May 1840 that the purpose of the periodical was to spread the truth, gather Israel, and be as a star of light for the faithful to prepare for the second coming of Jesus Christ.[24]

Within its pages, the *Star* created the feeling that the Second Coming was nigh at hand. The first article of the opening issue dealt with the doctrinal topic of the Millennium and reviewed the teachings of ancient prophets regarding the restoration and gathering of Israel in the last days.[25] "God will set his hand the second time to restore the house of Israel. . . . They will gather out from every nation under heaven, . . . employing the ships, steam-boats, railroad carriages, canal-boats, litters, horses, mules, camels, and swift beasts, and every kind of conveyance which the nations can furnish."[26] Articles such as this fueled a burning desire in the converts' hearts to gather to Zion.

Continual guidance was given in minute detail for each and every aspect the emigrants faced on their journey to Zion. For example, in August 1841, the *Star* published an article entitled, "Information to Emigrants." After furnishing several pages of general information regarding immigration to North America, the following practical counsel guided the Latter-day Saint emigrants on what they should take on their voyage:

THE *LATTER-DAY SAINTS' MILLENNIAL STAR*

We shall now proceed to give such particulars in regard to the journey as may be needful.

Those intending to emigrate will do well to take no furniture with them except the necessary articles of beds, bedding, wearing apparel, pots, cooking utensils, &c., which will come in useful both on the ship and on the steam-boat, and after they arrive. Do not be encumbered with old bedsteads, chairs, tables, stands, drawers, broken boxes, worn out bedding, soiled clothing, rusty tools, &c.; but provide a great plenty of good and substantial wearing apparel, bedding, &c., consisting of every necessary article of manufactured goods both for men and women, because these things are much dearer in Western America than in

England, and no duties will be charged by the American government of wearing apparel already made up, even if each passenger
has several suits of clothes. Every thing which is not designed for
use on the passage should be carefully packed in strong boxes or
trunks. Emigrants will not have to pay any thing for freight of
their usual household goods and furniture on the ocean; but it
will cost something for freight up the Mississippi River for every
article except a certain quantity which is allowed each passenger
free as travelling luggage.[27]

Articles also advised on the best route to take, including specific
guidelines for purchasing tickets, comparing travel costs, and avoiding
extra lodging costs:

New Orleans is by far the cheapest route for emigrants to Illinois;
and much more money may be saved by emigrating in large
companies. Those who wish to avail themselves of these advantages,
and who are intending to emigrate this autumn, are informed that
the name and age of each passenger, together with money to pay
their passage to New Orleans and to purchase provisions, must be
forwarded to Brother Amos Fielding . . . at least 10 days previous to
the time of sailing, so that a ship may be chartered and provisions
purchased according to the number of passengers, and thus avoid
all hurry and confusion. The money and names being forwarded
ten days previous to the time of sailing, the passengers and goods
need not arrive till two or three days before the time of sailing.
Thus when all things are prepared, they can go immediately on
board, and begin to arrange the berths, beds, provisions, &c., and
avoid the expense of living a while in the town of Liverpool.

Perhaps the passage money and provisions for each passenger
from Liverpool to New Orleans will be not far from four
pounds. Children under fourteen years of age, half-price; under
one year nothing. . . .

When the ship arrives in New Orleans the company will need to
send their foreman, or leader, or committee, to charter a steam

boat for Nauvoo or St. Louis, which will probably be from 15s.
[shillings] to 25s. per head, and provisions to be purchased for
about two weeks; so the whole passage money from Liverpool to
Nauvoo will probably be from £5 to £7.[28]

LATTER-DAY SAINT-CHARTERED VOYAGES

In 1891, Andrew Jenson published an article on Church emigration during the Nauvoo period in which he lists thirty-two Latter-day
Saint companies that left England for Nauvoo between June 1840
and January 1846, with the possibility of another unknown voyage in
1846. Further research suggests there were thirty-four Mormon

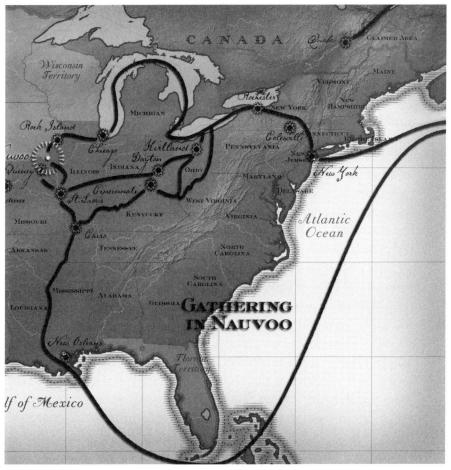

Map of Latter-day Saint Maritime Migration Routes to Nauvoo.

company voyages and at least thirteen additional Latter-day Saint voyages not chartered by the Church, but rather small groups of families or individuals.[29] James Linforth, in his book *Route from Liverpool to Great Salt Lake Valley*, notes that although the main Latter-day Saint immigration route from Liverpool to New Orleans had been chartered during the Nauvoo years, "numerous individuals have sailed between the seasons to New York, Philadelphia, Boston, and other American ports."[30] Jenson estimates that five thousand British Saints gathered to Nauvoo during these years.[31] These statistics suggest over one-fourth of the Saints who gathered to Nauvoo before the 1846 Mormon exile were British converts.[32]

In 1841, probably for logistical reasons, three separate groups of Saints chose to depart from the port of Bristol and enter North America at Quebec before making their way to Nauvoo via the St. Lawrence River and the Great Lakes.[33] All other Latter-day Saints company voyages destined for Nauvoo embarked from Liverpool. British immigrants embarking from Liverpool on three early voyages entered the United States through the port of New York and made their way through canals and on the Ohio River before steaming up to Nauvoo.[34] All other Latter-day Saint-chartered voyages disembarked at the port of New Orleans.[35]

Apparently, the decision to use the American port of New Orleans (commencing in December 1840) instead of the port of New York was influenced by a letter the Prophet Joseph Smith sent to the Twelve in England in October 1840. Therein he mentioned, "I think that those who came here this fall, did not take the best possible route, or the least expensive."[36] Six months later the *Millennial Star* published an "Epistle of the Twelve," wherein counsel was given regarding when and how British converts should immigrate to Nauvoo: "It is much cheaper going by New Orleans than by New York. But it will never do for emigrants to go by New Orleans in the Summer on account of the heat and sickness of the climate. It is, therefore, advisable for the Saints to emigrate in Autumn, Winter, or Spring."[37] The Saints had enough hardships to deal with in their journeys without having to cope with the intense heat and threat of disease of a New Orleans summer.

POETRY AND SONG: BALM FOR THE SOUL

Regardless of the season for travel, the emotional feelings created from tearing away from family, friends, and home were poignant. Brave men and women were in dire need of solace and comfort as they began their voyages. Poetry and song became the ointment for their pain and the balm for their souls. In a poem published in 1842 in the *Millennial Star*, Latter-day Saints convert J. Riley poetically proclaimed the invitation to gather:

> Come ye Saints of ev'ry nation,
> Flee to Zions's safe abode;
> Hail with joy the great salvation,
> Offer'd you by Christ the Lord.
>
> Glide across the mighty ocean,
> Bid the winds your canvass swell;
> Put the gallant ship in motion,
> Anchors weigh, and hoist your sail.[38]

Such words of inspiration were often sung by the Saints as they fled Babylon and embarked for Zion. For example, the *Millennial Star* noted that while on the 1843 voyage of the *Metoka*, "Saints on board gave expression to their feelings in various hymns, which they sang as the vessel was towed into the river."[39] The following year, Ann Pitchforth described her feelings when the *Fanny* left the docks of Liverpool. "When the farewell hymn was sung on ship-board, I felt what it was like to leave all for the truth."[40] Singing the hymns of Zion together had a unifying magic over the Saints. Long idle hours gliding across the Atlantic could become but moments of rejoicing when heart and voice found expression through song.

HYGIENE AND ORDER

Latter-day Saint company voyages were also known for their exemplary hygiene and order. Robert Reid, a Mormon passenger on the 1843 voyage of the *Swanton* described the condition of the ship:

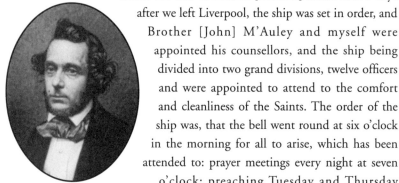

We had on board between two and three hundred passengers, under the care of brother [Lorenzo] Snow. A few days after we left Liverpool, the ship was set in order, and Brother [John] M'Auley and myself were appointed his counsellors, and the ship being divided into two grand divisions, twelve officers and were appointed to attend to the comfort and cleanliness of the Saints. The order of the ship was, that the bell went round at six o'clock in the morning for all to arise, which has been attended to: prayer meetings every night at seven o'clock; preaching Tuesday and Thursday nights, and twice on Sunday, with the church meeting in the afternoon.[41]

LORENZO SNOW

This exceptional organization was recognized by both Latter-day Saints and gentile passengers. In fact, a decade later (1854), the Liverpool emigration agent (Elder Stephen Richards) was questioned by the British House of Commons concerning the superior way in which the Latter-day Saints transported their people across the Atlantic. As a result of the interview, it was acknowledged in their records that the Mormons were capable of crossing the Atlantic in the most economical, and surest way.[42]

OBSTACLES ON THE ATLANTIC

In spite of their superior emigration system, these Latter-day Saint converts encountered the same obstacles that other immigrants faced, which included a long voyage across the treacherous Atlantic and the ever-present probability of seasickness. James Palmer, who voyaged in 1842 on the *Hanover* recalled how the sea suddenly changed its motion: "This company left the dock singing and rejoicing . . . and shortly the passengers became sick and all their mirth was turned into sadness."[43]

1842 PASSENGER ACT

Although seasickness could not be avoided for the most part, the general conditions of sea-bound passengers were slightly improved with the 1842 Passenger Act. This act came as a result of parliamen-

STORM AT SEA.

tary recommendations based on suggestions made the previous year by the Colonial Land and Emigration Commission. Their objective was fourfold:

> 1st. To regulate the number of emigrants conveyed in the different vessels, and to provide for their proper accommodations on board; 2ndly. To ensure a proper supply of provisions and water; 3rdly. To provide for the seaworthiness of the vessels; and, 4thly, to afford the poorer class of emigrants protection from the numerous frauds practiced upon them before they leave this country; to provide for their being carried to their stipulated destination; and to secure them a reasonable time for making arrangements before they are landed from the ship.[44]

This new and improved British law stipulated the following requirements:

> Each passenger to be given weekly seven pounds of bread, biscuit, flour, oatmeal, or rice, or the equivalent in potatoes. This was to be supplied uncooked, and was intended as no more than

an insurance against starvation. Passengers were expected to
bring their own sea-store [and the Mormons certainly did!].

Emigrants to be paid 1s. [shilling] a day subsistence money if the
vessel did not sail on the date stipulated on the contract ticket.

Passenger brokers and agents to be licensed.
Only three steerage passengers to be carried for each five tons of
the vessel's registered tonnage. Each passenger to have at least ten
square feet of space between decks.

Two children under fourteen to count as one statute passenger.
Children under one year not to be counted at all.

Drinking water to be carried in sweet containers [three quarts of
fresh water per passenger for each day].

Spirits to be neither sold nor drunk on board, on pain of a fine
of up to £100.

At those ports where emigration officers were stationed, they and
not the customs officers were responsible for carrying the Act into
effect—for inspecting water and provisions, assessing the seaworthiness of the vessel, and prosecuting for breaches of the Act.[45]
In addition, Jay Ray Davis notes that each passenger was allowed
a berth that could not be less than six feet long and eighteen inches
wide. Vessels were inspected for seaworthiness; two to four life boats
were required. Passage brokers also had to be licensed, and passengers
were to be issued money receipts.
Davis observes, however, that the commissioners' goals fell short of the
legislative expectations: "The statutory space requirements were not very
commodious. Required provisioning was monotonous and inadequate.
Steerage passengers needed lifeboats in the event of trouble as much as did
cabin passengers. Doctors could have helped in cases of injuries or disease.
Nothing was said about personal security, light, or ventilation."[46]
Therefore, most emigrants, including the Latter-day Saints, still
had some personal concerns over lodging conditions, provisions,

deadly disease,[47] and severe angry storms which affected them in a variety of ways. Possibly these challenges were lessened in their minds as they recalled the inspiring accounts of the British pilgrims who had likewise left their homeland centuries before, viewing themselves as a covenant people with a determined eye of faith. Their distant voices seemed to cry, "May not, and ought not, the children of these fathers right[l]y say, Our fathers were Englishmen, which came over this vast ocean, and were ready to perish, . . . but they cried unto the Lord, and he heard their voice, and . . . hath delivered them."[48]

DELIVERANCE AT SEA

Returning home from his mission to Great Britain with a shipload of converts, Woodruff noted on 28 April 1841, "This was a day that caused many mixed sensations of pleasure & pain graudeur & solemnity hope & fear to many." Elder Woodruff described "a great Storm & tempest which scenery I have not language to describe. . . . The raging of the tempest & the wonders of the deep & the movements of the ship which was the greatest seenery I ever beheld upon the water."[49] Sometimes the Atlantic tempests required great faith to control. Mary Ann Weston Maughan, who crossed the Atlantic in 1841, recalled one memorable storm:

MARY ANN WESTON
MAUGHAN

> When near the banks of Newfoundland we had a dreadful storm. Our Main Mast broke off below deck, and the jib boom also broke, and as it came round on deck struck a sailor on his head nearly killing him. They carried him below and he was kindly nursed by his comrads the Captain was very kind to him. It was a close call, but he got well in time. This was the only Accident we had on Board our ship during this dreadful Storm. The Captains stood on deck day and night with his Glass, for a Pilot Boat at length one answered our signal. They were two young men. The Captain Engaged one of them, and the other went away in his little boat and was soon out of sight soon after our Mast broak a young man in our Company took off his shoes and went on deck

going to the fore part of the ship he raised his right hand to
Heaven and in the name of Jesus Christ rebuked the Wind and
the Waves and Prophesied that the storm should abate and the
good ship *Harmony* [italics added] would carry her load of Saints
in safety to their destination and this came true for we all landed
safe in Quebeck.[50]

The same year these British Saints were miraculously delivered,
the *Millennial Star* published an article entitled "Narrow Escape."
This article noted that whereas two hundred Saints under the direction of Elder Hiram Clark arrived successfully (aboard the *Sheffield*),
another vessel had embarked from England the same month, named
the *Governor Fenner* and had collided with a steamer in the Irish
Channel. One hundred and twenty-two lives were lost. One elderly
man named Whitehead informed the British Mission office that he
would have been aboard the lost vessel, but instead had converted to
the Latter-day Saints Church and decided to go with Elder Clark on
the *Sheffield*, and thus his life was spared.[51]

In a letter to her homeland, Ann Pitchforth also reported her
lively Atlantic crossing in 1845, including what she perceived to be
divine intervention:

To be short, the Lord opened my way [to go to Nauvoo], I knew
beforehand by prophesy that it would be so. I sailed in the ship
Palmyra [italics added], and left a kind father and friends. When the
farewell hymn was sung on ship board, I felt what it was to leave all
for the truth; I had before gone through much persecution as many
of you know. Unkindness in all its forms I could cheerfully bear,
but to leave a kind and aged parent was almost more than I could
endure. Well did St. John say, "These are they who have come
through great tribulation,"&c. We had soon something else to
think of than farewells, friends, or any thing else, for the winds
arose, and our fears with them; wave dashed on wave, and storm on
storm, every hour increasing; all unsecured boxes, tins, bottles,
pans, &c., danced in wild confusion, cracking, clashing, jumbling,
rolling, while the vessel pitched, and tossed, and bounced till people
flew out of their berths on the floor, while others held on with diffi-

culty; thus we continued for eight days—no fires made—nothing cooked—biscuits and cold water; the waves dashed down the hold into the interior of the vessel, hatchway then closed, all in utter darkness and terror, not knowing whether the vessel was sinking or not; none could tell—all prayed—an awful silence prevailed— sharks and sins presenting themselves, and doubts and fears; one awful hour after another passing, we found we were not yet drowned; some took courage and lit the lamps; we met in prayer, we pleaded the promises of our God—faith prevailed; the winds abated, the sky cleared, the fires were again lit, then the luxury of a cup of tea and a little gruel. Oh! how ungrateful are we for our mercies, because they are so common. We soon sailed joyfully and pleasantly along, rescued a sinking vessel with nine human beings from a watery grave; they had been seventeen days up to their waists in water, sleeping by turns, held up by the others. Oh! we wept for joy to be the means of saving them, remembering our own perilous condition. We arrived at New Orleans. The sight of land caused every face to smile, though on a foreign shore.[52]

These captivating accounts demonstrate the ability of foreign converts to overcome the danger of angry storms through their collective faith. At the same time such experiences serve as a reminder of God's power over the deep. As the psalmist wrote:

They that go down to the sea in ships, that do the business in great waters; These see the works of the LORD, and his wonders in the deep. For he commandeth, and raiseth the stormy wind, which lifteth up the waves thereof. They mount up to the heaven, they go down again to the depths: their soul is melted because of trouble. They reel to and fro, and stagger like a drunken man, and are at their wits' end. Then they cry unto the LORD in their trouble, and he bringeth them out of their distresses. He maketh the storm a calm, so that the waves thereof are still. Then are they glad because they be quiet; so he bringeth them unto their desired haven. Oh that *men* would praise the LORD *for* his goodness, and *for* his wonderful works to the children of men! (Ps. 107:23–31).

HUMAN TEMPESTS

Aside from the frequent brooding of raging winds and angry sea, the potential human tempests often threatened each vessel as well. During an Atlantic storm on the 1841 voyage of the *Rochester,* it was observed that a cook had his hands full fighting with the Irish.[53] Enclosing several different nationalities in tight quarters under adverse conditions for an extended period of time was a dynamite formula with a very short fuse.

The human element often created a perilous condition for others. Alexander Neibaur wrote that the captain of the 1841 voyage of the *Sheffield* told his Latter-day Saints passengers that the ship was in a state of mutiny when one of his crew threatened him.[54] William Clayton observed human nature often overrides professed beliefs when, on board the 1840 voyage of the *North America,* he described that "some are not saints who profess to be."[55] He further related the challenge the brethren had of keeping female Church members away from the sailors. Surely those indiscretions were two-sided. The crew greatly resented such interference from the Latter-day Saints men.[56]

Despite these examples, most voyages ran fairly smoothly and generally the captains and crew looked upon transporting Mormons favorably. Upon reaching the port of New Orleans in 1844, William Kay, Latter-day Saints company leader on the *Fanny,* shared similar feelings in reporting his voyage: "I believe no people that ever crossed the Atlantic ever had a more prosperous voyage. . . . such a captain and crew for kindness I believe could scarcely be met with; his liberality exceeds all that ever came under our notice; indeed I am at a loss for words to express the respect he has manifested to all."[57]

WILLIAM KAY

RECREATION AT SEA

Some captains even took time to play with the children. Mary Haskin Parker Richards recalled her 1840 voyage on the *Alliance*: "Our Captain was an American. and was very kind. to us. He would often bring a cuple of Chairs out of the Cabin' for Ann' and me' to sat on. in the Portch of the Cabin door. and would then give each of us a rope from the Mast wich stood in front of us' to ballance ourselfs by. and would then Ask us if we ever enjoyed a nicer Rocking then we was then taking."[58]

While on the 1842 voyage of the *Sidney*, George Cannon described the comradery:

Perhaps a more agreeable ship's company, both of the Saints and seamen, never crossed the Atlantic. The Captain and officers are kind and humane men, and so far from disputes or hard feelings that the sailors say they never saw a family who agreed better: and they wonder how a company of people who were many of them strangers to each other can bear and forbear in the manner they do. One of the sailors, an intelligent man, told me that he had been in the passenger line of shipping for years and never saw anything like it: in general the Captain kept his distance and did not allow of freedoms from the passengers; but here he allowed them every indulgence, took pleasure in having the children round him on the quarter-deck and would play with them as if they were his own. May the Lord bless him for his kindness![59]

MARY HASKIN PARKER RICHARDS

The adults also allowed time for recreation with singing, dancing, and by other means. On the 1841 voyage of the *Rochester*, Apostles Orson Pratt, Heber C. Kimball, and Wilford Woodruff made time to try their hand at climbing the rigging and, though inexperienced, they seemed to have "known the ropes."[60] Woodruff, an avid fisherman, took time to observe marine life on several occasions. On 5 May 1841 he wrote, "We saw a large School of porposes." Two weeks later he recorded, "Saw a school of Mackerel." A few days later he penned, "We saw 50 fishing smack waiting for bait."[61]

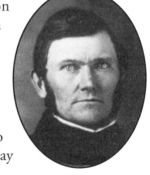

WILFORD WOODRUFF

FISHERS OF MEN

Occasionally there was even time to be engaged as fishers of men. Opportunities to preach to fellow passengers occurred when chartered Latter-day Saint voyages lacked the numbers needed to reach the full capacity of the ship and so various non-Latter-day Saints passengers were allowed to fill the vacancies. Immigrant accounts also provide evidence of blessings given to Saints and non-Mormons alike while crossing the Atlantic. In 1843, Elder Lorenzo Snow blessed the steward of the *Swanton*, who was at death's door. His miraculous recovery led to the conversion of several others, including the first mate.[62]

NOTES TO CHAPTER THREE

1. W. W. Phelps, "My Native Land, Farewell," in Kate B. Carter, comp., *Heart Throbs of the West,* 12 vols. (Salt Lake City: Daughters of Utah Pioneers, 1943), 4:153.

2. Wilbur S. Shepperson, "The Place of Mormons in the Religious Emigration of Britain, 1840–1860," *Utah Historical Quarterly* 20, no. 3 (July 1952): 207–209.

3. Maurine Carr Ward, ed., *Winter Quarters: The 1846–1848 Life Writings of Mary Haskin Parker Richards* (Logan: Utah State University Press, 1996), 60.

4. Thomas Callister, Collection HDA, fd. 1,1.

5. Kate B. Carter, comp., *Our Pioneer Heritage* (Salt Lake City: Daughters of Utah Pioneers, 1973), 16:505.

6. Priscilla Staines, in Edward W. Tullidge, *The Women of Mormondom* (1877; reprint, Salt Lake City: n.p., 1975), 288.

7. Robert Pixton, *Autobiography of Robert Pixton* HDA, 19.

8. John Q. Cannon, *George Cannon: The Immigrant: Isle of Man, 1794–St. Louis, U.S.A., 1844* (Salt Lake City: privately printed, 1927), 110.

9. Robert Crookston, *Autobiography of Robert Crookston* HDA, 5. Note that Babylon, once a cosmopolitan city in the ancient world, became a symbol to Latter-day Saints for the world and worldly influence. See for example D&C 1:16.

10. Over 80 percent of all Latter-day Saint immigrant voyages to America in the nineteenth century embarked from Liverpool.

11. Conway B. Sonne, "Liverpool and the Mormon Emigration" (paper presented at the Mormon History Association Conference, Liverpool, England, 10

July 1987), 4–5.

12. Herman Melville, *Redburn: His First Voyage* (Boston: St. Boltolph Society, 1924), 160–161.

13. Terry Coleman, *Passage to America: A History of Emigrants from Great Britain and Ireland to America in the Mid-Nineteenth Century* (London: Hutchinson of London, 1972), 65, explains that Hawthorne received his appointment from President Franklin Pierce, for whom he wrote a campaign biography. In his introduction to *The English Notebooks* by Nathaniel Hawthorne, (New York: Modern Language Association of America, 1941), ix-x, Randall Stewart explains that during these four years, the only literary work Hawthorne was engaged in was his journal, which comprised more than 300,000 words. Hawthorne once remarked that this journal was written "with so free and truth-telling a pen that I never shall dare to publish it." However, he finally consented to have his journals published sometime after the year 1900. Stewart also observes (in his preface to *The English Notebooks)* the singular nature of Hawthorne's private writings, noting that "the English notebooks are an important contribution to the comparative study of the English and the American modes of life. No other American man of letters has studied the respective characteristics of the two countries so painstakingly."

14. Coleman, *Passage to America,* 65–66.

15. Hawthorne, *English Notebooks,* 18.

16. Terry Coleman, *Going to America* (New York: Pantheon Books, 1972), 67–68.

17. "Epistle of the Twelve," *Millennial Star* 1, no. 12 (April 1841): 311.

18. "Information to Emigrants," *Millennial Star* 2, no. 4 (August 1841): 61.

19. *Millennial Star* 4, no. 1 (May 1843): 16.

20. "Emigration," *Millennial Star* 4, no. 4 (August 1843): 63–64.

21. *Millennial Star* 5, no. 1 (June 1844): 13.

22. *Millennial Star* 5, no. 1 (June 1844): 13. In another article titled "Emigration," *Millennial Star* 4, no. 10 (February 1844): 159, there was another reminder concerning "not omitting the names of the infants, as both the laws of England and America count by souls or heads, and very unpleasant circumstances have arisen sometimes through the neglect of not sending the names of the infants."

23. The British Mission Manuscript History, 16 January 1844 HDA, cited in Philip A.M. Taylor, "Mormons and Gentiles on the Atlantic," *Utah Historical Quarterly* 24, no. 3 (July 1956): 204.

24. Parley P. Pratt, "Prospectus" *Millennial Star* 1, no. 1 (May 1840): 5–6.

25. *Millennial Star* 1, no. 1 (May 1840): 4–8. Alan K. Parrish, "Beginnings of

the Millennial Star: Journal of the Mission to Great Britain," in *Regional Studies in Latter-day Saint Church History: British Isles,* ed. Donald Q. Cannon, (Provo, Utah: Department of Church History and Doctrine, Brigham Young University, 1990), 133, notes that the *Millennial Star* was "published as a monthly, biweekly, or weekly publication for 130 years, . . . the longest continuous publication in the history of the Church, terminating in 1970, along with *The Improvement Era, The Instructor,* and *The Relief Society Magazine.*" It is also of interest to note that the name of the periodical certainly fits the scriptural theme contained in the Doctrine and Covenants 29:8, wherein it is stated that one purpose of gathering the faithful to one place is "to prepare their hearts and be prepared in all things against the day when tribulation and desolation are sent forth upon the wicked."

26. "Prospectus," *Millennial Star* 1, no. 1 (May 1840): 5–6.

27. "Information to Emigrants" *Millennial Star* 2, no. 4 (August 1841): 60.

28. Ibid., 60–61.

29. Andrew Jenson, "Church Emigration," *Contributor* 12, no.12 (October 1891): 441. While my research generally parallels that of Jenson's, a notable exception is that while he lists only one Latter-day Saints voyage from Bristol in 1841, there were in fact three voyages. Jenson accurately lists 181 Saints who embarked from Bristol on what he refers to as an unnamed ship in February 1841. This ship was the *Caroline*. It is also probable that the *Caroline* brought another group of about 100 Saints in August of the same year. The ship *Harmony* also carried a group of approximately 50 Saints across the Atlantic in 1841. The 1846 unknown voyage Jenson notes may be the *Windsor Castle*, which embarked from Liverpool on 17 February 1846. See Appendix A for further details.

30. James Linforth, ed., *Route from Liverpool to Great Salt Lake Valley,* 1.

31. Jenson, "Church Emigration," 441. M. Hamblin Cannon, "Migration of English Mormons to America," *American Historical Review* 52, (October 1946–July 1947): 441, maintains that from 1840–1846, 4,733 British Saints gathered to Nauvoo from the 16,241 people who were baptized into the Latter-day Saints Church from the British Mission. The number of emigrants can be broken down by years as follows: 240 (1840); 1,135 (1841); 1,614 (1842); 769 (1843); 623 (1844); 302 (1845) and 50 (1846). See also Richard L. Evans, *A Century of "Mormonism" in Great Britain* (Salt Lake City: Publisher's Press, 1937), 243–245. Mormon immigration historian Richard L. Jensen, "Transplanted to Zion: The Impact of British Latter-day Saint Immigration on Nauvoo," *BYU Studies* 31, no. 1 (Winter 1991): 77–78, estimates that between 1840–1846 there were at least 4,600 Latter-day Saints immigrants, and that 90 percent of them gathered to Nauvoo before the

martyrdom of Joseph and Hyrum Smith on 27 June 1844. Linforth, *Route From Liverpool*, 14–16, estimates that there were 4,750. Wilbur S. Shepperson, "The Place of the Mormons in the Religious Emigration of Britain, 1840–1860," *Utah Historical Quarterly* 20, no. 3 (July 1952): 214, estimates that the figure is about 5,000. However, Shepperson cites *The Potters' Examiner and Workman's Advocate*, 1, no. 8 (20 January 1844): 64, as evidence that these numbers are questionable as "emigration letters often directed friends to come with the Latter-day Saints as the cheapest and most satisfactory means of traveling."

32. Allen and Leonard, *Story of the Latter-day Saints*, 2d ed., 160. Probably following the research of M. Hamblin Cannon above, these authors also accept the figure of 4,733 British Saints who gathered to Nauvoo before the exile, which thus boosted the population over 25 percent. Susan Easton Black, "New Insights Replace Old Traditions: Membership of the Church in Nauvoo, 1839–1846" (paper presented at the Brigham Young University symposium "Nauvoo, the City of Joseph," Provo, Utah, 21 September 1989), 1–2, indicates that 26 percent of the Latter-day Saints Church membership from 1830–1848 originated in England.

33. As noted above, the names of the ships which voyaged from Bristol, England, to Quebec were the *Caroline* (embarking February 1841), a second voyage on the *Caroline* (8 August 1841), and the *Harmony* (10 May 1841).

34. The names of the three ships debarking in New York were the *Britannia* (41 Saints, departing 6 June 1840), the *North America* (201 Saints, departing 8 September 1840) and the *Rochester* (130 Saints, departing 21 April 1841). These three combined voyages brought a total of 372 Saints.

35. Of the thirteen voyages which did not travel with an Latter-day Saints company, twelve disembarked in New Orleans and one in Philadelphia. In 1845, the Forsyth family of four voyaged on the *Susquehanna* before making their way up the Delaware to Philadelphia. See Grace Meldrum Smith, comp., John Irwin Forsyth, typescript (story adapted from the original manuscript "Life of John Irwin Forsyth" written by Jane Barker Forsyth Snyder, "Life of John Irwin Forsyth," the original manuscript with additional research by Mary E. Forsyth and Mildred A. Mercer [DUP Archives, Salt Lake City], and material taken from personal research done by Lily Meldrum Marchant and Grace Meldrum Smith), p. 1.

36. *HC* 4:230.

37. "Epistle of the Twelve," *Millennial Star* 1, no. 12 (April 1841): 311.

38. J. Riley, "Poetry, on Emigration," *Millennial Star* 2, no. 10 (February 1842): 160.

39. "The Metoka," *Millennial Star* 4, no. 5 (September 1843): 80.

40. Ann Pitchforth, "To the Saints in the Isle of Man," *Millennial Star* 8, no. 1 (15 July 1846): 12.

41. Robert Reid, "Letter from Robert Reid," *Millennial Star* 4, no. 1 (May 1843): 15.

42. Linforth, *Route from Liverpool,* 18.

43. James Palmer, Reminiscences of James Palmer HDA, 63

44. Colonial Land and Emigration Commissioners, *Report on Necessity of Amending the Passenger's Act* (22 July 1841), 3, cited in Ray Jay Davis, "Law and the Nineteenth-Century British Mormon Migration," in *Mormons in Early Victorian Britain,* ed. Richard L. Jensen and Malcolm R. Thorp (Salt Lake City: University of Utah Press, 1989), 245.

45. Coleman, *Passage to America,* 288. Davis, "Law and British Mormon Migration," 246, informs us that the law could not be properly enforced as only one officer and an assistant were stationed at Liverpool.

46. Davis, "Law and British Mormon Migration," 246.

47. There were only 25 total deaths mentioned out of 90 first-person Latter-day Saints immigrant accounts examined during the Nauvoo years. By comparison, there were an estimated 670 Mormon deaths between 1847–1869 crossing the oceans. See "I Have A Question," response by Susan Easton Black, et al., including Fred E. Woods, *Ensign,* July 1998, 41.

48. "Modern Representatives of Ancient Families," *Utah Genealogical and Historical Magazine* 25 (1934): 103.

49. Scott G. Kenney, ed., *Wilford Woodruff's Journal,* 1833–1898, typescript (Midvale, Utah: Signature Books: 1983), p. 2, 94–95.

50. Mary Ann Weston Maughan, *Journal and Autobiography of Mary Ann Weston Maughan,* HDA, 16.

51. Parley P. Pratt, "Narrow Escape," *Millennial Star* 2, no. 2 (June 1841): 23. It is also of interest to note that over 500 voyages with Latter-day Saints aboard all safely crossed the Atlantic between 1840–1890. This is in sharp contrast to the fact that at least 59 immigrant vessels sunk between 1847–1853 which were not carrying companies of Saints. However, on the Pacific, there was one known accident. The *Julia Ann* wrecked in 1855, with 28 Mormons among her 56 passengers. Of those 28, only 5 were drowned, while the remainder spent two months on an uninhabited island until they were rescued. See Conway B. Sonne, *Saints on the Seas: A Maritime History of Mormon Migration, 1830–1890,* 138; John Devitry-Smith, "The Wreck of the Julia Ann," *BYU Studies* 29, no. 2 (Spring 1989):5–29.

52. Pitchforth, "To the Saints in the Isle of Man," 12–13.

53. Kenney, *Wilford Woodruff's Journal,* 2:98.

54. Alexander Neibaur, *Journal of Alexander Neibaur,* L. Tom Perry Special Collections Library, Harold B. Lee Library, Brigham Young University, Provo, Utah, 6.

55. William Clayton, *Journal of William Clayton,* HDA, 77.

56. Ibid., 78–79.

57. William Kay, "Extract of a Letter from Elder William Kay," *Millennial Star* 4, no. 12 (April 1844), 202.

58. Ward, *Life Writings of Mary Haskin Parker Richards,* 61.

59. John Q. Cannon, *George Cannon, the Immigrant,* 111–112.

60. Kenney, *Wilford Woodruff's Journal,* 2: 99.

61. Ibid; 2:97, 100–101.

62. Jenson, "Church Emigration," 447. See also Lorenzo Snow, *Journal of Lorenzo Snow,* HDA, 82–83. The first mate was Louis Gaulter. For his own recounting of his conversion see *Journal of History,* (RLDS, now Community of Christ), 10, no. 3 (July 1917): 328–329.

CHAPTER FOUR

Up the Mississippi

"The voyage on the Mississippi is more dangerous than a passage on the ocean."
—MICHAEL CHEVALIER, FRENCH TRAVELER

THE SANDBAR

As the seagoing Saints concluded the Atlantic leg of their voyages and entered the Gulf Coast region, they were confronted with the obstacle of crossing the sandbar at the mouth of Old Man River. This was the point at which the mighty Mississippi emptied into the vast ocean. Considerable effort was required to pull the sailing vessels over this stretch of sandbar to the deeper, free flowing waters of the river. Patience was required for this venture, and some made better use of their time than others. The 1842 Latter-day Saints voyages of the *Sidney* and the *Medford* were each stuck on the bar at the mouth of the Mississippi for nearly a day and a half.[1] Much to the delight of the Saints on board the *Sidney*, Alexander Wright made the best of the situation by catching enough catfish for all who desired them.[2]

ALEXANDER WRIGHT

THE BALIZE

Some Saints had terrible misfortunes awaiting assistance over the sandbar. The challenge of crossing the sandbar in this region was remedied by steam-powered tugboats, which pulled the sea vessels across the bar and towed them about one hundred miles into port. The tugboats were manned by pilots who resided at what was referred to as the Balize. A. A. Conway describes this uninviting habitation that the Mormons were subjected to as they entered America in the early 1840s:

> The Balize, as it was known, where the pilot stations were established was little more than a mud bank situated a short distance above the North East Pass. One such station contained sixteen or eighteen houses built upon piles in the midst of the morass. The houses were connected one with the other by raised walks or bridges, laid on the mud, constructed of timber, logs and wrecks of vessels. The pilots at each station were mostly ex-merchantmen, chiefly English with some Americans, French and Spaniards. The monotonous existence at these stations resulted in the deterioration of the conduct of their inhabitants and they became notorious for the frequent occurrences of riots and brawls.[3]

Once a sufficient number of ships had gathered at the mouth of the river a towboat would pull six ships at a time upstream. The standard procedure was to join one ship on either side of the towboat and pull four behind. This allowed easy communication from one ship to another.[4] James Palmer, who voyaged on the ship *Hanover* in 1842, described this process.

> The first mate was on the look out for land and soon discovered from the main gallant topsail, that we are sailing directly towards the mouth of the Mississippi river shortly we saw a vessel approaching from our left, that came from Germany and a steam tug came booming over the bar to meet us thay threw their large cables and made fast to our ship and soon we ware anchored safely in the mouth of that king of all rivers, and soon our German friends were made fast along side and we were booming up towards New Orleans.[5]

In 1842 the notorious Captain Pierce commanded the *Henry*. The first two or three weeks after leaving Liverpool he was quite kind to company leader John Snyder and the 157 Saints under his leadership. After those weeks, however, he abused and insulted the Saints in every possible way. On several occasions contention arose between Elder Snyder and him. Captain Pierce swore he would keep the Saints on board until they starved to death.

True to his threat, when they reached the Balize he kept the Saints on ship for six miserable days. His only aim seemed to be to provoke his passengers as much as possible. A boarding officer at the Balize named Captain Taylor was waved down by Captain Pierce and boarded the ship. Pierce then produced the logbook in which he had recorded charges of mutiny against Elder Snyder and James Morgan.[6] According to a report of this incident from the *Liverpool Mercury*, Captain Pierce informed the boarding officer that, "the passengers were then, and had been, in a state of mutiny, from the time they were three days out from Liverpool."[7] Captain Taylor was then obliged to take these two men prisoners and lead them ashore. Fortunately, they were soon released and able to continue their journey with the Saints.[8]

JOHN SNYDER [SNIDER] (ON FAR LEFT) AND FAMILY

THE RIVER TRIP

Eager to position their feet on solid ground after more than two months on board, the immigrants were no doubt jubilant about the hundred-mile river trip from the mouth of the Mississippi to New Orleans. Each nautical mile north took them further away from the distastefulness of the Balize and closer to the metropolis of New Orleans where they could at last disembark from their sailing vessels and board a steamboat for St. Louis.

Mormon immigrants were delighted with the favorable change in scenery along the river banks. George Whitaker, who voyaged on the *Palmyra* in 1845, noted the panoramic views along the lush banks of this stretch of the river leading to New Orleans. He described the beautiful banks of the river: "I thought I never saw anything so beautiful as the sights going up the river. This was in the beginning of March. Everything looked fresh and green—the oranges were hanging on trees. I thought I would very much like to live there."[9]

CHARLES SMITH

DOCKING AT NEW ORLEANS

Arriving at any North American port was a shared relief to all seagoing Saints after the long voyage. At the conclusion of more than two months with a company of Saints aboard the *Swanton* (1843), Charles Smith remembered docking at New Orleans, "I seemed quite rejoicing to think that we were once more on land."[10] New Orleans was established as the principal port of arrival during the Nauvoo period and remained so until the spring of 1855.[11] All but nine voyages during this fifteen-year period arrived at New Orleans, which accounted for about eighteen thousand Saints.

During the sailing era of the 1840s, the voyages from Liverpool to New York averaged about five weeks. Sailing to the port of New Orleans took an average of nineteen days longer.[12] Why would anyone choose New Orleans over New York or a closer port? One, traveling through New Orleans was less expensive, and two, New Orleans provided convenient access to the Mississippi River which provided a direct route to Nauvoo.[13] Later, with the exile from Nauvoo in 1846 and the problems with yellow fever and cholera on the Mississippi, the Saints were rerouted to ports on the East Coast.[14]

FINANCING TRAVEL

Throughout the Nauvoo era, some immigrant Saints who had arrived in New Orleans were delayed in their travels to Nauvoo due to economic challenges. Others were detoured because of the negative

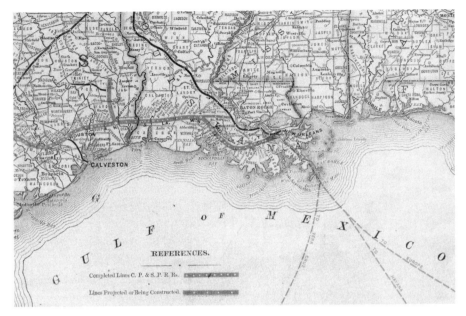

NEW ORLEANS, AT THE MOUTH OF THE
MISSISSIPPI RIVER ON THE GULF OF MEXICO.

reports from disgruntled Nauvoo Saints. Arriving at New Orleans, George Whitaker noted:

> This was the first time I had set my foot on land for about seven or eight weeks. We stayed there one day. I sold some of my shawls and got a good price for them. We met some of our brethren from Nauvoo, who had come to work there through the winter. They did not give a very pleasing account of things at Nauvoo, which discouraged some few of the Saints, and they remained there.[15]

Many were not as fortunate as Whitaker in their economic circumstances and were forced to stay for a time in New Orleans or elsewhere along the river. The *Millennial Star* informed the seagoing Saints that it was better to reach the American shores (Zion), than to stay in Europe (Babylon) and that they should be content "to make their way by degrees."[16] One British convert was not content to remain temporarily at New Orleans. Arriving penniless with his family in the spring of 1843, George Spilsbury described his determined efforts to find immediate resources to bring his stranded family up the Mississippi to Nauvoo, despite the adverse conditions he faced:

> We were in a strange land and in a hot place and with no money to buy our provisions nor to pay our fare on the steamboat. My wife wept like a child at our humiliating circumstances. Nevertheless I did not feel discouraged. Another ship load of Latter-day Saints arrived on the morrow after us, and I went on board and found a man going to Nauvoo. I borrowed the money from him to pay our fare by giving him my clothes for security. Thomas Bullock loaned us money to bring our provisions to Nauvoo. So by hard struggling and the blessing of the Lord I accomplished the desire of my heart in getting to Nauvoo and seeing the Prophet of the Lord and shaking hands with the man who had seen God face to face.[17]

GEORGE SPILSBURY

NEW ORLEANS

The detriment of insufficient funds was not unique to Latter-day Saint immigration through New Orleans, or any other port for that matter. A. A. Conway explains the three options that presented themselves to immigrants disembarking at New Orleans:

> If he possessed sufficient money to pay his passage upstream, he could immediately tranship himself with his luggage to a river steamboat and continue his journey inland. If he had insufficient funds to pay his passage, he could take a position at New Orleans until such time as he had accumulated sufficient money to defray the cost of transportation upstream. If he landed destitute, there was no alternative, but to look for employment and to trust to charity to support him in the meantime.[18]

LAND SHARKS

In addition to the financial concern of securing enough money for the passage, there was also a continual threat of land sharks (river thieves) who waited to rob gullible immigrants as they passed into the Crescent City which was, at this time, the fourth largest city in America. When Mormon emigration commenced from Liverpool to New Orleans in 1840 there was little protection offered the immigrants once they reached the United States ports. As Ray Jay Davis notes, "At that time no federal legislation regulated immigration into the United States. Consequently, the only restriction upon entrance into the country was one enacted by the Louisiana legislature. An 1842 law assessed a head tax of $2 each upon passengers coming from foreign ports. The proceeds supported operations of the charity hospital of the City of New Orleans."[19]

Security generally did not pose a problem when Latter-day Saint emigrants departed from Liverpool due to the careful protection and direction of Church agents. However, Church agents were not assigned to New Orleans during the Nauvoo period. Lucius Scovil, the first Latter-day Saints agent assigned to New Orleans described the problems the Saints faced there in 1848, which were no doubt magnified without Mormon agents during the early 1840s. Scovil provides a colorful account of the river thieves' tactics at New Orleans:

Yesterday, I fell in with one of those sharks, his name is Cook, and the head one of a company of ten in number, who are engaged in taking out permits and re-shipping passengers. They speak five or six languages, and are determined to monopolize the business. . . . they would send some person . . . on board to make confusion . . . bringing bills from some boat, and saying that they were captain or clerk of said boat, and would carry them for one dollar to St. Louis. . . . On this account the last company had to stop here six days, just because they were bamboozled by these runners. I consider that there is but one way to do business for the best good of the Saints, and that it is for one person to do all of the business, and the rest remember the Mormon Creed. Those sharpers are threatening me all the time, but I do not fear them. I am satisfied that the church has not known the extent of their speculations from them, and yet were soaping them all the while.[20]

Lucius N. Scovil

SLAVERY

Just as travelers secure souvenirs and mementoes along their trip, so the immigrants gathered experiences and impressions that shaped their ideologies and perspectives during the course of their journey. Slavery was one grave reality that demanded reckoning with. Alfred Cordon, arriving in the Delta City in November 1842, remembered, "There were a many slaves working in the streets chained together both men and women."[21] Depending on their initial exposure to slavery, the Saints did not always develop the same perspective of this institution. The reaction of William Staines, who immigrated to Nauvoo at age twenty-four in the spring of 1843, is especially noteworthy. Orson F. Whitney explains:

When about nine years of age he had been informed that these [American] slaves all worked in chains upon rice and sugar plantations in the Southern States. His sympathies were so aroused by the woeful tale that he refrained from eating sugar in order that the money thus saved might go to a fund that was being raised in England for the emancipation of slaves in America. Concerning his observations at New Orleans and along the Mississippi, he says: "Here to my surprise I found them driving fine mule teams, being trusted with cartloads of valuable merchandise, taking the same to all parts of the city and country, apparently equal with the free white man, except in being slaves and owned by someone. I found them working as porters, warehousemen, firemen on steamboats, etc., and their food was as good as that of white men performing like labor. I must confess that this surprised me, and for the first time I regretted that I had quit eating sugar to help to free the negro. I found him in slavery having all the sugar he needed and with a better breakfast than any farm laborer in England could afford to eat."[22]

For others, slavery did not appear as sweet as Staines here implies. Another Latter-day Saint who later passed through the region of New Orleans summarized her experience of watching hundreds of sun-baked Negroes on plantations by simply stating, "Oh! Slavery, How I hate Thee!"[23] This reaction was probably more common for most passing Mormon immigrants. Even though Staines succumbed to sugar, he was not relieved of his repugnant feelings towards the institution of slavery in general.[24]

RIVER TOWNS

As they steamed up the Mississippi, Latter-day Saints immigrants met another new adventure. On 1 April 1842, Alexander Neibaur described the Saints boarding the steamboat *Moravian* for Quincy, Illinois, and provided a vivid portrait of life along the river towns. Neibaur described Natchez as "a neat town" where they stopped to take wood for fuel. Vicksburg he portrayed as "an imposing town built upon rising ground; court house built upon a hill. Numerous turtles upon the shore." Memphis was "a neat little place on a hill." However, a change in daylight and weather conditions could produce a drastically different observation. Neibaur's description illustrates:

At midnight it thundered and the lightning illuminating the objects around us for many a mile. At the same time a terrific storm shook the boat, the captain and his men being frightened out of their wits, sparks of fire flying about in the steerage. Many of the passengers were awakened by the fear of fire. The captain gave orders to stop the engine and make for the land until daylight appeared, the cooks window being blown out of the kitchen. It was terrifying. Broke all the windows in the tophouse (wheel house).[25]

Mormon migrants did not hold a monopoly on recording impressions. Several newspaper articles articulated the local opinions regarding these maritime Mormons. One local newspaper, under the caption "Fresh Emigrants," published a positive view of this load of Saints as they arrived at St. Louis:

The emigrants by the *Moravian* [italics added], of whom we spoke yesterday, are not all of them Mormons, though such as not avowedly so, belong to families, the heads of which belong to the sect of the religionists. They are chiefly from Lancashire.

VICKSBURG.

Few of them are advanced in years, but such as are look hale and hearty. There are among them ninety children under 14 years of age. The females are comely—and some of them handsome and delicate, reminding us of the stories told of the "Lancashire witches," who are now-a-days

MEMPHIS.

St. Louis.

understood to be simply beautiful women. They are all excellent
health; and have not lost only two of their number on the passage—
(children) whose loss was repaired by as many accessions in the usual
way. They have an honest as well as a healthy look;—and they go
where we hope they will preserve their health and their morals.[26]

Unfortunately, the tide of favorable opinion from the river towns
often transformed to swells of prejudice. At times the Mormon immi-
grants had to reckon with a thunderous hatred directed against them.
Certainly this was the case two years later when they steamed up the
Mississippi on the Church-owned steamboat *Maid of Iowa*.[27] William
Adams describes the following vivid experience he encountered
March of 1844:

> We were very much anoyed, also persecuted in towns along the
> River. News went ahead that a Boat filled with Mormons were
> on their way to Nauvoo necessity caused the Boat to land to get
> supplys. Men would rush on to the Boat calling us foul names.
> "Joes Rats" was a common salutation we received. Natches, a

town on the east side of the River set the Boat on fire. It was not
discovered to [till] we had lef the place over half an hour and the
side of the Boat was a blaze also several Beds and bedding. The
fire was extenguished in a short time with the loss of several
feather Beds and bedding it was a narrow escape for the screw
[crew] and passengers also the Boat.[28]

Priscilla Staines explained that the fire was started by "some villain
[who] placed a half consumed cigar under a straw mattress."[29] She
also recalled the following incident, which soon followed.

At another landing a mob collected and began throwing stones
through the cabin windows, smashing the glass and sash, and
jeopardizing the lives of the passengers. This was a little too
much for human forbearance. The boat was in command of the
famous Mormon captain, Dan Jones; his Welsh blood was now
throughly warm; he knew what mobs meant. Mustering the
brethren, with determined wrath he ordered them to parade with
loaded muskets on the side of the boat assailed. Then he
informed the mob that if they did not instantly desist, he would
shoot them down like so many dogs; and like so many dogs they
slunk away.[30]

CAPTAIN DAN JONES

William Adams, a second witness to this
episode adds the following:

Another town that we landed late in the evening
Captain Jones ordered that no Person be allowed
aboard the Boat but men came rushing aboard
and would not be held back. Br. James Haslem
went on the herricon [hurricane] deck and fired off
a gun in hope it would be a warning to the mob that
we would not be run over by them, but in
quelling them they ran for firearms and fired off
several shots. Things looked serious Steam was got up as speedily
as possible and the Boat was shoved off and they landed three
miles up the River and lay over till the next morning, but we were

NATCHEZ.

not molested. . . . I will state one incident where the company was in eminent danger of looseing their lives and sinking the Boat, [which] also shows their hadred against the Latter-day Saints. The lower Mississippi had quite a number of First class steamboats running between St. Lewis and New Orleans that made the round Trip every week each time they passed the *Maid of Iowa* [italics added] we would have a grand salute by cheering and laughing and calling us bad names. One of those Boats I forget her name tried to run us down and would if Captain Jones had not been on the Herricon [hurricane] Deck as he was always on duty, made them shear off by hollowing and threating to shoot the Pilot this took place at night when the Company were in there Beds.[31]

PERILS OF RIVER TRAVEL

In addition to these challenges, there were the normal obstacles of river travel, including sandbars, snags, currents, and ice. One early French traveler named Chevalier noted such obstacles: "The voyage on the Mississippi is more dangerous than a passage across the ocean. . . . In the former, you are exposed to the risks of explosions, and of fire, and in ascending, to that of running against snags and planters . . . the danger of your boat falling afoul of another, running in an opposite direction in a fog, to say nothing of the inconvenience of getting aground on sand-bars."[32]

Mormon immigrants from the 1842 voyages of the *Medford* and the *Sidney* took the steamboat *Alex Scott* upriver and ran aground and were therefore stuck for three weeks ninety miles below St. Louis, because the water was so low. By the time they got to St. Louis, the river had frozen over, and here they had to spend the winter of 1843.[33] However, evidence reveals that they did not all cluster together in the city of St. Louis, but migrated to different pockets of the St. Louis region. For example, David Candland, one of the passengers on the *Medford*, spent the winter with a portion of his

company across from St. Louis on the Illinois side of the Mississippi. He wrote, "We had a good passage, and arrived Safe in New Orleans. Left thence in a steamer for St. Louis called 'Alex Scott' and located ourselves at Alton about 25 miles above St. Louis for the winter in consequence of severe weather."[34]

Another Latter-day Saint company that crossed the Atlantic a month later on the *Emerald* was detained in the river cities of Alton, Chester, and St. Louis for three cold winter

DAVID CANDLAND

THE GRAND TURK.

months due to the ice on the Mississippi.[35] Parley P. Pratt, the company leader of the *Emerald,* decided against St. Louis on the following grounds: "I landed with my family in Chester, Illinois—eighty miles below St. Louis. The company continued on to St. Louis. My reason for landing here was, that I would not venture into Missouri after the abuses I had experienced there in former times."[36] Who would blame Pratt for such a decision, as he had spent over eight miserable months locked up in Missouri jails![37]

PARLEY P. PRATT

ST. LOUIS DELAYS

A major factor for migrant Saints' delays in St. Louis was lack of finances. This was the case with Latter-day Saint converts aboard the 1844 voyage of the *Norfolk.*[38] At this time, St. Louis was a place that most Nauvoo-bound immigrating Saints wanted to pass through in a hurry. Cholera or yellow fever, was an ever-present threat, and the hardness in the hearts of the St. Louis apostates seemed to be as cold as the winter ice on the Mississippi.[39] Such hardness sometimes influenced the Mormon immigrants on their way to Nauvoo. Hiram Clark, who gathered to Zion with a group of 181 Saints in 1841, noted that about 30 of his group had been "disaffected through false reports" and therefore chose to tarry at St. Louis.[40]

Thomas Wrigley, who gathered to Nauvoo in 1843 to prepare the way for his British family, received opposition on two fronts. When he visited his sister's family, who were not members of the Church, he related that "they tried their best by every means to persuade me to give up my faith."[41] When he returned to St. Louis the following year to bring his family up the Mississippi he was delayed there for a season. He described the dark conditions then present in the city:

> We for some time felt afraid of the exterminating orders of Governor Boggs, which were still in force, but our numbers began to increase in that city and we took courage and a few met in a private house and organized a branch of the Church and the Lord blest the faithful but it was sometimes hard work having to

contend with the prejudice of the people of the world and every apostate that left Nauvoo came there and did their best to bring persecution on us.[42]

Joseph Fielding, company leader for more than two hundred Saints on the 1841 *Tyrian* voyage, summarized in a letter his view on the apostate spirit in St. Louis as follows:

At St. Louis we found a number of Saints, at least who have a name among the Saints, some of these prove a trial to those who call there. They tell you many evil tales; I wish they would stop all who are like themselves. The faithful need not be troubled at them; let them talk and have all they can get, they seem afraid to suffer affliction with the people of God, and so go to Missouri, where there are none, thinking also to get a little more money.[43]

In his journal, Fielding added: "Here we saw some poor, faithless Saints something like spiders webs set to catch flies they came to us with fair Words as our best Friends, but their counsel was that of Enemies, but did not prevail to stay any of our Company except two."[44]

JOSEPH FIELDING

THE NAUVOO RECEPTION

It was the stalwart Saints who were able to withstand the numerous bombardments of deceptions and discouragement encountered at St. Louis. Their determined spirit urged them on to their desired haven in Nauvoo. One can hardly imagine the inexpressible relief and joy which greeted the weary travelers as they at last set foot in their much-anticipated Zion. After crossing the Atlantic on the *Metoka* in 1843 and finally reaching Nauvoo that fall, William Rowley described the pleasant surprise he found there:

You may suppose we were most pleasingly surprised, after having had our ears continually assailed with the doleful accounts of "the wretchedness of the place," its "log and mud" built "cabins," its "knee deep" muddy streets, the "poverty and starvation" that awaited us, the "villainy and roguery" of its inhabitants, the "awful delusion of Mormonism," "beware of old Joe Smith," and a thousand other such like salutations; you may judge then, how much we were gratified at beholding the striking contrast, while gazing with rapturous delight, first upon the "Temple," which already assumes a lofty bearing from the commanding eminence on which it is being erected; then the "Nauvoo House;" the "Mansion House," (the residence of him of whom the world is not worthy); the Masonic, Music, and public halls; some completed, and others are being so, besides numerous well-built and substantial brick stores, and private dwellings. The whole site and aspect of the city, presenting a most cheering picture of the enterprise and industry of its inhabitants, exhibiting a remarkable difference to many of the western towns which we passed in coming up the Mississippi, of far longer standing and origin.[45]

The Saints were greeted not only with the makings of a beautiful city, but also with the outstretched arms of the Nauvoo brethren who seem to have soothed the wounds of immigrating. Hiram Clark, who gathered in 1841, was grateful for the reception he received, which no doubt illuminated his night voyage: "We landed at Nauvoo on the 18th of April, about eleven o'clock in the evening, yet many of the brethren stood on the shore to welcome us on our arrival."[46]

HIRAM CLARK

Another example of a warm welcome is found in a letter to the *Millennial Star* wherein Heber C. Kimball relates the reception that the Twelve and over a hundred immigrating Saints received the summer of 1841: "We landed in Nauvoo on the 1st of July, and when we struck the dock I think there were about three hundred Saints there to meet us, and a greater manifestation of love and gladness I never saw before. President Smith was the first one that caught us by the hand."[47]

The Nauvoo residents anticipated newly arriving converts as parents would welcome a long-since departed child. James Burgess, who left Liverpool for Nauvoo in the fall of 1842, remembered, "When our boat arrived at the city [Nauvoo] there were hundreds to welcome us."[48] As new converts to a religion which claimed to be a restoration of God's ancient covenant church complete with apostles and prophets, the thrill of being greeted by the Prophet Joseph Smith must have been over-whelming. Robert Crookston testified, "As we approached the landing place to our great joy we saw the Prophet Joseph Smith there to welcome his people who had come so far. We were all so glad to see him and set our feet upon the promised land so to speak. It was the most thrilling experience of my life for I know that he was a Prophet of the Lord."[49]

JOSEPH SMITH JR.

The Prophet himself described what it was like for him to greet a boatload of Saints who had crossed the Atlantic on the *Emerald*.

> I was present at the landing and the first on board the steamer, when I met Sister Mary Ann Pratt (who had been in England with Brother Parley,) and her little daughter, only three or four days old. I could not refrain from shedding tears.

> So many of my friends and acquaintances arriving in one day kept me very busy receiving their congratulations and answering their questions. I was rejoiced to meet them in such good health and fine spirits; for they were equal to any that had ever come to Nauvoo.[50]

The *Maid of Iowa* also ferried other Saints up the Mississippi who had crossed the Atlantic on the *Fanny* in 1844. When this group of British converts reached the shores of Nauvoo, many recorded their endearing first encounters with the Prophet Joseph Smith. William Adams recalled the exquisite joy of being greeted by Joseph and Hyrum Smith along with two hundred Nauvoo Saints.[51] Priscilla Staines, a fellow passenger, felt that notwithstanding the masses who had assembled to greet the incoming Saints, she would be able to recognize the Prophet Joseph Smith. Staines remembered: "I felt impressed by the spirit that I should know him. As we neared the pier the prophet was standing among the crowd. At the moment, however, I recognized him according to the impression, and pointed him out."[52] Thomas Steed said he recognized the prophet by his "noble expression." He recorded, "The Prophet Joseph Smith was at the pier. At first glance I could tell it was him. . . . He came on board to shake hands and welcome us by many encouraging words, and express his thankfulness that we had arrived in safety."[53] It appears there were no published photographs of the Prophet available to these converts, therefore it makes these experiences all the more significant. British convert

THOMAS STEED

Christopher Layton remembered this day as a day of rejoicing. He described, "There stood our Prophet on the banks of the river to welcome us! As he heartily grasped our hands, the fervently spoken words 'God bless you,' sank deep into our hearts, giving us a feeling of peace such as we had never known before."[54]

After being torn from kindred and homeland, having sailed thousands of watery miles and possibly losing a family member, British Saints saw the Prophet for the first time. There he stood, before their faces—the noble embodiment of their faith. The Spirit bore witness to his holy calling as God's prophet and seer to all the world. Joseph Smith succored these weary Saints and greeted them with the warmest possible affections.

CHRISTOPHER LAYTON

Having their faith strengthened and the desire of their hearts realized, they were now ready to meet the challenges and trials which would confront them during the Nauvoo era.

LANDING NEAR NAUVOO HOUSE.

NOTES TO CHAPTER FOUR

1. Andrew Jenson, "Church Emigration," *Contributor* 12, no. 12 (October 1891): 445.

2. Alexander Wright, *Journal of Alexander Wright*: March 1839–January 1843, HDA, 398-399.

3. A. A. Conway, "New Orleans as a Port of Immigration, 1820–1860" (master's thesis, University of London, 1949), 79. The earliest mention of the Balize occurs in a letter by Phineas H. Young in *Journal History of the Church of Jesus Christ of Latter-day Saints,* hereafter cited as *Journal History,* (14 December 1842), 2, wherein Young describes the arrest of John Snyder by the boarding officer at the Balize. As previously noted, Snyder was the Latter-day Saints company leader of the ship *Henry,* which came into port in New Orleans in 1842. A year later, Thomas Bullock, who voyaged on the *Yorkshire,* indicates that he came in sight of the Balize on 8 May 1843 in 27th Quorum 70's Record, *Autobiography of Thomas Bullock,* HDA, 14.

4. Conway, "New Orleans as a Port of Immigration," 79–80.

5. James Palmer, Reminiscences of James Palmer, HDA, 66. See also Richard

Rushton, *Journal of Richard Rushton,* HDA, 10–11, who relates how in this same year, another group of immigrating Saints aboard the ship *Hope* were towed with another vessel up the Mississippi.

6. Alfred Cordon, Reminiscences and Journal of Alfred Cordon HDA, 162–163.

7. "Mormon Mutiny," *Liverpool Mercury* 32, no. 1650 (23 December 1842): 2.

8. John Snyder was a Canadian convert who was one of the first seven Latter-day Saints missionaries to serve a mission in Great Britain.

9. George Whitaker, *Autobiography of George Whitaker,* HDA, 7.

10. Charles Smith, *Reminiscences and Diary of Charles Smith* HDA, 11.

11. For an excellent article on the Mormon episode in New Orleans during this era, see David Buice, "When the Saints Came Marching In: The Mormon Experience in Antebellum New Orleans, 1840–1855," *Louisiana History* 23, no. 3 (Summer 1982): 221–237.

12. Conway B. Sonne, *Saints on the Seas: A Maritime History of Mormon Migration,* 1830–1890 (Salt Lake City: University of Utah Press, 1983), 69.

13. Church leaders issued an epistle to the British Saints on 15 November 1841, directing them when immigrating to the United States to use the port of New Orleans, rather than Montreal, New York, or Philadelphia, because it was the least expensive and also afforded convenience for water travel to Nauvoo, cited in *Journal History* 15 November 1841, 3. Several years later, Latter-day Saints Liverpool emigration agent Reuben Hedlock again reminded the Saints that fares to the East-Coast ports were higher than fares to New Orleans. See "Conferences," *Millennial Star* 5, no. 10 (March 1845): 155.

14. In a letter from Brigham Young to Franklin D. Richards dated 2 August 1854, "Foreign Correspondence," *Millennial Star* 16, no. 43 (October 1854): 684, Brother Brigham stated, "You are aware of the sickness liable to assail our unacclimated brethren on the Mississippi river, hence I wish you to ship no more to New Orleans, but ship to Philadelphia, Boston, and New York, giving preference in the order named." However, again for economic reasons, the port of New York became the primary port on the East Coast until the close of the nineteenth century.

15. Whitaker, *Autobiography of George Whitaker,* 7.

16. Editorial, *Millennial Star* 5, no. 3 (August 1844): 46.

17. Viva Skousen Brown, ed. and comp., *The Life and Posterity of Alma Platte Spilsbury* (Provo, Utah: privately printed, 1983), 40.

18. Conway, "New Orleans as a Port of Immigration," 98–99.

19. Colonial Land and Emigration Commission, *Report on Necessity of*

Amending the Passenger's Act (22 July 1841), 3, cited in Ray Jay Davis, "Law and the Nineteenth-Century British Mormon Migration," *Mormons in Early Victorian Britain,* ed. Richard L. Jensen and Malcolm R. Thorp (Salt Lake City: University of Utah Press, 1989), 247.

20. Lucius N. Scovil, "Letters to the Editor," *Millennial Star* 11, no. 5 (1 March 1849): 72.

21. Alfred Cordon, *Reminiscences and Journal of Alfred Cordon,* HDA, 165.

22. Orson F. Whitney, *History of Utah* (Salt Lake City: George Q. Cannon and Sons Co., 1904), 4:117.

23. Jean Rio Griffiths Baker, *Diary of Jean Rio Griffiths Baker,* transcript, HDA, p. 9. Griffiths voyaged to America on the *George W. Bourne* in 1851.

24. Whitney, *History of Utah,* 4:117.

25. Alexander Neibaur, *Journal of Alexander Neibaur,* typescript, L. Tom Perry Special Collections Library, Harold B. Lee Library, Brigham Young University, Provo, Utah, p. 9–10.

26. "Fresh Emigrants," *Quincy Whig* 3, no. 52 (24 April 1841): 1, cited in Newbern Issac Butt, comp., 4 vols., Mormons in Ohio, Illinois, Missouri, etc. Newspaper clippings, 1831–1848, typescript, Americana Collection, L. Tom Perry Special Collections Library, Harold B. Lee Library, Brigham Young University, Provo, Utah, p. 1: 205.

27. For an excellent article on this topic see Donald L. Enders, "The Steamboat *Maid of Iowa:* Mormon Mistress of the Mississippi," *BYU Studies* 19, no. 3 (Spring 1979): 321–335.

28. Williams Adams, *Autobiography of William Adams,* typescript, HDA, p. 4.

29. Priscilla Staines, in Edward W. Tullidge, *The Women of Mormondom* (1877; reprint, Salt Lake City: n.p., 1975), 289. Staines thought the town was Memphis instead of Natchez, yet according to Samuel Cummings's early river guide, the *Western Pilot* (Cincinnati: N and G Guilford and Co., 1834), 108, Natchez seems more likely to be the place of this foul event. Although Cummings describes Natchez as the largest town in Mississippi and "romantically situated on a very high bluff," he acknowledges a much darker picture in the lower part of the city known as "under the hill," where the river business was transacted. Cummings noted that it was "a repulsive place, being the resort of all that is vile from the upper and lower country. Great number of boats are always lying here, and the place is filled with boatmen, mulattoes, houses of ill fame, and their wretched tents–and too often the scene of drunkenness and debauchery."

30. Priscilla Staines, in Edward W. Tullidge, *The Women of Mormondom,* 290–291.

31. Adams, *Autobiography of William Adams,* p. 4.

32. George W. Givens, *In Old Nauvoo: Everyday Life in the City of Joseph* (Salt Lake City: Deseret Book Co., 1990), 37.

33. Jenson, "Church Emigration," 445–446.

34. David Candland, *Journal of David Candland,* typescript, HDA, p. 1.

35. Jenson, "Church Emigration," 446.

36. Parley P. Pratt, *Autobiography of Parley P. Pratt* (Salt Lake City: Deseret Book Co., 1985), 285.

37. Parley P. Pratt, *Autobiography of Parley Parker Pratt* (Salt Lake City: Deseret Book Co., 1980), 189, 246. Page 189 notes that Elder Pratt was first arrested on 31 October 1838. Having spent months in the Richmond jail, he spent additional time incarcerated in Columbia and was not released until 4 July 1839 (p. 246).

38. Jenson, "Church Immigration," 450. Matthias Cowley indicated that the previous year his father James was offered ten dollars per day to stay and work in St. Louis. His father emphatically said "No!" He added, "I started from home to go to Nauvoo, to see the Prophet of the Lord, Joseph Smith, and I'm going, bless your souls. I would not stop here for all of St. Louis." Matthias Cowley, *Reminiscences of Matthias Cowley,* typescript, HDA, p. 1.

39. However, Stanley B. Kimball, "The Saints and St. Louis, 1831–1857: An Oasis of Tolerance and Security," *BYU Studies* 13, no. 4 (Summer 1973): 489–519, presents a broader picture of St. Louis in recounting how this city was used as a Mormon refuge, despite the 1838 extermination order by the governor of Missouri. He also points out that many Saints fled to St. Louis following the Nauvoo exile (1846) and demonstrates how this inland city was an important stop for poor Mormon immigrants who, after receiving needed employment, continued their journey on the Missouri River from 1846–1855 to the West.

40. Hiram Clark, "Extract from Elder Hiram Clark's Journal, and Address to the Saints in the British Islands," *Millennial Star* 4, no. 10 (February 1844): 147.

41. Thomas Wrigley, in Kate B. Carter, comp., *Our Pioneer Heritage* (Salt Lake City: Daughters of Utah Pioneers, 1962), 5:496.

42. Ibid., 497.

43. Joseph Fielding, "Joseph Fielding's Letter," *Millennial Star* 3, no. 4 (August 1842): 77.

44. Joseph Fielding, *Journals of Joseph Fielding,* HDA, 5:2–3.

45. W. Rowley, "Letter from W. Rowley," *Millennial Star* 4, no. 12 (25 January 1844): 193.

46. Clark, "Extract from Elder Hiram Clark's Journal," 147.

47. Orson F. Whitney, *Life of Heber C. Kimball: An Apostle—The Father and Founder of the British Mission,* 9th ed. (Salt Lake City: Bookcraft, 1979), 313.

48. James Burgess, *Journal of James Burgess,* HDA, 65.

49. Robert Crookston, *Autobiography of Robert Crookston,* typescript, HDA, p. 6.

50. HC 5:354.

51. Adams, *Autobiography of William Adams,* p. 4.

52. Priscilla Staines, in Edward W. Tullidge, *The Women of Mormondom,* 291.

53. Thomas Steed, *The Life of Thomas Steed from His Own Diary, 1826–1910,* (n.p.: privately printed, 1935), 8.

54. Myron W. McIntyre and Noel R. Barton, eds. *Christopher Layton* (n.p.: Christopher Layton Family, 1966), 11.

VIEW OF NAUVOO FROM BLUFF PARK.

CHAPTER FIVE

Assimilation and Beautification

*"We would wish the Saints to understand that, when they
come here, they must not expect perfection."*
—JOSEPH SMITH JR.

Just before stepping onto the covenant land of America, Puritan
leader John Winthrop told his congregation while still aboard the
ship *Arbella*, "Wee must be knitt together in this worke as one man."
He urged, "Wee must entertaine each other in brotherly affeccion,
wee must be willing to abridge our selues [selves] of our superfluities,
for the supply of others necessities . . . alwayes haueing [having]
before our eyes our Commission and Community in the worke."[1]

Two centuries later these same words applied beautifully to the
diverse conglomeration of Saints stepping onto the covenant land of
Nauvoo. The unity required for the task of erecting a temple and a
city would also require a test of faith. Many centuries earlier, ancient
Israel had also been cautioned, "God did not choose the people for
the lands sake, but the place for the peoples sake" (2 Macc. 5:19). For
many covenant Saints, Nauvoo proved to be a testing ground.

TEMPORARY LODGINGS

Most British converts had been forewarned of the harsh realities
awaiting them at the new covenant city of Nauvoo. For example, in a
Millennial Star editorial entitled, "Information to Emigrants," it was

clear what the foreign converts should expect with regard to temporary lodging:

> When emigrants arrive in Nauvoo they must expect to undergo many inconveniences: they cannot expect to rent houses and enter at once on a comfortable living, but must pitch their tents, and build themselves temporary cottages. About 30 or 40 yards of calico will make a very good tent, and the value of four or six week's work, with little or no expense, will erect a small cottage, which the new settlers in that country consider both comfortable and respectable.[2]

Arriving at Nauvoo with his family on 3 November 1843, Benjamin Ashby recalled, "My father and Bro. John Grag rented a room in a stone house near the landing, for a few days and then we moved into a log house belonging to Joseph B. Noble where we lived until our house was finished, which we occupied about the last of January."[3] Other immigrants stayed in a structure that came to be known as "Widow's Row."

WIDOW'S ROW, WHERE LDS MIGRANTS TEMPORARILY LODGED.

HELPFUL NEWS TO BRITISH EMIGRANTS

The previous year, Francis Moon, one of the first British converts to voyage to Zion on the *Britannia,* frankly apprised his fellow countrymen through a letter published in the *Millennial Star* regarding the American costs, employment opportunities, and wages. In this letter published February 1841, Moon also made suggestions as to how conditions might be improved:

> Some may want to know the price of things. A man that works on the farms is paid a dollar per day or something equal to it, 100 cents make one dollar, and 5 dollars one English pound. If a man be employed in digging potatoes, he receives one-fifth of what he digs, if he goes to cutting corn he receives one-eighth; for making a pair of boots (and the maker does not find leather) they give about a dollar and-a-half. A pig a month or five weeks old is sold for 25 cents—a good cow about 14 dollars. Flour is about 4 dollars and fifty cents per barrel, a barrel weighs 196 lb., potatoes are sold for 20 cents per bushel, good beef is sold for 3 cents per lb., pork at the same; butter at about 10 to 14 cents, sugar at 12 cents per lb. If any one is disposed to keep a cow (and but few are without two or three) they may keep them free of expense, by sending them out to graze on the neighbouring plains, and for the winter's keep they are at liberty to cut as much grass as they please. But after all this it is a new country, we have no factory as yet, but we want means to build corn mills, and not having much machinery we have to do at home what would be done at factories if we had them. What we want is some persons with property for to raise these places, and then men to work them, and then the clothing would be at a less rate, and we English would feel more at home.[4]

DISAPPOINTMENTS AND CAUTIONS

The following month the *Millennial Star* republished an epistle that first appeared in the *Times and Seasons,* entitled, "A Proclamation of the First Presidency of the Church to the Saints Scattered Abroad, Greetings." Among other things it explained that Nauvoo was a Hebrew word that signified "a beautiful situation, or place, carrying with it, also, the idea of *rest*; and is truly descriptive of this most delightful situation," in spite of its reputation for sickness.[5] This letter continued with a caution:

> We would wish the Saints to understand that, when they come here, *they must not expect perfection,* [italics added for emphasis] or that all will be harmony, peace, and love; if they indulge these ideas, they will undoubtedly be deceived, for here there are persons, not only from different states, but from different nations, who, although they feel a great attachment to the cause of truth, have their prejudices of education, and consequently it requires some time before these things can be overcome: again, there are many that creep in unawares, and endeavor to sow discord, strife, and animosity in our midst, and by so doing, bring evil upon the Saints. . . . Therefore let those who come up to this place, be determined to keep the commandments of God, and not be discouraged by those things we have enumerated, and then they will be prospered, the intelligence of heaven will be communicated to them, and they will eventually see eye to eye, and rejoice in the full fruition of that glory, which is reserved for the righteous.[6]

As might be expected, some of the incoming Saints were disappointed by the undeveloped region of Hancock County (Nauvoo lay within this boundary), and some were hurt by the lack of charity from a few prejudiced Church members. Others were pressed by economic problems because their industrial trades were invalid there. To help remedy these concerns, Church leaders throughout the Nauvoo period encouraged the Saints who had means to provide newly arrived labouring migrants with employment opportunities by establishing factories in Nauvoo.

Cautions were provided by Church leaders to guide naive incoming converts eager to purchase land and gain employment. At a Nauvoo conference held 16 August 1841, the Saints sustained the proposal that an individual, "who shall hereafter be found trying to influence any emigrants belonging to the Church, either to buy of them (except provisions) or to sell to them (except the Church agents), shall be immediately tried for fellowship, and dealt with as offenders, and unless they repent shall be cut off from the Church."[7]

Less than two years later (13 April 1843), the Prophet Joseph Smith warned some incoming migrants that, "some of the early arrivals had been victimized by unscrupulous speculators who sold them lands with defective titles. If the emigrants traded or dealt with anyone other than the Church agents, the Church was helpless to do anything for them."[8]

A case that illustrates this risk is that of Hugh Moon. As previously mentioned, Moon and a part of his family left Liverpool on the first British immigrant voyage to America (6 June 1840). Apparently they could not afford to complete their trip to Nauvoo and therefore rented a house in the Pittsburgh region, not arriving at their final destination until the end of 1841. Upon arrival in Nauvoo, Moon entered into a property transaction with a gentile land speculator. He recorded, "December 9th—We came to Montrose to a log house owned by Bates Noble; Myself and my brother John, and three sisters—Hannah, Dorothy and Alice lived in Montrose for two or three years. We rented land of a man by the name of Kilburn."[9]

Warnings also came from family members who had previously immigrated. One Latter-day Saint migrant who wrote home to his British parents in the summer of 1843 reminded them that although they were coming to Zion, they would still need to labor diligently by the sweat of their brows. He warned they would have a difficult time finding employment in which wages were paid in cash. The letter mentioned, "He cultivates his own land and is then his own master, *but not without many pinches* in the time if he has a family."[10]

Further, one *Millennial Star* article entitled, "Advice to Emigrants" stated, "But let it ever be remembered that this is a new country, so that those who come to this place should not be surprised nor murmur if some of them should have to make brick; if some should have to quarry stone, and prepare and put them in their place. . . . In short every man must purpose in his mind whatever his hands find to do, to do it with all his might."[11]

Church leaders and members provided as much aid as possible to the incoming British Saints. But as James Linforth points out, "the continual law-suits which the Saints in Nauvoo were engaged in to

WATER STREET IN NAUVOO.

defend the Prophet Joseph; and the effects of speculation in land, by
some monied men from without, who bought lands at a low rate, and
sold them again at enormous prices, exhausted the pockets of the
Saints."[12] Later, economic stresses were compounded with the political turmoil which beset the Saints when they became a perceived
political and economic threat in their region.[13]

   Even with all these obstacles, most met and rose above these challenges. Writing home to the Saints in England, British immigrant
Joseph Fielding reported in January 1841 from Nauvoo that "some
Saints have died who came from England, and some have left the
faith, but not at all a great proportion of those that have come."[14]

NEGATIVE REPORTS
   A few Saints who gathered to Nauvoo apparently were not willing
to work to build the holy city and thus never discovered the Zion
which lay inside Nauvoo's borders nor within themselves. These few
found assimilation difficult, if not impossible. The *Quincy Whig*

reported, "We understand that great dissatisfaction exists at Nauvoo, amongst those who have lately arrived from England. It is said that many have determined to leave—and that letters have been sent to England, warning their friends, who had designed to emigrate, of the sad state of things in the City of the Church."[15]

In 1840, one of the first Latter-day Saint converts to emigrate from England to Nauvoo had predicted that such a thing would occur. He compared faithless converts who sent back derogatory reports of Nauvoo with the ancient Israelite spies who had returned negative reports of the promised land of Canaan. In a letter home to his fellow Saints came the warning: "You will be tried by the reports of those who have gone to behold the good land, some you will find who will speak evil of the place and all that appertain to it."[16]

Concerning these dissatisfied souls, a convert from Preston, Sister Melling, offered incisive insight as well as candid advice to her fellow British Saints in a letter she wrote back to her homeland: "In gathering to this land many shake out by the way, and others after they arrive. . . . Do not persuade any barren soul to come here—we want men of faith, who can sacrifice their all for Christ's sake and the Gospel's. . . . There are many fallen that came from England, and some will return, and spread all manner of evil. The reason is because they know neither the Father nor the Son."[17]

Gentiles also spread disparaging tales concerning Nauvoo which were circulated at home and abroad. One curious, non-Mormon British citizen named W. Aitken, of Ashton-under-Lyne, journeyed all the way from his homeland to spy out the land of Nauvoo and the covenant people, whom he assessed to be rather peculiar. Among other things, he described what he considered to be difficult living conditions for newly arrived British converts and admonished potential migrants "to avoid Nauvoo, as they would the city of a plague." Although he viewed Nauvoo through jaundiced eyes, his writings present a rare economic and cultural perspective from a British non-Mormon:

> We came to the English portion of the city, which consisted of huts of the meanest description; and in wet weather, the place must be a complete swamp.

Into one of these huts I entered with my companion, and inquired if any English people lived there; and a young man answered, "Yes, there's two here."

Two boxes, which contained their clothes and other things when they left home, were their sitting utensils; and a bed, perched upon some home-made bedsteads, of the rudest construction, with two tins and an iron pot, were all the visible household goods and gods. When we got in, the place was full, so its size may be judged of. Light was admitted at a home-made window frame, some hay supplying the place of glass in many of the quarrels.

The young man who sat upon the box had despair written in his countenance. His name was Greenhalgh—came originally from Bolton, and was by trade a turner and filer. He stated that there was no such thing as getting money for work done, the truck system being in full operation. He had been working three days for a man, and he wanted him to take shingles (wood used instead of slate for houses and cut into proper sizes) in return for his labour; but as he could neither eat them, nor sell them, he of course had not taken them. He had not seen a coin for five weeks, and wanted ill to get away if he knew how. The young gentleman who was with me stated that he was building some houses, and that if he was willing to labour at any thing he could do, he would give him a liberal allowance of wages to go with him, pay his fare in the cabin down to St. Louis, the expenses to be stopped out of his wages.

He seemed as glad as any culprit could do, when he is informed that his life will be spared.

A very nice looking woman came in during our controversy, and she had come from Bolton with her husband, deeply impregnated with doctrines of Mormonism; but the eden of the west had vanished into woe, want and misery. She stated that her husband was nothing behind with his tenths,— that is, he had worked regularly every tenth day at the temple and hotel [Nauvoo House]. Her husband had had a good situation at home and in St. Louis; but when in the latter place, they were afraid of giving offence to the church, and they had removed to the city, since which time they had never enjoyed any comfort.

Her husband and she lived in a hut similar to the one we were in; and she stated that if any one had told them it was such a place as it was, they would not have believed it.

They both gave Smith a good character; and stated that if those who had money amongst the church would do as he wanted them, the poor would be better off. She also complained of the operations of the truck system; and stated that her husband had been working for some man who gave him city scrip—a species of paper money—and that they had to pay an exorbitant per centage for all goods they got with it; and the same in all instances where truck was in existence.

We left these to go and see if we could not find some little oasis on which the eye could rest with pleasure, in this "holy city" of the west.

But the same appearances every where presented themselves— miserable huts, and tales of wretchedness from the inmates. The murmur of discontent arose from the dwellings; and the dissatis-fied, without money and spiritless, had no means to get away. But I appeal to the commonest comprehension, and ask what else could be the result of thousands coming suddenly into one place, destitute of capital themselves, and nearly all that went, similarly situated.

Let an emigration of that description take place in one of our towns, in which is an abundance of capital, and what would be the result? However well intentioned the inhabitants might be, it would be impossible to find them food and employment; and a great amount of misery must be the inevitable consequence.

> I would advise the individuals who are impregnated with the doctrines of Mormonism, if they have any respect for their comfort, to avoid Nauvoo, as they would the city of a plague.

> I went to see and judge for myself; and have written these pages to dispel the delusion under which I know too many are labouring.[18]

Despite this rather negative published account and other disparaging tales spread by various Saints and non-Mormons alike, the stream of migrants continued to flow. Notwithstanding the great distance of the emigrants' journeys, the costs of travel, and the discomforts and apparent moments of discontent, most converts at home and abroad considered the privilege of gathering to Zion priceless. Thousands of foreigners assembled in Nauvoo from 1840–1846, and they migrated to Utah by the tens of thousands through the remainder of the nineteenth century.[19] In a letter written in October 1840, Brigham Young informed his brother Joseph, "The Saints have got a start for to gether to America and goe they will, and nothing can stop them. . . . They have so much of the spirit of getherin that they would goe if they knew they would die as soon as they got there."[20] That is precisely what some of them did.

DEATH PLAGUES NAUVOO

Some of the adverse rumors were in fact grounded in legitimate concerns. Many deaths occurred from disease which continually plagued the gathered Saints, notably with their initial entrance onto this malaria-infested swampland. On reaching Nauvoo in the summer of 1839, Benjamin Johnson noted, "Nearly all were down with typhoid or malarial fever which it almost seemed would sweep the place with death, for among all the families of the saints it was rare to find one who was able to wait upon and care for another."[21]

Lorenzo Brown, who arrived with his family in Nauvoo, 6 June 1839, described this sickly season, which apparently was compounded

BENJAMIN F. JOHNSON

with the suffering previously inflicted by the Missouri exodus: "The Saints this season were inflicted a great deal with sickness occasioned by their previous hardships and exposures through which they had passed in Missouri. . . . People living in wagons and tents before they could build a log house would be taken sick and perhaps shake two or three months with ague or burn with fever."[22]

His father, Benjamin Brown, compared the suffering caused by the Missouri persecutions to the debilitating condition the Saints faced at this time in Nauvoo:

> Many of them were sick, and they had no house to enter when they arrived. The nature of the climate, combined with the hardships they had endured, soon made those ill who were not so previously. Numbers of the sick and dying had to lie on the ground, with only a blanket over them. No springs or wells were handy, and the Mississippi waters were unfit to drink, so that many had to go miles for water to give to the afflicted. Sometimes one would go on horseback with a jug, and fetch a little for the sick, and take it round to them. It was frequently declared that the persecutions in Missouri were small matters compared to the miseries endured at this period in Nauvoo.[23]

William Draper portrayed the horrifying appearance of the Commerce community when he attended a Church conference there, 6 October 1839: "I went and another such sight my eyes never beheld. That portion of the assembly that had lived in Commerce during the Summer looked more like ghosts that had neither flesh nor blood or but very little of both. Yet they seemed to be satisfied and glad to think they were able to attend conference."[24]

British convert Jacob Peart anguished in his sorrow after having family members stripped from his bosom due to a scourge which afflicted them shortly after arriving in Nauvoo in the spring of 1841. Three weeks after his arrival, his sickly wife passed away. Peart lamented, "My

JACOB PEART

oldest daughter, Ann, took sick about the time we landed in Nauvoo and died 5 days after her mother. My daughter Fanney, and youngest daughter, Marry died a short time after."[25]

One of the most heartrending situations which sometimes befell these vulnerable residents occurred when the entire family lay ill and their only nursing fell upon the shoulders of a sick child. Such was the dreadful fate of Mosiah Hancock:

We were so sick at times that we knew not what to do! Sometimes my parents were so ill they could hardly move, and I would take a quart cup and fill it with water from the spring that was about 60 yards from the house. Then, I being weak, would crawl on my arms and knees, and place the cup of water ahead of me and crawl to it each time I reached it, until I reached the house. Then because of father's feverish distress, I would usually give it to him. The water would disappear before anyone could get scarcely a taste, and looking at the heroic face of my mother, and the innocent face of my little sister Amy, I would repeat the pilgrimage until my knees and elbows would be worn near the bone![26]

MOSIAH L. HANCOCK

Mormon historian, H. Dean Garrett, explains that the bulk of such sickness was due to the swampy, unhealthy conditions caused by a combination of the river and the many streams and springs that flowed down from the bluffs. Even though the Saints dug a ditch for drainage, the threat of disease was not entirely removed. The mosquitoes continued to hover around Nauvoo, and malaria (referred to by the Nauvoo Saints as the "ague" or the "fever") persisted to plague the Saints throughout their stay. Such a bleak condition was sustained by the continual threat of other diseases incubated by the constant arrival of emigrants from Great Britain and from the States.[27] Two years after the Saints had arrived at Nauvoo (1841), and after hundreds of British converts had gathered, the malaria epidemic reached such proportions that it became expedient for Sidney Rigdon to preach a general funeral sermon instead of conducting individual funerals.[28]

ENVISIONING NAUVOO THE BEAUTIFUL

These harsh, sickly conditions appear to be precisely the reason why the Prophet Joseph chose the name Nauvoo, to emphasize the city's *envisioned* beauty. In an article first published in the *Times and Seasons* 15 January 1841 and reprinted for the British Saints in the *Millennial Star* two months later, the First Presidency issued a proclamation to the "Saints Scattered Abroad." In this treatise Joseph infused a spirit of encouragement to Nauvoo inhabitants and incoming migrants: "The name of our city (Nauvoo) is of Hebrew origin, and signifies a beautiful situation, or place, carrying with it, also, the idea of *rest*; and is truly descriptive of the most delightful situation. . . . This place has been objected to by some, on account of the sickness which has prevailed in the summer months."

Joseph further expressed his hope that the afflictions resulting from ague and fever could be "easily remedied by draining the sloughs on the adjacent islands in the Mississippi."[29] When John Butler first visited Commerce, he recalled, "I asked Brother Joseph what kind of a place it was. He said it was a low, marshy, wet, damp, and nasty place, but that if we went to work and improved it, it would become more healthy and the Lord would bless it for our sakes."[30]

Although such unfavorable conditions were for some a severe trial, they forged the character and beautified the inner nature of the Mormon converts. Furthermore, the word of the Lord provided consolation for those Saints who found Nauvoo to be a place of final rest for their loved ones: "Blessed is he that keepeth my commandments, whether in life or in death; and he that is faithful in tribulation, the reward of the same is greater in the kingdom of heaven. . . . For after much tribulation come the blessings" (D&C 58:2,4). The Lord would later reveal, "My people must be tried in all things, that they may be prepared to receive the glory that I have for them, even the glory of Zion" (D&C 136:31).

Eventually conditions in Nauvoo began to improve. William Cahoon observed shortly after his move to Nauvoo in the spring of 1842, "The Saints began to gather from all parts of the world and from the surrounding States in great numbers. Houses began to be built in all directions and the city of Nauvoo constantly increased in number and enlarged her boundaries and under the wisdom and direction of God's Prophet Joseph Smith, Zion was greatly blessed."[31]

TRANSITION INTO NAUVOO SOCIETY

Some, as previously noted, discovered the beauty of Zion immediately upon their arrival as they were warmly welcomed by the hospitality of Church leaders and fellow Saints. One who gathered with his family from England was Alexander Neibaur, who, upon reaching Nauvoo noted, "A number of the Br. [brethren] was ready to receive us; they kindly offered their houses, many slept in a large stone building belonging to one of the Br. . . . [A] number of the Br. came to Inquire whether all of us had obtained habitations. We got in very comfortably with a Br."[32] Such brotherly love, especially at a time of transition, helped newly arriving immigrants forget the trials of the journey.

ALEXANDER NEIBAUR
(LOWER LEFT) AND SONS.

Neibaur's intellectual assets aided his transition into Nauvoo society. As the first male Jewish convert to Mormonism, a sketch of his assimilation into Nauvoo culture is certainly warranted. A few months after he arrived in Nauvoo, a Nauvoo newspaper published by the Church, the *Times and Seasons,* announced the formal opening of his dental practice and noted the kindness of Brigham Young in allowing Alexander to open up a business from Young's home:

ALEXANDER NEIBAUR, SURGEON DENTIST, From Berlin, in Prussia, late of Liverpool and Preston, England. Most respectfully announces to the ladies and gentlemen and the citizens of Nauvoo as also of Hancock county, in general, that he has permanently established himself in the city of Nauvoo, as a dentist, where he may be consulted, daily, in all branches connected with his profession, Teeth cleaned, plugged, filed, the Scurva effectually cured, children's teeth regulated, natural or artificial teeth from a single tooth to a whole set inserted on the most approved principle. Mr. N. having had an extensive practice both on the continent of Europe, as also in England, for the last 15 years, he hopes to give general satisfaction to all those who will honor him with their patronage.

Mr. B.[Brigham] Young having known Mr. N. (in England) has kindly consented to offer me his house to meet those ladies and gentlemen who wish to consult me. Hours of attendance from 10 o'clock in the morning to 6 at evening. . . .

Charges strictly moderate.[33]

In addition to his professional skills, there is also evidence that Neibaur's linguistic talents facilitated his assimilation into the Latter-day Saints community. Neibaur's diary mentions that he read German with Joseph Smith at the Smith home.[34] The writings of Joseph Smith also acknowledge Neibaur's aid in helping the Prophet learn German. Joseph writes under the date of 18 March 1844, "I stayed at home to recite German with Brother Neibaur."[35] In a similar entry dated 3 June 1844, Joseph recorded, "At 5 p.m. I read German with Alexander Neibaur."[36]

Dr. Neibaur was not only fluent in German and English, but was also familiar with Latin, Greek, French, Spanish, and Hebrew. There is evidence from the personal writings of the Prophet Joseph Smith that Neibaur also tutored him in the Hebrew language. On 23 May 1844, Joseph noted, "Read Hebrew with Neibaur."[37] In an autobiographical sketch, Neibaur wrote, "In the fall of 1843, had the honor of instructing the Prophet Joseph Smith, until he went to Carthage, in German and Hebrew, from which text he preached several times to large congregations."[38]

While Alexander Neibaur tutored the Prophet in languages, he also humbly received instruction from him. One especially rare and precious diary entry records Joseph Smith relating his 1820 "first vision" experience to Neibaur shortly before the Prophet's martyrdom. According to Mormon historian James B. Allen, "this is the only contemporary diary known to Mormon scholars that contains such an account."[39] Among other things, Neibaur recalled that Joseph said he went "into the woods to pray, kneels himself down . . . saw a fire toward heaven came near & nearer; saw a personage in the fire, light complexion, blue eyes, a piece of white cloth drawn over his shoulders, his right arm bear; after a while a other person came to the side of the first."[40] It speaks volumes of the Prophet Joseph's relationship of respect and trust with Alexander Neibaur that he was willing to share intimate details of this sacred experience with him.

ASSIMILATION THROUGH TEMPLE CONSTRUCTION

Assimilation of British and American culture was greatly enhanced by the cooperative effort required to build the Nauvoo Temple. The walls of prejudice and cultural misunderstandings crumbled as the Saints sweated side-by-side to raise the walls of the temple. The unity necessary in a Zion community was forged as these Saints gave their best efforts in the construction. While the First Presidency did not expect immediate perfection from the Saints who gathered to Nauvoo, they did require unity, sacrifice, and a very concerted effort to serve one another and build the city, especially the temple. One letter from the First Presidency admonished the following:

> In order to erect the Temple of the Lord, great exertions will be required on the part of the Saints, so that they may build a house which shall be accepted by the Almighty, and in which His power and glory shall be manifested. Therefore let those who can freely make a sacrifice of their time, their talents, and their property, for the prosperity of the kingdom, and for the love they have to the cause of truth, bid adieu to their homes and pleasant places of abode, and unite with us in the great work of the last days, and share in the tribulation, that they may ultimately share in the glory and triumph.[41]

Like Neibaur, those who had aptitude towards specialty skills assimilated more quickly into the Nauvoo community. If an individual

Nauvoo , Illinois. Temple on the Hill ca. 1846.

coupled his useful discipline with a disposition of consecration and sacrifice, the formula almost certainly ensured successful assimilation. One such man was William Player, a dedicated British proselyte who came to Zion wholly determined to participate in the temple construction. Player was an expert stonecutter who immigrated to Nauvoo by June 1842. He was immediately appointed principal stone setter and worked diligently until the last stone was laid. Noted for his dedication, he continued to labor on the temple walls in spite of harsh, winter weather and sickness in which he nearly lost the use of his limbs.[42]

Another British convert, Charles Lambert, also skilled in stonecutting received a far less amiable reception. He had emigrated from Yorkshire, England, in his twenty-eighth year, voyaging to Zion on the *Fanny* in 1844.[43] Although he had been employed in Britain as a building contractor, he did not immediately earn the respect of his American brethren who labored on the Nauvoo Temple. When he arrived at the temple grounds, penniless and without an acquaintance, he was abruptly informed that no money was available to pay the workmen, though work on the Temple had previously sustained the poor.[44] Lambert wrote of this experience:

CHARLES LAMBERT

The day after I arrived . . . I went up to the [Nauvoo] Temple and saw there was work for me, but my dress and general appearance did not bespeak that of a working man. I inquired for those in charge. Reynolds Cahoon presented himself and some others. They tried me very much and sought to make game of me. They took me for a crank and enthusiast. R. Cahoon at last said, "If you can work, we can do with your work, but we have nothing to give you." I replied sharply, "I have not come here to work for pay, I have come to help to build that House," pointing to the [Nauvoo] Temple. Then they laughed. At this time I had not one penny and [was] an entire stranger.[45]

Lambert had only the traveling clothes on his back. His garb consisted of a nice suit, an apron and a cap, and a fine high silk hat.

His superior apparel must have incited the sport they made of him. The Americans apparently felt some contempt for this British craftsman, perhaps inheriting the disdain, in part, from the two previous generations in which America and Great Britain opposed each other both in the Revolutionary War and the War of 1812. To demonstrate their antagonism, the Americans made sport by throwing chips of stone at Lambert's British "stove pipe" hat as it hung at the work site and eventually destroyed it. Lambert wisely determined to ignore this act of persecution and continued to work as if it had never occurred. His example of forgiveness and his superior work soon won the respect and admiration of his fellow workmen.[46]

THE SPIRIT OF SACRIFICE

William Player and Charles Lambert sacrificed greatly as they labored day after day on the temple. These two craftsmen became particularly concerned when many fellow laborers quit to find gainful employment. How would the temple become a realization? After discussing the situation they resolved that regardless of nonexistent salaries, each would give his pledge to see the temple through to its completion. This they did, but not without great sacrifice. But they felt the inner assurance that after the trial of their faith and because of their consecration, the Lord would pour out His blessings upon them and minister to their needs.

Lambert never could have guessed that the test of his faith would present itself in such a peculiar manner. One day a stranger introduced himself as Higgins, from Missouri. The gentleman, dressed in fine attire, proposed an offer which was difficult for Lambert to refuse. The strange encounter is provided in its entirety:

> "I have heard of your skill as a workman, and want you to go to Missouri and work for me. You are not appreciated or properly paid here. If you will quit the Temple and go and work for me you can name your own price and you will be sure of your pay. You see I have plenty of money with which to pay you." Suiting the action to the word, he thrust his hand into his pocket, and drew it out full of $10.00 and $20.00 gold pieces, which he displayed in a tempting manner, and urged him to accept his offer

and not to submit any longer to the unfair treatment accorded him at the Temple. With a gesture of impatience called forth by the intimation of unfairness, Father Lambert thanked the stranger for his offer, but said he couldn't think of accepting it. He said he had no complaint to make of his treatment at the Temple, and the price others would pay for work they wished done would not influence him in the matter, as he intended to continue on at the Temple from principle. Bidding the stranger "Good-day" he turned to continue his walk along the street, but almost immediately the query arose in his mind as to how the stranger knew his name, and where he got his information from about this skill as a mechanic, and turned to take a final look at the stranger, when lo! he was nowhere to be seen. He had disappeared as completely as if the ground had opened and swallowed him, and yet he had not had time by any ordinary means of locomotion to get out of sight. His opinion then was, and remained so up to the day of his death, that he had been talking with no other than Satan, the prince of tempters, and though he had not yielded to his tempting offer he was vexed with himself for listening to him at all, and especially to his insinuations about the Temple management.[47]

Several others caught the spirit of sacrifice as they helped in building the house of the Lord. Elijah Funk Sheets was one among a hundred others who committed to labor on the Nauvoo temple for a period of six months without pay.[48] Wandle Mace recalled that during the post-martyrdom period, "Men were as thick as blackbirds busily engaged upon the various [temple] portions all intent upon its completion."[49] Brigham Young remembered that tremendous sacrifice was extended, some temple workers laboring without adequate shoes or clothing.[50]

While the Nauvoo Temple was under construction, all male Church members were required to tithe one day in ten in order to complete the work of this holy edifice as well as the Nauvoo House.[51] Even with his incredibly busy schedule, the Prophet Joseph Smith did not think himself above this time commitment. His example to others in the community was laudable. An encounter occurring near one of the quarries on a temple tithing day demonstrates Joseph's effect on others:

THE NAUVOO TEMPLE.

It was Temple Tithing Day. . . . [Brother Bybee] had hitched his team to his wagon and with his son had gone to the quarry to load a large stone into the wagon; then, they started for the temple. Pulling out of the quarry with its stone floor was no problem, but when they started across the "Flat" their wagon became stuck in a mud hole. . . .

[Brother Bybee] had just stepped off the wagon when [he saw] a man walking along the side of the street. . . .

The man wadded into the mud [to help dislodge the wagon]. . . .

The wagon moved a bit, and the horses were able to keep it going. After going about a hundred feet onto dry ground the boy let the team rest. . . . [Brother Bybee] called out, "Thank you, Brother Joseph."

The boy was greatly impressed that a prophet of the Lord . . .
was not above wading in mud halfway to his knees and getting
his shoulder covered with mud to help another man in distress.[52]

Saints were also encouraged to contribute to the erection of the temple by financial donations. Aside from these collections, in July 1845, the British Saints were invited to provide donations for a temple bell. The Saints in Liverpool not only provided money for the bell, but in addition, they wished to contribute a clock.[53] In December 1845, Elder Wilford Woodruff spoke at a special Manchester conference held prior to his departure from England, "The British Saints have come forward nobly, when called upon to assist the brethren in the building of the Temple. Some £220 has been donated since we called for the assistance for the bell and clock; this is well, and I feel convinced that you will continue your efforts."[54]

Sacrifice was a common denominator in the Nauvoo equation. Transforming a swampland into a charming city and raising a magnificent temple would not have been possible without extreme sacrifices extracted from the community. Sacrificing deepened their faith and commitment to the cause of Zion. It was a unifying bond that melded the Saints into one body.

MUSIC: THE UNIVERSAL LANGUAGE

Another contribution to the spirit and edification of Nauvoo was made through music, the universal language. One gifted musician was William Pitt, a British convert from the village of Dymock in Gloucestershire. When Pitt emigrated, he brought a large collection of music specifically arranged for brass instruments. In 1842, this refined musician, who specialized in playing the clarinet, became the leader of a group of British musicians known as the Nauvoo Brass Band. This band, formed at the call of the Prophet Joseph, not only played in the Nauvoo Legion to help with military drills, but was also summoned to play at picnics, concerts, and excursions, including one pleasure cruise aboard the steamboat *Maid of Iowa*.[55]

Perhaps one of their most memorable experiences occurred at 6:22 A.M. on 24 May 1845, when the capstone on the Nauvoo Temple was pronounced set and the brass band played the "Capstone March,"

composed by William Pitt for this solemn occasion.
Following the rendition of this special composi-
tion, Brigham Young pronounced, "The last
stone is now laid upon the Temple and I pray
the Almighty in the name of Jesus to defend us
in this place and sustain us until the Temple is
finished and we have all got our endowments."[56]

WILLIAM PITT

THE POWER OF THE TEMPLE
From the day of groundbreaking until its
completion, the temple brought a sense of
reverence to Nauvoo. Joseph Fielding recalled
his impressionable experience the day he arrived at the Temple site at
the close of 1841: "We soon passed the sacred Place, and Foundation
of the Temple, the Arches of the Vault Windows were not all finished,
The Sight of this though by the Light of the Moon, only gave me
peculiar feelings, the Idea that it was done at the special Command of
the Almighty was a new thing in this Age, it seemed to fill the mind
[with] Solemnity, and to give a sacredness to the whole Place."[57]

Building the temple provided a shared focal point for the diverse
population of Nauvoo. Social interaction and cooperation were
required to accomplish this lofty undertaking. Assimilation was
further promoted as the Saints entered into common covenants with
God and each other. Yet in a few short years, the tranquility of this
sacred setting would be jolted when the scenery suddenly changed.

NOTES TO CHAPTER FIVE

1. Perry Miller and Thomas H. Johnson, eds., *The Puritans: A Sourcebook of Their Writings* (New York: Harper and Row, 1963),198–199, cited in Leonard J. Arrington, Feramorz Y. Fox, and Dean L. May, *Building the City of God: Community and Cooperation among the Mormons*, 2d ed. (Urbana: University of Illinois Press, 1992), 1.

2. "Information to Emigrants," *Millennial Star* 2, no. 4 (August 1841): 61.

3. Benjamin Ashby, *Autobiography of Benjamin Ashby*, L. Tom Perry Special

Collections Library, Harold B. Lee Library, Brigham Young University, Provo, Utah, 7.

4. Francis Moon, "Important from America: Interesting Letter from Elder Moon, Who Lately Emigrated from England to America," *Millennial Star* 1, no. 10 (February 1841): 255.

5. Joseph Smith, Sidney Rigdon, and Hyrum Smith, "A Proclamation of the First Presidency of the Church to the Saints Scattered Abroad, Greetings, *Millennial Star* 1, no. 11 (March 1841): 270.

6. Ibid., 274.

7. *HC* 4:403–404.

8. "History of Joseph Smith," *Deseret News* (20 August 1856), cited in M. Hamlin Cannon, "The 'Gathering' of British Mormons to Western America: A Study in Religious Migration" (Ph.D. diss, American University, 1950), 77.

9. Hugh Moon, *Autobiographical Sketch of Hugh Moon*, HDA, 3. The Kilburn mentioned here is undoubtedly David Kilbourne who was a business rival of Isaac Galland. He had been sent with Henry Austin by the New York-based financiers of the Demoine Land Association to oust Galland from his position as agent in the acquisition of claims to land in the Half-Breed Tract.

10. "Letter from Nauvoo," *Millennial Star* 4, no. 6 (October 1843): 88.

11. "Advice to Emigrants," *Millennial Star* 2, no. 10 (February 1842): 151.

12. James Linforth, ed., *Route from Liverpool to Great Salt Lake Valley Illustrated with Steel Engravings and Wood Cuts from Sketches Made by Frederick Piercy* , 2.

13. Allen and Leonard, *Story of the Latter-day Saints*, 2d ed. (Salt Lake City: Deseret Book Co., 1992), 165.

14. Joseph Fielding, "Joseph Fielding's Letter," *Millennial Star* 3, no. 4 (August 1842): 80.

15. *Quincy Whig* 4, no. 5 (29 May 1841): 2, noted in Newbern Issac Butt, comp., 4 vols., Mormons in Ohio, Illinois, Missouri, etc. Newspaper clippings, 1831–1848, typescript, Americana Collection, L. Tom Perry Special Collections Library, Harold B. Lee Library, Brigham Young University, Provo, Utah, p. 1: 208–209.

16. Francis Moon, "Important from America. Interesting Letter from Elder Moon, Who Lately Emigrated from England to America," *Millennial Star* 1, no. 10 (February 1841): 253.

17. "Extract of a Letter from Sister Melling, Who Lately Emigrated from Preston, England, to Nauvoo, United States," *Millennial Star* 2, no. 6 (October

1841): 96.

18. W. Aitken, *A Journey up the Mississippi River, from Its Mouth to Nauvoo, the City of the Latter-Day Saints,* (Ashton-under-Lyne, England: John Williamson, n.d.), 37–38, courtesy of the Missouri Historical Society, St. Louis, Missouri. According to Wilbur S. Shepperson, "The Place of the Mormons in the Religious Emigration of Britain, 1840–1860," *Utah Historical Quarterly* 20, no. 3 (July 1952): 213, "In most [non-Mormon] journals, derogatory remarks were the rule rather than the exception when referring to Mormon emigration. Claiming to have visited Nauvoo, returning [British] emigrants told fanciful stories which grew with circulation of its unfriendliness, chaotic social system, economic austerity, and general mismanagement." Notwithstanding, the British converts continued to immigrate to America.

19. It is estimated that out of about 90,000 Latter-day Saint foreign converts who gathered to America during the nineteenth century, roughly 55,000 were British or 61 percent of the total converts. As previously noted, about 25 percent of Nauvoo's population by 1845 was British. However, Richard L. Jensen, "Transplanted to Zion: The Impact of British Latter-day Saint Immigration upon Nauvoo," *BYU Studies* 31, no. 1 (Winter 1991): 84–85, points out that "British immigrant Latter-day Saints maintained a relatively low profile in Nauvoo. . . . Most of the immigrants had been Latter-day Saints for only a relatively short period. During this interlude it was necessary for these immigrants to establish their roots more firmly. . . . [Yet] in time, many of the British Latter-day Saint immigrants whose growth in Nauvoo had been less evident would become fully productive participants in the Mountain West and in missions further afield."

20. Extract of Brigham Young's letter cited in Leonard J. Arrington, *Brigham Young: American Moses* (New York: Alfred A. Knopf, 1985), 94.

21. Benjamin F. Johnson, *My Life's Review: Autobiography of Benjamin Franklin Johnson* (Provo, Utah: Grandin Book Co., 1997), 49.

22. Lorenzo Brown, *Journal of Lorenzo Brown* 1823–1900, 2 vols., typescript, L. Tom Perry Special Collections Library, Harold B. Library, Brigham Young University, Provo, Utah, p. 1: 6–7.

23. Benjamin Brown, *Testimonies for the Truth: A Record of Manifestations of the Power of God, Miraculous and Providential, Witnessed in the Travels and Experience of Benjamin Brown, High Priest in the Church of Jesus Christ of Latter-day Saints, Pastor of the London, Reading, Kent, and Essex Conferences,* (Liverpool: S.W. Richards, 1853), Americana Collection, L. Tom Perry Special Collections Library, Harold B. Lee Library, Brigham Young University, Provo, Utah, 18–19.

24. William Draper, Life of William Draper, typescript, L. Tom Perry Special Collections Library, Harold B. Lee Library, Brigham Young University, Provo, Utah, p. 8.

25. Jacob Peart, Sr., *Autobiographical Sketch of Jacob Peart Sr.,* typescript, Family History Library, Salt Lake City, p. 5.

26. Mosiah Hancock, *The Life Story of Mosiah Lyman Hancock,* Americana Collection, L. Tom Perry Special Collections Library, Harold B. Lee Library, Brigham Young University, Provo, Utah, 14.

27. H. Dean Garrett, "Disease and Sickness in Nauvoo," in *Regional Studies in Latter-day Saint Church History: Illinois,* ed. H. Dean Garrett (Provo, Utah: Department of Church History and Doctrine, Brigham Young University, 1995), 172. Herein, Garrett also adds that other diseases which afflicted the Nauvoo Saints were "dysentery, typhoid, brain fever (meningitis), scarlet fever, and diphtheria, which were all communicable."

28. *Journal History,* 25 July 1841, HDA, notes, "In the afternoon Elder Sidney Rigdon preached a general funeral sermon, designed to comfort and instruct the Saints, especially those who had been called to mourn the loss of relatives and friends." Allen and Leonard, *Story of the Latter-day Saints,* 157, suggest that the general funeral sermon was necessitated by the malaria epidemic which had struck again in 1841.

29. J. Smith, Rigdon, and H. Smith, "A Proclamation to the Saints Scattered Abroad," 270.

30. John Butler, *Autobiography of John Lowe Butler: 1808–1861,* typescript, L. Tom Perry Special Collections Library, Harold B. Lee Library, Brigham Young University, Provo, Utah, p. 21.

31. Stella Cahoon Shurtleff and Brent Farrington Cahoon, comps. and eds., *Reynolds Cahoon and His Stalwart Sons* (Salt Lake City: Paragon Press, 1960), 87.

32. Alexander Neibaur, *Journal of Alexander Neibaur,* typescript, L. Tom Perry Special Collections Library, Harold B. Lee Library, Brigham Young University, Provo, Utah, p. 12.

33. "Alexander Neibaur," *Times and Seasons* 2, no. 19 (2 August 1841): 502.

34. Neibaur, *Journal of Alexander Neibaur,* p. 15–16, wrote, "Caled at J. Smith 10 oclock . . . took dinner, read German." Another account dated 2 June 1841 states, "saw Mr. S. [Joseph Smith] all forenoon, wife sick. Read German all forenoon."

35. *HC* 6: 267.

36. Ibid., 6:426. Joseph Smith, *Teachings of the Prophet Joseph Smith,* selected and arranged by Joseph Fielding Smith (Salt Lake City: Deseret Book Co., 1976), 349, states, "I have been reading the German [New Testament] and find it to be the

most [nearly] correct translation, and to correspond nearest to the revelations which God has given to me for the last fourteen years."

37. Ibid., 6:402.

38. Alexander Neibaur, *Autobiographical Sketch of Alexander Neibaur*, Seventies Record, 5th Quorum, Biographies, HDA, 15.

39. James B. Allen, "Eight Contemporary Accounts of Joseph Smith's First Vision: What Do We Learn from Them?" *Improvement Era*, April 1970, 6. According to a phone conversation with Dr. Allen on 30 November 2001, this is still the only contemporary diary which records this sacred event.

40. Neibaur, *Journal of Alexander Neibaur*, p. 15.

41. *HC* 4:273.

42. *Journal History*, 11 October 1842 HDA.

43. *Latter-day Saint Biographical Encyclopedia: A Compilation of Biographical Sketches of Prominent Men and Women in the Church of Jesus Christ of Latter-day Saints*, s.v. "Lambert, Charles," 2: 779.

44. *HC* 6:58. In a public address delivered in Nauvoo on 15 October 1843 the Prophet Joseph stated, "Some say it is better to give to the poor than build the Temple. The building of the Temple has sustained the poor who were driven from Missouri, and kept them from starving; and it has been the best means for this object which could be devised."

45. Charles Lambert, *Autobiography of Charles Lambert*, typescript HDA, p. 9–10.

46. "Lambert Reminiscence," in *Faith Promoting Series*, book 17 of *Gems of Reminiscence* (Salt Lake City: Geo. C. Lambert), 172–173.

47. Ibid., 174–175.

48. *Latter-day Saint Biographical Encyclopedia*, s.v. "Sheets, Elijah Funk," 1:614.

49. Wandell (Wandle) Mace, *Journal of Wandell (Wandle) Mace*, 1809–1890, L. Tom Perry Special Collections Library, Harold B. Lee Library, Brigham Young University, Provo, Utah, 185–186.

50. *Deseret News* (14 October 1863), 96–97, cited in *Journal of Discourses*, (Liverpool: Daniel H. Wells, 1865), 10: 252.

51. The Lord revealed that the Nauvoo House was to be built where "the weary traveler may find health and safety while he shall contemplate the word of the Lord" (D&C 124:23). However, due to the forced exodus which suddenly came upon the Saints, they could not finish the Nauvoo House, but rather chose to complete the Temple before they migrated west.

52. Richard Neitzel Holzapfel and T. Jeffrey Cottle, *Old Mormon Nauvoo and*

Southeastern Iowa: Historic Photographs and Guide (Santa Ana, CA: Fieldbrook Productions, 1991), 69, cited in T. Edgar Lyon, "Recollections of 'Old Nauvooers' Memories from Oral History," *BYU Studies* 18, no. 2 (Winter 1978): 147–148. Orson F. Whitney, *Life of Heber C. Kimball* 8th ed. (Salt Lake City: Bookcraft, 1978), 68, explains how Joseph Smith was also engaged in working on the Kirtland Temple. He quotes Elder Kimball: "The Prophet, being our foreman, would put on his tow frock and tow pantaloons and go into the quarry." On 1 September 1834, the Prophet Joseph Smith wrote, "I acted as foreman in the Temple stone quarry, and when other duties would permit, labored with my own hands." See *HC* 2:161.

53. Wilford Woodruff, "Letter to the Editor," *Millennial Star* 6, no. 3 (July 1845): 43.

54. "Special Conference," *Millennial Star* 7, no. 1 (January 1846): 5.

55. Horace G. Whitney, "The Nauvoo Brass Band," *Contributor* 1, no. 6 (1880):135.

56. *HC* 7:417–418.

57. Andrew F. Ehat, "'They Might Have Known That He Was Not a Fallen Prophet,'—The Nauvoo Journal of Joseph Fielding," *BYU Studies* 19, no. 2 (Winter 1979): 141.

CHAPTER SIX

Nauvoo Exodus

"Early this month we'll leave Nauvoo
And on our journey will pursue
We'll go and bid the mob farewell
And them let them go to heaven or hell."

—FIRST VERSE OF SONG, *EARLY THIS SPRING WE'LL LEAVE NAUVOO,*
UNKNOWN MORMON AUTHOR
GEORGE BOOSINGER PAPERS, HENRY F. HUNTINGTON LIBRARY, SAN MARINO, CA.

In less than seven years (1839–1846), thousands of Saints had marched into Nauvoo resolute in their dream to erect a magnificent city. Amidst the deathly air, thick with malaria-carrying mosquitoes, they shoveled mud from the swamps of Commerce and baked the moist soil into brick to fashion their homes and shops. A bustling city had risen from the marsh through the sweat and tears of noble men and determined women. Tragically, these selfless, faithful pioneers would now be required to forsake all of their endeavors and migrate once again. Leaving behind their temple and homes, they wearily gazed towards the unproven westward territory where they would once again attempt to build Zion.

MANIFEST DESTINY

For some incoming Saints it was a jolt to enter the beautiful city of Nauvoo and then abruptly be required to abandon it. Softening the blow and making their exodus conceivable was the pervasive nine-

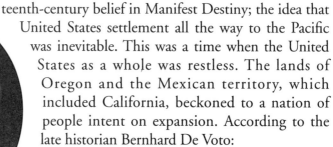

teenth-century belief in Manifest Destiny; the idea that United States settlement all the way to the Pacific was inevitable. This was a time when the United States as a whole was restless. The lands of Oregon and the Mexican territory, which included California, beckoned to a nation of people intent on expansion. According to the late historian Bernhard De Voto:

PRESIDENT
JAMES K. POLK

> The Americans had always devoutly believed that the superiority of their institutions, government, and mode of life would eventually spread, by inspiration and imitation, to less fortunate, less happy peoples. That devout belief now took a new phase: it was perhaps the American destiny to spread our free and admirable institutions by action as well as by example, by occupying the territory as well as by practicing virtue.[1]

The Native Americans were among those deemed "less fortunate and less happy," and thus were swept away in the tidal momentum of Manifest Destiny.

DRIVING OUT THE NATIVE AMERICANS

Removing the Native Americans from their homelands began when explorers and colonists first set foot on North American shores. By the time Manifest Destiny was coined, United States expansion had already forced thousands of Native Americans from their lands. Manifest Destiny salved the consciences of men and women intent on gaining land and riches. After all, neither they nor Native Americans could change what was written in the stars.

Of course Native Americans did not see it that way. In reference to the forked tongue of the white man, one anonymous native perhaps said it best: "They made us many promises, more than I can remember, but they never kept but one; they promised to take our land, and they took it."[2] Commencing in the 1840s, Americans focused on the West with dreams of new land and fortune, with little regard for those who had inhabited it for centuries. For many, the ravenous appetite of greed swallowed up whatever conscience existed. Nevertheless, with the removal of Native Americans and with western expansion in vogue, the way was prepared for the Saints to push on.

REASONS FOR EXPULSION

In Nauvoo, Church members journeyed west, not out of greed, but out of necessity. The Saints were not wanted. In the space of a few short years, they had emerged into a very powerful city which had become a menace to the local inhabitants of Hancock County, due to the Saints' newfound economic and political power. With the Mormons voting as a unit, they had the potential of taking control of the county or possibly even the state. They embraced a peculiar religion, not understood by others. The citizens of Hancock County and the Nauvoo Saints were suspicious of each other and accused each other of local crimes. The influence of contentious apostates fueled the flames of persecution mounted against the Saints.[3] The federal government refused to protect them, and they could not protect themselves. The Nauvoo Charter, which had basically afforded the

CROSSING THE MISSISSIPPI ON THE ICE.

Saints the privileges of self-government, had been revoked January 1845, leaving the Saints vulnerable to unbridled persecution—again.

PROPHECIES OF CHURCH EXPANSION TO THE ROCKY MOUNTAINS

Though the necessity of an exodus was agonizing, some early converts to Mormonism were comforted by the Prophet Joseph's earlier prophesies concerning a Latter-day Saint movement west. One who remembered well was Wilford Woodruff, who recalled a prophetic experience that took place in Kirtland as early as 26 April 1834. According to Woodruff, Joseph had told a small group the following:

> I want to say to you before the Lord, that you know no more concerning the destinies of this Church and kingdom than a babe upon its mother's lap. You don't comprehend it. . . . It is only a little handfull of Priesthood you see here tonight, but this Church will fill North and South America—it will fill the world. . . . It will fill the Rocky Mountains. There will be tens of thousands of Latter-day Saints who will be gathered in the Rocky Mountains, and there they will open the door for the establishing of the Gospel among the Lamanites. . . . This people will go into the Rocky Mountains; they will there build temples to the Most High. They will raise up a posterity there, and the Latter-day Saints who dwell in these mountains will stand in the flesh until the coming of the Son of Man. The Son of Man will come to them while in the Rocky Mountains.[4]

Just two years later, Lorenzo Dow Young was told through a blessing given him by Hyrum Smith that he would be restored to health and "live to go with the Saints into the bosom of the Rocky Mountains to build up a place there."[5] Other instances occurred establishing the inevitability of the journey west,[6] but none so complete as one given in Montrose, Iowa, on 6 August 1842. After crossing the Mississippi into Iowa Territory, Joseph recorded the experience as he viewed it:

LORENZO DOW YOUNG

I prophesied that the Saints would continue to suffer much affliction and would be driven to the Rocky Mountains, many would
apostatize, others would be put to death by our persecutors or lose
their lives in consequence of exposure or disease, and some of you
will live to go and assist in making settlements and build cities and
see the Saints become a mighty people in the midst of the
Rocky Mountains.[7]

Anson Call provided his own invaluable and
detailed account of this same prophetic occasion:

ANSON CALL

I had before seen him in a vision, and now saw
while he was talking his countenance change to
white; not the deadly white of a bloodless face,
but a living brilliant white. He seemed absorbed
in gazing at something at a great distance, and said:
"I am gazing upon the valleys of those mountains." This was followed by a vivid description
of the scenery of these mountains, as I have since become
acquainted with it. Pointing to Shadrach Roundy and others, he
said: "There are some men here who shall do a great work in that
land." Pointing to me, he said: "There is Anson, he shall go and
shall assist in building up cities from one end of the country to
the other, and you," rather extending the idea to all those he had
spoken of, "shall perform as great a work as has been done by
man, so that the nations of the earth shall be astonished, and
many of them will be gathered in that land and assist in building
cities and temples, and Israel shall be made to rejoice."

It is impossible to represent in words this scene which is still vivid
in my mind, of the grandeur of Joseph's appearance, his beautiful
descriptions of this land, and his wonderful prophetic utterances as
they emanated from the glorious inspirations that overshadowed
him. There was a force and power in his exclamations of which the
following is a faint echo: "Oh the beauty of those snow-capped
mountains! The cool refreshing streams that are running down
through those mountain gorges!" Then gazing in another direc-

tion, as if there was a change in locality: "Oh the scenes that this people will pass through! The dead that will lay between here and there!" Then turning in another direction as if the scene had again changed: "Oh the apostasy that will take place before my brethren reach that land!" "But," he continued, "the priesthood shall prevail over its enemies, triumph over the devil and be established upon the earth, never more to be thrown down!" He then charged us with great force and power, to be faithful in those things that had been and should be committed to our charge, with the promise of all the blessings that the Priesthood could bestow. "Remember these things and treasure them up. Amen."[8]

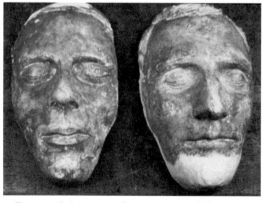

GEORGE H. GODDARD

Joseph not only saw the eventual destination of the Saints, but apparently knew the route they would take as well. In Nauvoo, George H. Goddard remembered that Joseph had taken a piece of chalk and drawn the way the Saints would go in order to reach the Great Basin.[9] Mosiah L. Hancock also noted that one day Joseph Smith entered the carpenter shop of Levi W. Hancock, and after taking a map out, stated, "Now . . . I will show you the travels of this people," wherein Joseph drew a line west through Iowa and then said, "Here you will make a place for the winter . . . and here you will become a great and wealthy people in that land."[10]

DEATH MASKS OF JOSEPH AND HYRUM.

THE MARTYRDOM

Neither Joseph nor his brother would ever go west. Like Moses, Joseph was privileged to view the promised land, but was not be able to enter it. Sealing their testimonies with their blood, Joseph and Hyrum completed their missions and entered into a far greater land of promise. Their martyrdoms on the infamous day of 27 June 1844 draped the city of Nauvoo with a shroud of darkness. Harvey Cluff recalled, "The martyrdom of these men of God cast a gloom over the people so intense at the time . . . no cyclon or dark cloud of persicution inflicted upon the Saints in the past seemed so black and fatal. Forced into the wilderness among savages, was supposed by the enemy, to prove the final destruction of the Church of Jesus Christ of Latter-day Saints."[11] Their assumption was that not only had the Saints lost their beloved prophet, but they now had to find a way to continue the great work for which he had but laid a foundation. No one believed the beleaguered religion could survive such obstacles.

WHO WOULD LEAD ISRAEL TO THE PROMISED LAND?

Without a prophet and with mobs ever circling, the question reverberating throughout the discouraged city was, "Who will lead Israel to the promised land?" The answer soon became clear: the Saints would follow the Twelve, and Brother Brigham would take the role of a Joshua. Brigham would lead the Saints across the river and, like Abraham, would bring the Lord's covenant people through a modern day Mesopotamia. This time, however, it would be the difficult Iowa trek between the Mississippi and the Missouri Rivers.

EARLY PLANS FOR A SPRING DEPARTURE

As early as 19 March 1845, Hosea Stout noted that he and Brigham Young had discussed the possibility of settling somewhere in the "interior of the country between the head waters of the Arkansas and the head waters of the Colerado of the West."[12] In time, the plan for a westward movement and the time for relocating would be refined. Plans for a spring exodus in 1846 were firmly made after a committee, representing nine counties in the Hancock region, met in Carthage 1–2 October 1845 to determine definite measures for a Mormon expulsion.[13] The committee adopted the following resolution:

> *Resolved,* That it is the settled and deliberate conviction of this
> convention that it is now too late to attempt the settlement of

the difficulties in Hancock county upon any other basis than that of the removal of the Mormons from the state; and we therefore accept and respectfully recommend to the people of the surrounding counties to accept the proposition made by the Mormons to remove from the state next spring, and to wait with patience the time appointed for removal.[14]

When Governor Ford learned of this resolution, he dictated a letter he desired to have published in the *Nauvoo Neighbor*. Among other things, Ford stated, "I fear that they [the Mormons] will never be able to live in peace with their neighbors of Hancock and surrounding counties. There is no legal power in the state to compel them to leave, and no such power will be exercised during my administration." The governor further noted, "I desire that you will impress these facts upon the Mormons, and that you will counsel and promote any peaceable means of accommodation, whereby the Mormons may be induced to leave the state. . . . Is it not better that they should do so voluntarily, than to have a state of continual war."[15]

SPLINTER GROUPS AND DISAFFECTION

Some Saints had already left Nauvoo, due to various personal trials ranging from doctrinal disillusionment and deadly disease, to economic stress and political turmoil. Sometimes those who were disaffected took others with them. Sidney Rigdon, for example, chose to return to the East as a result of his 8 September 1844 excommunication stemming from his false claim the previous month that he had been appointed by Joseph Smith as the "guardian" of the Church.[16] Four days later, the *Burlington Hawkeye* announced, "Sidney Rigdon has left Nauvoo for Pittsburgh and it is expected that a large number of the English Mormons will follow him."[17]

SIDNEY RIGDON

Just one week later, the *Hawkeye* further noted that Rigdon was passing through St. Louis on his way to the East.[18] In another article entitled, "Leaving the City," the *Warsaw Signal* indicated that "the

Ospres [probably the Osprey] passed down yesterday, having on board Sidney Rigdon and about 100 other Mormons."[19] Although somewhat suspect, such evidence suggests the possibility that Rigdon did not leave Nauvoo alone, but rather a cluster of British Saints went to the East with him. The press paid meticulous attention to the departing Saints, which may be indicative of the high interest these departures held for the citizens in the vicinity.

JAMES J. STRANG

Another would-be leader at the time of the 1844 succession dispute was James J. Strang, a very charismatic person who claimed that Joseph had appointed him his successor by letter. Mormon historian Richard E. Bennett explains Strang's ability: "His particular genius, however, centered in his enormous self-confidence and unbridled ambition, his persuasive speaking and writing abilities, his opportunistic sense of timing, and his uncanny ability to capitalize on the fear and discontent among the people."[20]

By the year of the Nauvoo exodus (1846), Strang had led hundreds of vulnerable Church members away from the bulk of the westward-bound Saints. The *Lee County Democrat* reported, "The Mormons we learn are now daily crossing the Mississippi in large numbers en route for their anticipated home in Oregon or California. Some are seceding from the Church and returning to the east; and dispersing throughout the country; while many are wending their way to the city of Voree, in Wisconsin, to place themselves under the head and guidance of . . . James J. Strang."[21]

Despite these defections, the larger body of faithful Saints remained united in their determination to press forward under the steady guidance of God's chosen leaders—Brigham Young and the Quorum of the Twelve.

NAUVOO COVENANT

Church leaders agreed it best to leave Nauvoo in the spring of 1846, but neither Brigham nor the Twelve were anticipating a rushed exodus. Plans were carefully laid to lead all who desired to go safely

BRIGHAM YOUNG

out of Nauvoo. To accomplish this awesome task the leadership of the Church knew they needed to enlist the help of the faithful and strong members.

On 6 October 1845, general conference was held in the Nauvoo Temple. In this covenant setting, Elder George A. Smith reminded the congregation that when they were driven from Missouri, they had "entered into a covenant not to cease their exertions until every saint who wished to go was removed, which was done." Elder Smith then emphasized that the Lord "wants to see the same principle carried out now, that every man will give all to help to take the poor; and every honest industrious member who wants to go." President Brigham Young moved with a resolution that "we take all the Saints with us, to the extent of our ability, that is, our influence and property." He next pronounced a prophecy concerning the deliverance of the Saints: "If you will be faithful to your covenant, I will now prophesy that the great God will shower down means upon this people, to accomplish it [the resolution] to the very letter."[22]

SUPREME EFFORTS TO COMPLETE THE TEMPLE

Two days later, the Twelve issued an "Epistle to the brethren of the Church of Jesus Christ of Latter-day Saints, scattered abroad through the United States of America," in which the exodus was announced:

> You will perceive from the foregoing interesting Minutes of the General Conference, just held in the Temple in this place not only the unparalleled union of the great body of the saints convened, but also that a crisis of extraordinary and thrilling interests has arrived. The exodus of the nation of the only true Israel from these United States to a far distant region of the west, where bigotry, intolerance and insatiable oppression lose their power over them—forms a new epoch, not only in the history of the church, but of this nation. . . .

It is our design to remove all the saints as early next spring as the first appearance of thrifty vegetation. In the meantime the utmost diligence of all the brethren at this place and abroad will be requisite for our removal, and to complete the unfinished part of the Lord's House.[23]

Since the paramount reason why so many had forsaken native lands and kindred and made the expensive and arduous journey to Nauvoo was not only to be numbered among the "only true Israel," but most especially to partake in the ordinances of the holy temple, the completion of the temple before their departure became urgent. By November 1845 the Saints were steadily engaged in completing the temple in order to receive their endowments prior to the impending exodus. On 10 December 1845, the full endowment was administered in a Latter-day Saint temple for the first time in this dispensation. By 7 February 1846, the endowment had been administered to over 5,600 Saints. During this brief, two-month period, Church members worked long hours to administer this sacred ordinance and to perform sealings for as many Saints as possible before leaving the city and temple they had built.[24] On 1 January 1846, Elder Parley P. Pratt wrote, "I continued to minister in the Temple night and day, with my President and the rest of the Twelve, until early in February."[25]

A touching scene occurred on 3 February 1846, when Brigham Young informed a large group of Saints at the temple that the administration of ordinances had come to an end because time was short and physical preparations for the exodus must commence in earnest. He reassured them that more temples would be built in the future wherein the Saints could again receive the endowment. After walking some distance from the temple, Brigham assumed the crowd had dispersed. To his astonishment, when he returned to the temple he found the house of the Lord overflowing. As he gazed upon the congregation he perceived their desire to receive as much spiritual food as they could consume before the famine. Here was a people hungering and thirsting for God's greater word as revealed in the ordinances. The brethren were moved with compassion and "continued at work diligently in the House of the Lord."[26]

One sister who administered temple ordinances alongside her husband (Charles C. Rich) throughout those winter months was

Sarah Pea Rich. She later reflected on the great comfort and strength which the endowment had provided for the westward journey:

> The devil was mad, and the lives of many of our brethren were sought by the mob that had assassinated our brethren, Joseph and Hyrum. But many were the blessings we had received in the House of the Lord, which [h]as caused joy and comfort in the midst of all our sorrows, and enabled us to have faith in God, knowing He would guide us and sustain us in the unknown journey that lay before us. For if it had not been for the faith and knowledge that was bestowed upon us in that Temple [Nauvoo] by the influence and help of the Spirit of the Lord, our journey would have been like one taking a leap in the dark, to start out on such a journey in the winter as it were, and in our state of poverty, it would seem like walking into the jaws of death. But we had faith in our Heavenly Father, and we put our trust in Him, feeling that we were His chosen people and had embraced His gospel; and instead of sorrow we felt to rejoice that the day of our deliverance had come.[27]

A HASTY EXIT

Three maps hung on the temple walls, a constant reminder to the thousands who passed by of the imminent flight. Members of the Twelve had begun a study of John C. Fremont's 1842–1844 Rocky Mountain exploration reports. President Brigham Young made a careful study of both Fremont's maps and the recently published, Lansford Hasting's *Emigrants' Guide to Oregon and California*.[28] An orderly plan was laid out calling for twenty-five companies consisting of one hundred families each. However, despite their careful plans for a spring removal, two factors compelled a hasty exit. First, Brigham Young and several members of the Twelve had been falsely indicted for the crime of counterfeiting. If the long arm of the law succeeded in incarcerating these Church leaders, who could lead the Saints to safety?

JOHN C. FREMONT

The second reason was that they had been warned by Governor Thomas Ford that federal troops from St. Louis had threatened to intercept and destroy them.[29] Therefore, a heightened sense of urgency pressed down upon the leadership to hasten their departure.

A CALL TO ASSIST

On 1 January 1846, the *Millennial Star* carried the minutes of a special conference held in Manchester, England, before the departure of Wilford Woodruff to America. In this meeting, Elder Woodruff noted Brigham Young's intent that the Church assist fifteen to twenty-thousand people in their departure from Nauvoo. Elder Woodruff wrote, "These have to be provided for with food for some twelve months, waggons, &c., and means to travel, and it will be a mighty struggle to deliver all the people, but they have determined to make the sacrifice. . . . We want the Saints in Britain, therefore, to assist us in this migration."[30] The British Saints willingly offered their American brothers and sisters much-needed aid. Due to the perilous travails of the community of Saints in the States, emigration from abroad all but halted for a season.[31]

CROSSING THE MISSISSIPPI

The withdrawal from Nauvoo occurred in waves. The Saints' dreams of the luxury of a spring exodus froze as the stark reality of stinging winter winds smote their cheeks on that bitter fourth day of February 1846. This sorrowful day initiated the first group's crossing of the cold Mississippi River.[32] The passage across the river was supervised by the Nauvoo police, under the direction of their chief, Hosea Stout. "They gathered several flatboats, some old lighters and a number of skiffs, forming all together quite a fleet, and were at work night and day, crossing the Saints."[33]

Ezra Benson left Nauvoo 9 February 1846. His diary elicits compassion from the reader as he wistfully lists his abandoned treasures. He recalled departing "in the dead of winter, leaving my pleasant home and fireside. I left my furniture standing in the house, such as chairs, tables, bedsteads and clock. . . . We crossed the Mississippi river, leaving our beautiful city and Temple, not knowing where we should go."[34]

EZRA T. BENSON

The Benson family camped a few miles west of the Mississippi River at Sugar Creek, along with many other Latter-day Saint families. Henry Bigler remembered that on 17 February 1846, "Brigham called the Saints together and proceeded to organize them into companies of hundreds, companies of fifties and tens, gave them considerable instruction relative to going west, preparing outfits, etc."[35]

David and Della Miller, Nauvoo historians, assert that Nauvoo's evacuation was an ongoing process from February to September 1846. They note that "a person's exit from Nauvoo did not bar him from returning for one reason or another such as an attempt to sell property or obtain additional items for the trek."[36] Yet by fall, most of the beleaguered citizens of Nauvoo had relinquished their homes forever and feared the hostile environment too much to return.

SCATTERED CONDITION OF THE SAINTS

Of deep concern to the Twelve was the scattered condition of the Saints as well as their temporal and spiritual circumstances. Ellsworth maintains that a high number "of the Nauvoo exiles returned to former places of residence in the East."[37] Other Saints just scattered from Nauvoo because of insufficient means to travel with the body of the Church heading west. Many faithful Saints who did not go west in 1846 went south to St. Louis to find shelter from angry mobs and to earn necessary funds for the continuation of their journey to the Rockies at a later date. It is estimated that nearly 1,500 Saints gathered to St. Louis at this time.[38]

One Nauvoo Saint who yearned to go on the trek west but lacked the initial funds to do so was William Adams. Adams spent three years at various places of employment before he could raise enough money to begin his journey to Utah in 1849. He left Nauvoo in March 1846 and spent the first summer in Catona building houses.[39] In the fall he quarried stone in New Diggins, Wisconsin. During the spring of 1847 he worked in St. Louis for the gas works. He then began a six-month contract as a cook near Springfield, Illinois, earning a mere twenty dollars a month. Adams then labored on the Illinois State House in Springfield from the spring of 1848 until the spring of 1849.[40] Adams recalled:

> My wife and I had been saving with our means and had saved four or five hundred dollars in money, and considered that now was the time to make a move to gather with the Saints.
>
> I had felt very uneasy and troubled at being so far away from the gathering place of the Saints. I reparied to a sacred spot and made a covenant with the Lord that as soon as I got means I would gather with the Saints, and I asked Him to prosper me and bless me in my labors. He answered my prayer, and I was determined to fulfill my part. My eldest brother Thomas had arrived from Ireland, and pressed me not to go to Utah but stop an[d] go into business, as it looked very favorable for making money in Springfield, but nothing would stop me. I bought a new wagon, one yoke of good cattle and six cows. I spent a couple of weeks breaking the cows, to work, and got them used to be handled and yoked. Close to the first day of May, 1849, I started on my journey to Utah in company with Thomas Judd and family.[41]

THE IOWA CROSSING

Hundreds of families with the immediate means to join one of the various pioneer companies leaving Nauvoo experienced a very laborious crossing of Iowa in the winter and spring of 1846. During this haunting year of extremity, thousands of Saints straggled across the vast inhospitable Iowa Territory with little progress, taking 131 days to travel three hundred miles.[42]

Three factors significantly contributed to the excruciatingly slow journey across Iowa, the first being a completely inadequate food supply. Some of this deficit was due to the anxious parties who hastily fled the city without adequate preparations or provisions in their consternation to keep up with able leaders. They feared being left behind and getting separated from competent leaders among the Twelve who could take them over the unknown trail. Many, with their lack of planning and inaccurate assessment of their own needs, depleted the personal supplies of generous leaders like Brigham

Young. As a result of these shortages many men were forced to leave family and wagon in search of temporary employment in order to secure food. The second factor in the slow crossing was disorganization. Some of the company leaders were independent, competitive, and disobedient to Brigham Young. They pushed on ahead without care or concern for others. Finally, the very wet spring with melting snows and near-continual rain reduced travel, at times, to a miserable half mile a day! The quagmire made it exceedingly difficult to drive the wagons and even the wind retarded progress.[43]

An example of the hardship and frustration caused by such conditions was reported by Henry Bigler. On 18 March 1846, he recorded the frustrating situation that presented itself at Richardson's Point,[44] where his company had been stalled for ten days because of marshy conditions. He explained that although the brethren tried to improve their unpleasant circumstances, the lengthy encampment on private property proved somewhat costly: "Owing to the wether being so wet and the road mudy many of the brethren made rails for the Gentiles for provisions. . . . The man on whose land we are now encampted upon by the name of Cox presented a bill of ten dollars damage sustained by the horses gnawing the oak and ash trees."[45]

HENRY BIGLER

A few weeks later, on the anniversary of the establishment of the restored Church (6 April 1846), Hosea Stout recorded that it was "of all mornings the most dismal dark and rainy." Further:

HOSEA STOUT

> This day capped the climax of all days for travelling. The road was the worst that I had yet witnessed up hill & down through sloughs on spouty oak ridges and deep marshes raining hard the creek rising. The horses would sometimes sink to their bellies on the ridges teams stall going down hill. We worked and toiled

more than half the day and had at last to leave some of our waggons and double teams before we could get through.[46]

A BOOST IN MORALE

In light of such trying circumstances, the Nauvoo Brass Band sought to rally the sinking morale of others. Fifteen members of the band and their families left Nauvoo in mid-February 1846, and President Young permitted the group to travel together. At Sugar Creek (in Iowa Territory), the band members pledged to assist each other through the arduous journey that lay ahead. William Clayton, who played violin in the band, recorded in his journal in the spring of 1846 that he had extended to other members of the band four to five hundred pounds of bacon, twelve hundred pounds of flour, as well as other supplies.[47] As a united group, "they were not only able to sustain the Saints' morale with dances and musicales, but provided a much-needed boost to the Saints' faltering financial affairs by giving paid concerts at such Iowa settlements as Farmington and Keosagua [Keosauqua]."[48]

POOR SAINTS LEFT BEHIND—EXPELLED FROM NAUVOO

Tragically, a remnant of the poorest Saints were left behind in Nauvoo because they simply could not secure sufficient provisions and funds to leave with the rest of the community. By mid-August, fewer than 1,500 of them remained in Nauvoo. By 10 September 1846, a powerless group of 150 men were consigned to face an anti-Mormon force numbering about 800. Fortunately, the Quincy committee finally interceded and the Battle of Nauvoo, as it was called, lasted less than a week, at which time a treaty was made. The terms of the treaty included a pledge for arms to be surrendered, the sick and poor to be cared for, the Mormons to leave the state as soon as possible, a proper disposition of property, and for hostilities to immediately cease. In spite of the treaty, a belligerent mob brutally forced the pitiful remaining Saints across the Mississippi.[49]

The *Burlington Hawkeye* published a poignant eyewitness account of what Nauvoo looked like just following the Battle of Nauvoo in September 1846: "On either shore of the Mississippi may be seen a long line of tents, wagons, cattle, &c., with numberless wretched specimens of humanity. Since the armistice or 'treaty' the Mormons are crossing in almost breathless haste. Three or four 'flats' are running constantly, both day and night."[50]

This witness also provided a sobering view of the abandoned temple. The writer described soldiers rolled up in their blankets with "muskets, swords, cannon balls and terrible missiles of death. Verily, thought I, how are the holy places desecrated! I thought of old Oliver Cromwell, when he drove the horses of his army through the 'cloisters' of the Worcester Cathedral, and appropriated the Baptismal fount as a manger. . . . I left the Temple 'solitary and alone.'"[51]

THE POOR CAMP DELIVERED

By the fall of 1846, the poor refugees were stranded in Iowa Territory on the western banks of the Mississippi, faced with the impending cold weather and an alarming shortage of adequate provisions. The situation was bleak, and a more wretched condition of a broken people is hard to imagine. One non-Mormon happened upon this ill-fated band and penned the unsettling scene of a young mother suffering not only starvation near death, but heartbreak as well: "On the Montrose side of the Mississippi, many of the scenes were heart-rending. I stopped at the door of one tent, arrested by the subdued sobs of a young mother, whose heart was broken with grief. By her side lay her infant, a corpse."[52]

The cries of the innocent were heard by the great God in heaven and life-sustaining food was divinely delivered to these tormented people on 9 October 1846. On this provident day, numerous quail flew into the poor camp and miraculously fell upon their tables and among their tents. The suffering Saints were able to catch them alive and devoured the much-needed sustenance. Concerning this day of deliverance, Thomas Bullock recorded:

Friday 9 October 1846 . . . This morning we had direct manifestation of the mercy & goodness of God, in a miracle being performed in the Camp. A

THOMAS BULLOCK

POTTER'S SLOUGH, WHERE QUAIL MIRACLE OCCURRED.

large, or rather several large flocks of Quails, flew into Camp. Some fell on the Wagons—some under—some on the Breakfast tables. The boys & brethren ran about after them & caught them alive with their hands. Men who were not in the Church marvelled at the sight. The brethren & sisters praised God & glorified his name, that what was showered down upon the Children of Israel in the wilderness is manifested unto us in our persecution. The boys caught about 20 alive & as to the number that were killed—every man woman & child had quails to eat for their dinner.[53]

It is futile to ignore the obvious comparison which this scene of a modern camp of Israel mirrors with the biblical account of Moses leading a desperate people in their wilderness wanderings. One day, "it came to pass, that at even the quails came up, and covered the camp" (Ex. 16:13). Not only is this resemblance clear to the student of history today, but it was to the poor camp of Israel in 1846 as well.

HELEN MAR
WHITNEY KIMBALL

In reflecting upon the experience of the Nauvoo exodus, Helen Mar Whitney [Kimball] wrote, "Our experience, I think, comes nearest to that of the children of Israel after their departure out of the land of Egypt than any other people of whom we have any record. . . . And who have been as miraculously saved from death . . . And the same God has . . . brought us deliverance every time; and it is our wish and purpose to trust Him still."[54] During the Nauvoo exodus, the Lord stated, "I am he who led the children of Israel out of the land of Egypt; and my arm is stretched out in the last days, to save my people Israel" (D&C 136:22). This promise comforted and sustained the Saints and their leaders.

However, Brigham Young was a practical man and believed that God often fulfilled His promises to His covenant people through His servants. Therefore, when he heard of the suffering poor camp left behind, President Young counseled, "Let the fire of the covenant which you made in the House of the Lord, burn in your hearts, like flame unquenchable, till you, by yourselves or delegates . . . [can] rise up with [teams] and go straitway, and bring a load of the poor from Nauvoo. . . . This is a day of action."[55] Rescue teams were immediately dispatched to rescue the struggling Saints. Afterwards the redeemed poor were dispersed under the care of various camps throughout Iowa.

AN EMIGRATION REVELATION

With thousands of Saints strung out across Iowa, over 500 men (many of whom were able teamsters) enlisted in the Mormon Battalion to support the United States in the war with Mexico, and the unforseen travel hardships devouring so much precious time, Brigham Young decided against taking his company all the way to the Rockies that season.[56] In September he established Winter Quarters (situated on the west bank of the Missouri River) as the designated headquarters for the migrants to spend the fall of 1846 and the winter of 1847.

At Winter Quarters, on 14 January 1847, Brigham Young received a revelation that made clear not only how the Saints should conduct their travel, but also designated who was to lead them to the promised land. The revelation began, "The Word and Will of the Lord concerning the Camp of Israel in their journeyings to the West" (D&C 136:1). The Saints were to "be organized into companies, with a covenant and promise to keep all the commandments and statutes of the Lord" (D&C 136:2). Their companies (led by captains) of hundreds, fifties, and tens, were to be led "under the direction of the Twelve Apostles" (D&C 136:3). This statement clearly confirmed that the Lord was leading his covenant people under the direction of Brigham Young and the Twelve.[57] This truly was a modern-day camp of Israel.

COVENANTS—CATALYST FOR WESTWARD TREK

Instructions were given to the vanguard company which would prepare the way for others to gather to the Salt Lake Valley. This "emigration revelation" became a pattern for God's covenant people aiding others desiring to gather to Zion by sail, rail, or trail throughout the latter half of the nineteenth century. The words of

Winter Quarters.

President Young, "Let the fire of the covenant which you made in the House of the Lord burn in your hearts, like flame unquenchable," seemed to reverberate in this portion of the Winter Quarters revelation: "Let every man use all his influence and property to remove this people to the place where the Lord shall locate a stake of Zion. And if ye do this with a pure heart, in all faithfulness, ye shall be blessed" (D&C 136:10–11).

This covenant which thousands of Church members made in the Nauvoo Temple became the backbone that carried the Saints to Zion. At times the spine strained under the intense burdens it was required to carry, but it was the commitment to covenants that nourished and strengthened marrow to the bones. Limbs too weak to take another step were enlivened by God's promises connected with covenants, and these durable, faithful Saints received the enabling power to rescue the poorest and weakest among them who were stranded in Missouri and Illinois. Hundreds, even thousands, stood true to the covenants made in the Nauvoo Temple to evacuate all the poor, especially when it looked as if the extermination order would be enforced. Though wrestling with human weaknesses, these Saints strove to become an Enoch people, knit together with one heart and mind, with no poor among them.

In the bustling city of Nauvoo, a diverse migrant people became united by covenants they entered into with God and each other. This union of North Americans and British emigrants, refined by the elements of faith, endurance, and charity, forged a people bound and determined to build Zion once again. Molded from the malaria-infested swamps of Commerce and from the pressing spiritual labor at home and abroad, these covenant people prepared the way for others to establish Zion in the West.

NOTES TO CHAPTER SIX

1. Bernhard De Voto, *The Year of Decision: 1846* (1942; reprint with a foreword by Arthur Schlesinger, Jr., New York: Book-of-the-Month Club, 1984), 9–10.

2. Dee Brown, *Bury My Heart at Wounded Knee* (New York: Bantam Books

published by arrangement with Holt, Rhinehart and Winston, 1972), quotation taken from Geoffrey Ward of *Newsweek*, inside of front cover.

3. David E. Miller and Della S. Miller, *Nauvoo: The City of Joseph*, 2d ed., (Bountiful, Utah: Utah History Atlas, 1996), 130–141.

4. Wilford Woodruff, in *Official Report of the 68th Annual Conference of The Church of Jesus Christ of Latter-day Saints* (Salt Lake City: The Church of Jesus Christ of Latter-day Saints, 1898), 57-58.

5. James Amasa Little, "Biography of Lorenzo Dow Young," *Utah Historical Quarterly* 14, nos. 1-4 (1946): 46.

6. Hyrum L. Andrus, "Joseph Smith and the West," *BYU Studies* 2, no. 2 (1960): 129-147.

7. *HC* 5:85.

8. *Tullidge's Histories*, vol. 2 of *History of Northern Utah, and Southern Idaho*, biographical supplement, 271, cited in *HC* 5:86.

9. E. Cecil McGavin, Nauvoo the Beautiful (Salt Lake City: Bookcraft, 1972), 127.

10. Mosiah L. Hancock, *Life Story of Mosiah Lyman Hancock*, L. Tom Perry Special Collections Library, Harold B. Lee Library, Brigham Young University, Provo, Utah, 19.

11. Harvey H. Cluff, *Journal of Harvey H. Cluff*, 1836–1868, typescript, L. Tom Perry Special Collections Library, Harold B. Lee Library, Brigham Young University, Provo, Utah, p. 6–7.

12. Juanita Brooks, ed., *On the Mormon Frontier: The Diary of Hosea Stout*, 1844–1861 (Salt Lake City: University of Utah Press, 1964), 1:28.

13. Miller and Miller, *Nauvoo: The City of Joseph*, 188.

14. B. H. Roberts, *A Comprehensive History of the Church* (Salt Lake City: Deseret News Press, 1930), 2:505.

15. "Part of a Dispatch from the Governor," *Nauvoo Neighbor* 3, no. 23 (29 October 1845): 1.

16. Allen and Leonard, *Story of the Latter-day Saints*, 2d ed., 214–215.

17. "Mormon News," *Burlington Hawkeye* 6, no. 16 (12 September 1844), noted in Newbern Issac Butt, comp., 4 vols., Mormons in Ohio, Illinois, Missouri, etc., p. 2:11.

18. "Mormon News," *Burlington Hawkeye* 6, no. 17 (19 September 1844), p. 2:12.

19. "Leaving the City," *Warsaw Signal* 6 (19 June 1844), noted in Newbern Issac Butt, comp., 4 vols., Mormons in Ohio, Illinois, Missouri, etc. Newspaper clippings, 1831–1848, typescript, p. 2:227.

20. Richard E. Bennett, *We'll Find the Place: The Mormon Exodus*, 1846–1848 (Salt Lake City: Deseret Book Co., 1997), 13.

21. "The Mormons," *Lee County Democrat* 5, no. 245 (11 April 1846), noted in Newbern Issac Butt, comp., 4 vols., Mormons in Ohio, Illinois, Missouri, etc. Newspaper clippings, 1831–1848, typescript, p. 4:37.

22. *HC* 7:464–465.

23. *HC* 7:478–479.

24. Allen and Leonard, *Story of the Latter-day Saints*, 224.

25. *Journal History*, 1 January 1846, HDA.

26. Ibid., 3 February 1846, HDA.

27. Sarah De Armon Pea Rich, *Journal of Sarah De Armon Pea Rich*, typescript, L. Tom Perry Special Collections Library, Harold B. Lee Library, Brigham Young University, Provo, Utah, p. 42–43.

28. Allen and Leonard, *Story of the Latter-day Saints*, 227–228.

29. *Church History in the Fullness of Times*, 2d ed. (Salt Lake City: The Church of Jesus Christ of Latter-day Saints, 1993), 306.

30. "Special Conference," *Millennial Star* 7, no. 1 (1 January 1846): 5.

31. According to Andrew Jenson, "Church Emigration," *Contributor* 12, no. 12 (October 1891): 441, only two voyages of British converts embarked from Liverpool for Nauvoo during 1846. One named the *Liverpool* left on 16 January and carried about 45 emigrants; he had no information on the other. However, further research suggests that this other voyage was probably the *Windsor Castle*, which left Liverpool on 15 February.

32. It is intriguing that Latter-day Saints leader Sam Brannan and over 200 migrating Saints embarked that exact day from New York on a six-month voyage aboard the ship Brooklyn, sailing them to Yerba Buena (later San Francisco), California. For more information on this topic see Lorin K. Hansen, "Voyage of the Brooklyn," *Dialogue: A Journal of Mormon Thought* 21, no. 3 (Autumn 1988), 46–72.

33. *Journal History*, 9 February 1846, HDA.

34. Ezra Taft Benson, "Ezra Taft Benson, I," *Instructor* 80, no. 2 (May 1945), 215.

35. Henry W. Bigler, *Diary of Henry W. Bigler:* Volume 1, 1846–1850, typescript, L. Tom Perry Special Collections Library, Harold B. Lee Library, Brigham Young University, Provo, Utah, p. 15.

36. Miller and Miller, *Nauvoo: The City of Joseph*, 198.

37. Samuel George Ellsworth, "A History of Mormon Missions in the United States and Canada, 1830–1860" (Ph.D. diss., University of California, 1951), 299.

Ellsworth also points out that other nonexilic groups of Saints were scattered during this time such as those who followed Lyman Wight to Texas, the Brooklyn Saints in California and members of the Mormon Battalion. To this could be added scores of branches throughout the eastern and southern states.

38. For more information on the Church in St. Louis during this period, see Stanley B. Kimball, "The Saints and St. Louis, 1831–1857: An Oasis of Tolerance and Security," *BYU Studies* 13, no. 4 (Summer 1973), 489–519.

39. The location of Catona is not known. However, Adams may have meant Caton, Illinois.

40. William Adams, *Autobiography of William Adams*, 1822–1894, typescript, L. Tom Perry Special Collections Library, Harold B. Lee Library, Brigham Young University, Provo, Utah, p. 15–16.

41. Ibid., 16.

42. *Church History in the Fullness of Times*, 309. For comparison, a year later the 1847 vanguard pioneer company traveled over one thousand miles from Winter Quarters to the Salt Lake Valley in only 111 days.

43. Ibid., 311–312.

44. Bigler, *Diary of Henry W. Bigler*, p. 18. Bigler refers to this place as Richmond Point, it is most probably Richardson's Point. Andrew Jenson, in "*Encyclopedic History of The Church of Jesus Christ of Latter-day Saints*, s.v. "Richardson's Point," notes that "Richardson's Point in Van Buren County, Iowa, is the place were Pres. Brigham Young made his headquarters from March 7th to 20th, 1846, when traveling westward through Iowa en route for the Rocky Mountains."

45. Bigler, *Diary of Henry W. Bigler*, p. 18.

46. Brooks, *Diary of Hosea Stout*, 1:149.

47. William Clayton, "William Clayton's Journal," (Salt Lake City: *Deseret News*, 1964, 375), cited in William E. Purdy, "They Marched Their Way West: The Nauvoo Brass Band," *Ensign*, July 1980, 22.

48. Purdy, "They Marched Their Way West," 22.

49. Miller and Miller, *Nauvoo: The City of Joseph*, 202–203.

50. Che-Mo-Ko Mon, "Nauvoo. The Day After It Was Evacuated," *Burlington Hawkeye* 8 (24 September 1846), noted in Newbern Issac Butt, comp., 4 vols., Mormons in Ohio, Illinois, Missouri, etc. Newspaper clippings, 1831–1848, typescript, p. 4:31.

51. Ibid., p. 4:31–32. One local Fort Madison newspaper titled the *Lee County Democrat* 5, no. 248 (2 May 1846), noted in Newbern Issac Butt, comp., 4 vols., Mormons in Ohio, Illinois, Missouri, etc. Newspaper clippings, 1831–1848, type-

script, p. 4:38, suggests that a primary reason for wanting to drive the Mormons out of Illinois at this time was politically motivated. The article noted that the "Quincy Whig is constantly fanning the flames of discord, and makes manifest a determination, on the part of the whigs, to compel them all to leave prior to next fall's election—hoping thereby to secure the election of a whig Congressman."

52.Che-Mo-Ko Mon, "Nauvoo. The Day After It Was Evacuated," p. 4:33.

53. Will Bagley, ed., *The Pioneer Camp of The Saints: The 1846 and 1847 Mormon Trail Journals of Thomas Bullock* (Spokane: Arthur H. Clark Co., 1997), 76.

54. Helen Mar Whitney [Kimball], "Travels Beyond the Mississippi," *Woman's Exponent* 12 (1 May 1884): 182.

55. *Journal History*, 28 September 1846 HDA, 5–6.

56. Allen and Leonard, *Story of the Latter-day Saints*, 245.

57. Richard E. Bennett, *Mormons at the Missouri, 1846–1852: And Should We Die . . .* (Norman: University of Oklahoma Press, 1987), 157.

EPILOGUE

The Saints began gathering into Nauvoo in 1839, and less than seven years later they were driven out. Yet they left an imprint of their faith and sacrifice through the majestic monument of their holy temple, a tangible witness to their faith, sacrifice, and tenacity. On 9 October 1848, arsonists set fire to the temple. The *Keokuk Register* noted that the shooting flames "threw a lurid glare into the surrounding darkness. Great volumes of smoke and flame burst from the windows, and the crash of the falling timbers was distinctly heard on the opposite side of the river. The interior of the building was like a furnace, the walls of solid masonry were heated throughout and cracked by the intense heat."[1]

When Brigham Young heard of the burning of the temple he remarked, "I hoped to see it burned before I left, but I did not. I was glad when I heard of its being destroyed by fire, and of the walls having fallen in," and then he pronounced, "Hell, you cannot now occupy it."[2]

Some Latter-day Saint emigrants bound for Utah went out of

NAUVOO TEMPLE ON FIRE.

their way to visit these sacred ruins.[3] Could they have foreseen the rays of heaven shining again on Nauvoo and the temple rising again from the banks of the mighty Mississippi?

With the help of Church member Wilford Wood, The Church of Jesus Christ of Latter-day Saints began to acquire the Nauvoo Temple land in 1937. Wood was able to acquire most of the temple property for only nine hundred dollars from the Bank of Nauvoo. Professor Robert C. Freeman wisely observed, "What seems clear is that the early destruction that visited the temple had a silver lining. Because the fire and wind devastated the site soon after the Saints' exodus, the property was rendered less attractive to non-Latter-day Saints interests. Perhaps these early events made the reacquisition of the temple block in recent decades more attainable."[4]

A quarter century later, members of Nauvoo Restoration Inc., performed an archaeological excavation at the temple site and were able to find the temple foundation stones. In 1977 a bronze replica of the Nauvoo Temple was placed at the site enabling visitors to see what had once graced this sacred setting.[5] Then in the April 1999 general conference of The Church of Jesus Christ of Latter-day Saints, President Gordon B. Hinckley made the thrilling surprise announcement that the Nauvoo Temple would return. He said, "I feel impressed to announce that . . . we plan to rebuild the Nauvoo Temple. . . . It will stand as a memorial to those who built the first such structure there on the banks of the Mississippi."[6]

RUINS OF THE TEMPLE AT NAUVOO.

The dedication day for the Nauvoo Temple is set for 27 June 2002, in appropriate remembrance of the martyrdom of the Prophet Joseph Smith and of his loyal brother Hyrum. This sacred structure will stand not only

COMPLETED REBUILT NAUVOO TEMPLE.

as a memorial to those who initially built this sacred edifice, but as a reminder of those faithful converts who heeded the call to gather to Zion without delay. The story of their journey to and through Nauvoo is an old story of God gathering His people in any age to endow them with His greater light, truth, and power. Bound in His covenants they fashioned a city and a temple, while He fashioned their character. The latter-day Nauvoo Temple will forever stand as a monument to their inspiring story.

NOTES TO EPILOGUE

1. *Keokuk Registe*r, (12 October 1848), as cited in Robert C. Freeman, "Out of the Ashes: The Story of the Nauvoo Temple," *Religious Studies Newsletter* 14, no. 2 (January 2000): 2–3.

2. Brigham Young, in "Funds of the Church," *Journal of Discourses*, 26 vols. (Liverpool: George Q. Cannon, 1861), 8:203.

3. James Ririe, in Kate B. Carter, comp., *Our Pioneer Heritage* (Salt Lake City: Daughters of Utah Pioneers, 1966), 9:355; Sarah Birch Waters, in Kate B. Carter, comp., *Our Pioneer Heritage* (Salt Lake City: Daughters of Utah Pioneers, 1968), 11:164; and Jane Ann Folwer Sparks, *The Reminiscences and Diary of Jane Ann Folwer Sparks,* HDA, 14.

4. Freeman, "Out of the Ashes," 4–5.

5. Richard O. Cowan, "The Nauvoo Temple," in *A City of Refuge: Quincy, Illinois,* ed. Susan Easton Black and Richard E. Bennett (Salt Lake City: Millennial Press, 2000), 291.

6. President Gordon B. Hinckley, "Be a Little Better," *Official Report of the 169th Annual General Conference of The Church of Jesus Christ of Latter-day Saints* (Salt Lake City: The Church of Jesus Christ of Latter-day Saints, 1999), 117.

APPENDIX A[1]

British Latter-day Saint Voyages to America

	Date of Sailing	Port of Sailing	Name of Ship	Tons	Leader of Company	Total No.	Emigration Agent
1.	June 6th, 1840	Liverpool	Britannia		John Moon	41	Brigham Young
2.	Sept. 8th, 1840	Liverpool	North America		Theodore Turley	200	Brigham Young
3.	Oct. 15th, 1840	Liverpool	Isaac Newton		Samuel Mulliner	50*	Brigham Young
4.	Feb. 7th, 1841	Liverpool	Sheffield		Hiram Clark	235	Brigham Young
5.	February, 1841	Bristol	**Caroline**		**Thos. Richardson**	181*	Brigham Young
	August, 1841	**Bristol**	**Caroline**			?	Brigham Young
6.	Feb. 16th, 1841	Liverpool	Echo		Daniel Browett	109	Brigham Young
7.	March 17, 1841	Liverpool	Alesto		Thomas Smith	54	Brigham Young
8.	April 21st, 1841	Liverpool	Rochester		Brigham Young	130	Brigham Young
	May 10, 1841	**Bristol**	Harmony			?	Brigham Young
9.	Sept. 21st, 1841	Liverpool	Tyrean [Tyrian]		Joseph Fielding	207	P. P. Pratt and Amos Fielding
10.	Nov. 8th, 1841	Liverpool	Chaos		Peter Melling	170	P. P. Pratt and Amos Fielding
11.	Jan. 12th, 1842	Liverpool	Tremont			143	P. P. Pratt and Amos Fielding
12.	Feb. 5th, 1842	Liverpool	Hope			270	P. P. Pratt and Amos Fielding
13.	Feb. 20th, 1842	Liverpool	John Cummins			200*	P. P. Pratt and Amos Fielding
14.	March 12, 1842	Liverpool	Hanover		Amos Fielding	200*	P. P. Pratt and Amos Fielding
15.	Sept. 17th, 1842	Liverpool	Sidney		Levi Richards	180	P. P. Pratt and Amos Fielding
16.	Sept. 25th, 1842	Liverpool	Medford		Orson Hyde	214	P. P. Pratt and Amos Fielding
17.	Sept. 29th, 1842	Liverpool	Henry		John Snider	157	P. P. Pratt and Amos Fielding
18.	Oct. 29th, 1842	Liverpool	†Emerald		Parley P. Pratt	250	P. P. Pratt and Amos Fielding
19.	Jan. 16th, 1843	Liverpool	Swanton	709	Lorenzo Snow	212	Amos Fielding and H. Clark
20.	March 8th, 1843	Liverpool	Yorkshire	808	Thomas Bullock	83	Amos Fielding and H. Clark
21.	March 21, 1843	Liverpool	Claiborne	686		106	Amos Fielding and H. Clark
22.	Sept. 5th, 1842	Liverpool	Metoka	944		280	Amos Fielding and H. Clark

Date of Sailing	Port of Sailing	Name of Ship	Tons	Leader of Company	Total No.	Emigration Agent
23. Oct. 21st, 1843	Liverpool	Champion	729		91	Amos Fielding and H. Clark
24. Jan. 23rd, 1844	Liverpool	Fanny	529	William Kay	210	Reuben Hedlock
25. Feb. 6th, 1844	Liverpool	Isaac Allerton	594	**George Riser?**	60	Reuben Hedlock
26. Feb. 11th, 1844	Liverpool	Swanton‡	677		81	Reuben Hedlock
27. March 5th, 1844	Liverpool	Glasgow	594	Hiram Clark	150	Reuben Hedlock
28. Sept. 19th, 1844	Liverpool	Norfolk	661		143	Reuben Hedlock
29. Jan. 17th, 1845	Liverpool	Palmyra	691	Amos Fielding	200*	Reuben Hedlock
30. February, 1845	Liverpool				86*	Reuben Hedlock
31. Sept'mb'r, 1845	Liverpool	Oregon	650		125*	Reuben Hedlock
32. Jan. 16th, 1846	Liverpool	Liverpool	600	Hiram Clark	45	Reuben Hedlock
Miscellaneous	Liverpool	Miscellaneous		Miscellaneous	137	Reuben Hedlock
February, 1846	**Liverpool**	**(possibly the Windsor Castle)**				

*Approximate.

†There is a discrepancy in the number of souls on the *Emerald*. Elder Hiram Clark, who assisted to fit out the company, says she carried 314, but I have taken the number stated by Elder Pratt.

‡ *i.e.* Second trip made by that ship with "Mormon" emigrants.

Building on Jenson's work I have included in bold two additional chartered voyages as well as some previously missing information. Between 1840–1846, there were also 13 additional Latter-day Saint independent voyages.

The following detailed account of the thirty two companies has been compiled with great care, and with a special view to accuracy, from public and private documents, both in printed and manuscript form:

FIRST COMPANY.—*Britannia*, 41 souls. The following is recorded in the history of Joseph Smith:

"Saturday, June 6th, 1840, Elder John Moon and a company of forty Saints, to wit: John Moon, Hugh Moon, their mother, and seven others of her family, Henry Moon, (uncle of John Moon), Henry Moon, Francis Moon, William Sutton, William Sitgraves, Richard Eaves, Thomas Moss, Henry Moore, Nancy Ashworth, Richard Ainscough, and families, sailed in the ship *Britania* from Liverpool for New York, being the first Saints who have sailed from England for Zion."

The *Britannia* arrived in New York on Monday, July 20th, 1840, from whence the emigrants continued the journey to Nauvoo, Illinois.

SECOND COMPANY.—*North America,* about 200 souls. Saturday, September 5th, 1840, Apostles Brigham Young and Willard Richards went from Manchester to Liverpool, and in the evening organized a company of Saints bound for New York, by choosing Elder Theodore Turley, a returning missionary, to preside, with six counselors, among whom was Elder William Clayton, one of the earliest English converts. Apostles Brigham Young and Willard Richards went on board the *North America* on Monday the 7th, and remained with the Saints on board over night. On Tuesday morning, about nine o'clock, the vessel was tugged out by steamer. The Apostles accompanied the emigrants about fifteen miles, and then left them in good spirits.

The company had a prosperous voyage to New York, where they arrived in the beginning of October, and from there they continued the journey to Buffalo, New York. Owing to the expensiveness of the route many of the emigrants fell short of means to complete the journey to Nauvoo; they therefore divided at Buffalo, a part going to settle in and around Kirtland, Ohio, while the balance, under the leadership of Theodore Turley, continued the journey to Nauvoo, to which place Joseph the Prophet states he had the pleasure of welcoming about one hundred of them, about the middle of October, 1841.

THIRD COMPANY.—*Isaac Newton,* about 50 souls. This company, embracing the first Latter-day Saint emigration from Scotland, has not been noted before in Church history. The following particulars are gleaned from the private journal of Samuel Mulliner, who was the leader of the company:

"The ship *Isaac Newton* sailed from Liverpool October 15th, 1840, with a small company of Scotch Saints, under the direction of Elders Samuel Mulliner and Alexander Wright. The passage cost £2 17s 6d for adults, and 19s 3d for children. After a most pleasant passage of forty-eight and one half days, the company arrived in New Orleans in the evening of December 2nd. On the 4th they started on a steamboat for St. Louis, the fare being $4^{00} for an adult. The water in the river was low, and the emigrants were delayed several days in consequence thereof; but they finally arrived in St. Louis December 17th. Elder Mulliner was unsuccessful in his attempt to hire a boat to take the company to Nauvoo, and therefore a number of the emigrants remined at Alton, Illinois, until the following spring, when they reached Nauvoo in safety."

This was the first company of British Saints who emigrated by way of New Orleans.

FOURTH COMPANY.—*Sheffield*, 235 souls. The following is culled from the history of Joseph Smith:

Saturday, February 6th, 1841, a council meeting was held at Brother Richard Harrison's, seventy two Burlington Street, Liverpool, for the purpose of organizing a company of Saints going to New Orleans on a ship Sheffield. Captain Porter, Apostles Brigham Young, John Taylor and Willard Richards and other officers were present. Elder Hiram Clark was chosen president, and Thomas Walmsley, Miles Romney, Edward Martin, John Taylor, Francis Clark and John Riley, counselors to President Clark. Edward Martin was appointed clerk and historian of the company. President Clark and his counselors were blessed and set apart for their mission.

The *Sheffield* sailed from Liverpool, bound for New Orleans, with two hundred and thirty-five Saints on board, on Sunday the 7th. In the *Millennial Star*, Volume I, page two hundred and sixty-three, the following occurs:

"The emigrants were from Preston, Manchester and other towns of England, and were destined for the colonies of the Saints in the State of Illinois, and the Territory of Iowa. Among the company was a large proportion of the industrious poor, who were upon the point of starvation in this land (England), or who were working like slaves to procure a very scanty substance. By the kindness of their brethren they were enabled to escape worse than Egyptian bondage and go to a country, where they can by their industry obtain an inheritance and enjoy plenty for themselves and their children."

After a passage of fifty-one days the company landed in New Orleans; three deaths and two births having occurred on the voyage. On arriving at New Orleans, Elder Clark made a contract with a steamer to carry the company to St. Louis for two dollars and fifty cents each, including baggage. From St. Louis to Nauvoo they secured a passage on the *Goddess of Liberty* for one dollar each. About thirty of the emigrants who had become disaffected through false reports, tarried at St. Louis. The bulk of the company landed in Nauvoo, April 18th, 1841, about eleven o'clock in the evening. Notwithstanding the late hour, quite a number of the brethren stood on the shore to welcome these new arrivals from the old world.

FIFTH COMPANY.—181 souls. About the same time as the *Sheffield* sailed from Liverpool (February, 1841), another company of Saints from Herefordshire and the surrounding country sailed from Bristol, but I have been unable to learn the name of the ship, or the number of emigrants going on it. However, basing my calculation on Apostle Parley P. Pratt's statement to the effect that one thousand people had emigrated up to April, 1841, we have grounds for believing that about one hundred and eighty-one souls sailed from Bristol on that occasion.

SIXTH COMPANY.—*Echo.* 109 souls. According to the history of Joseph Smith, Apostles Brigham Young, Willard Richards and John Taylor met in council at 72 Burlington Street, Liverpool, Thursday, February 11th, 1841, and set apart, by the laying on of hands, Elder Daniel Browett, to take charge of a company of Saints about to sail for New Orleans, on the ship *Echo*, (Captain Wood); John Cheese, David Wilding, James Lavender, William Jenkins, Robert Harris and John Ellison were also set apart to be his counselors. Elder Browett was appointed clerk and historian of the company. The *Echo* sailed from Liverpool, bound for New Orleans, Tuesday, February 16th, 1841, with one hundred and nine Saints on board, but I have been unable to find any particulars about the voyage.

SEVENTH COMPANY.—*Alesto*, 54 souls. The ship *Alesto* sailed from Liverpool bound for New Orleans, with fifty-four Saints on board, under the direction of Elders Thomas Smith and William Moss. No particulars are at hand concerning the voyage.

EIGHTH COMPANY.—*Rochester*, 130 souls. Tuesday April 20th, 1841, Apostles Brigham Young, Heber C. Kimball, Orson Pratt, Wilford Woodruff, John Taylor, George A. Smith and Willard

Richards and family went on board the ship *Rochester*, Captain
Woodhouse, at Liverpool bound for New York, with a company of
one hundred and thirty Saints. Captain Woodhouse delayed his
sailing two days, to accommodate the Elders.

The *Rochester* sailed on the twenty-first and arrived at the quaran-
tine ground at New York May 19th, after a toilsome passage. At one
time she was beset with head winds and a tedious storm, when the
Apostles united in prayer, in answer to which the storm abated, the
sea became calm, and the voyage was continued with rejoicings. On
the twenty-eighth of April the ship encountered a tempest, shipped a
heavy sea in which Apostle Woodruff got thoroughly drenched, while
Willard Richards escaped under the bulwarks.

The *Rochester* arrived at the dock in New York about four o'clock
p.m., on Thursday, May 20th, but the passengers were prevented
from landing by the carters and rowdies until late in the evening.
Such was the confusion in New York at that time at the arrival of a
ship, steamboat or coach, that strangers were led to suppose that the
city was without mayor, marshal, police or any other office to keep
the peace.

The company remain[e]d in New York until the fourth of June,
when the journey was continued, under the direction of Brigham
Young, Heber C. Kimball and John Taylor, via Philadelphia to
Pittsburg by railway and canal transportation. They traveled on what
was then called the swift line, for which they paid fourteen dollars for
each adult; the slow line carried passengers for nine dollars. After
staying four days at Pittsburg, they set sail on the steamboat *Cicero*,
June 12th, and after having proceeded about fifteen miles the boat
ran on a sand bank, where it was detained three days; in fact the boat
ran aground several times, the water being very low, and the passengers were three weeks on board before they arrived in Nauvoo. The
weather was also extremely warm. Apostle Kimball, in a communication to the *Millennial Star*, advised future emigrants to come by way
of New Orleans, on which route the accommodations would be
better and the fare less, and he also recommended that British Saints
should sail in the cool part of the season.

The company finally arrived in Nauvoo July 1st, 1841, and was
met on the river bank by about three hundred Saints, who had come

down to meet the new-comers. A greater manifestation of love and gladness had perhaps never been witnessed among brethren in this dispensation than that which was exhibited on this occasion when the Prophet Joseph met his brethren of the Twelve, whom he loved so dearly. Joseph was the first person on board the steamer which brought the company in, and gave the immigrating Saints a warm and hearty greeting.

NINTH COMPANY.—*Tyrean*, 207 souls. On Tuesday, September 21st, 1841, the ship *Tyrean* sailed from Liverpool with two hundred and seven Saints bound for Nauvoo, via New Orleans, under the presidency of Joseph Fielding. By chartering the ship for the purpose, the company saved about six hundred dollars.

The *Tyrean* arrived in New Orleans in the early part of November, from whence the emigrants proceeded to Warsaw, Hancock County, Illinois, about twenty miles below Nauvoo, where they arrived November 24th. It was the intention to locate the newcomers on the site of Warren, a new settlement, which the Saints tried to locate one mile south of Warsaw, but difficulties arose with the old settlers, in consequence of which the British emigrants moved to Nauvoo about the middle of December, following. Some of them had previously moved thither.

TENTH COMPANY.—*Chaos*, about 170 souls. "On Monday, November 8th, 1841, the splendid ship, *Chaos*, sailed from Liverpool, bound for New Orleans, under the charter of the Latter-day Saints. She carried out nearly one hundred and seventy passengers. Cheerfulness and satisfaction seemed to pervade every heart as they bade farewell to their native shores, and launched forth toward the land of promise." (*Millennial Star*, Volume II, page 105.)

Patriarch Peter Melling was placed in charge of the company, which arrived in Nauvoo early in 1842, as Joseph Smith, under date of March 7th, 1842, records that "Peter Melling, the Patriarch, from England, brought to the office, thirteen dollars and thirty-seven and a half cents in cash, and sixty-five dollars' worth of clothing from Parley P. Pratt and Amos Fielding, of England." (*Millennial Star,* Volume XIX, page 135.)

ELEVENTH COMPANY.—*Tremont*, 143 souls. The ship *Tremont* sailed from Liverpool January 12th, 1842, with one hundred and forty-three passengers, mostly Saints, bound for Nauvoo via New Orleans. This was the first company that sailed in 1842.

Under date of Sunday March 27th, 1842, the Prophet Joseph records:

"I witnessed the landing of one hundred and seventy English Saints from the steamer *Ariel* under the presidency of Lyman Wight; also about three thousand dollars worth of goods for the Temple and Nauvoo House."

These must have been the passengers who crossed the Atlantic in the ship *Tremont*, and perhaps some that emigrated in the *Chaos* two months previous. It is likely that Peter Meeling [Melling] the leader of the *Chaos* company, pushed through with only a portion of his people, and that the others waited somewhere on the road to come on to Nauvoo with the *Tremont* passengers.

TWELFTH COMPANY.—*Hope*, 270 souls. The ship *Hope*, Captain Soule, sailed from Liverpool February 5th, 1842, with two hundred and seventy passengers, mostly members of the Church, bound for Nauvoo, via New Orleans. Under date of April 13th, 1842, the following is recorded in the history of Joseph Smith:

"About one hundred and fifty Saints from England, landed in Nauvoo from the steamer *Louisa*, and about sixty from the steamer *Amaranth*."

These were undoubtedly a portion of the emigrants who sailed in the *Hope*.

THIRTEENTH COMPANY.—*John Cummins*, about 200 souls. Previous to the sailing of this company, the following emigration notice appeared in the *Millennial Star*:

"The *John Cummins* is chartered for us, and is to sail on the twentieth of February 1842. Immediate application should be made by those who wish a passagePassage costs from £3 15s to £4, including provisions. Passengers find their own bedding and cooking utensils; and all their luggage goes free. On arriving at New Orleans, a passage can be obtained up the Mississippi River, fifteen hundred miles by steamer, for fifteen shillings, and freight free, as we have learned by letter from Elder Joseph Fielding, who sailed with two hundred passengers in the *Tyrean* last September."

The *John Cummins* sailed on the day appointed. (February 20th, 1842.) In the *Times and Seasons* of May 16th, 1842, the following appears in an editorial notice:

"Elder Amos Fielding has just arrived in Nauvoo with about one hundred and fifty emigrants from England; a ship load came some time ago."

The last sentence has very likely reference to the Saints sailing in the *John Cummins*.

FOURTEENTH COMPANY.—*Hanover*, about 200 souls. The ship *Hanover* sailed from Liverpool March 12th, 1842, with about two hundred Saints on board bound for Nauvoo, via New Orleans, in charge of Amos Fielding. After a prosperous trip Amos Fielding arrived in Nauvoo with about one hundred and fifty of his company, May 14th, 1842.

FIFTEENTH COMPANY.—*Sidney*, 180 souls. On Saturday, September 17th, 1842, the ship *Sidney*, Captain Cowen, sailed from Liverpool, with one hundred and eighty Saints on board, under the direction of Elder Levi Richards, bound for Nauvoo, via New Orleans. George D. Watt the first man baptized in England, who emigrated with this company, writes from New Orleans, under date of November 13th, 1842, as follows:

"We have had a passage of fifty six days—fine weather—with a kind captain and crew, who allowed us every reasonable privilege. There have been five deaths out of the company, and one sailor who fell from the yard arm and was killed. The dead are: Brother Yates' eldest child, Sister Cannon, (mother of President George Q. Cannon), Brother Browne's child and two children belonging to a man who is not in the Church. We stuck upon the sand bar at the mouth of the river (Mississippi) thirty four hours. About two hours after we got off, the *Medford* came on the bar, where she stuck thirty hours. We landed here (New Orleans) on the eleventh instant and the *Medford* arrived to-day the thirteenth. She lies about ten yards from us. * * * We have taken one of the largest and best steamboats in this port. We pay two dollars and fifty cents per head, and twenty-five cents per one hundred pounds above the weight allowed each person, which is one hundred pounds. We are all going up together; *i.e.* The *Sidney* and *Medford* passengers."

After tarrying three days at New Orleans, the emigrants embarked on the steamer *Alexander Scott* and made rapid progress till they had passed the mouth of the Ohio River, when they ran a-ground and remained fast three days. After getting clear again they continued the journey to within ninety miles of St. Louis, where the vessel had to remain three weeks for want of water. When the emigrants finally arrived at St. Louis, it was the dead of winter, and the river being frozen up above that city, it became necessary for the Saints to remain there for awhile until communication opened up again with the towns on the upper Mississippi. Without much difficulty houses and provisions were secured, and the remainder of the winter was spent quite comfortably in St. Louis. In April, 1843, the journey was continued to Nauvoo.

SIXTEENTH COMPANY.—*Medford*, 214 souls. On Sunday, September 25th, 1842, the ship *Medford*, Captain Wilber, sailed from Liverpool with two hundred and fourteen Saints bound for Nauvoo, via New Orleans, under the presidency of Apostle Orson Hyde, who was returning home from his mission to Jerusalem.

The *Medford* arrived in New Orleans, November 13th, 1842, after a fair passage, having had only two deaths on board. From New Orleans the emigrants continued the trip up the river in company with the passengers who had crossed the Atlantic on the *Sidney*, but were detained in St. Louis because of ice on the river, until the following spring, when the journey was continued to Nauvoo.

SEVENTEENTH COMPANY.—*Henry*, 157 souls. Thursday, September 29th, 1842, the ship *Henry*, Captain Pierce, sailed from Liverpool with one hundred and fifty-seven Saints bound for Nauvoo, via New Orleans, under the direction of John Snider.

Elder Snider arrived in Nauvoo January 23rd, 1843, but his company of emigrants were detained on the way because of ice on the

Mississippi River, and did not arrive in Nauvoo till the following spring.

EIGHTEENTH COMPANY.—*Emerald*, 250 souls. October 29th, 1842, the ship *Emerald*, Captain Leighton, sailed from Liverpool with two hundred and fifty Saints bound for Nauvoo, via New Orleans, under the direction of Apostle Parley P. Pratt who writes:

"We had a tedious passage of ten weeks and some difficulties, murmurings and rebellions; but the Saints on board were called together, and chastened and reproved sharply, which brought them to repentance. We then humbled ourselves and called on the Lord, and he sent a fair wind and brought us into port in time to save us from starvation. We landed in new Orleans early in January, 1843. Here I chartered a steamer called the *Goddess of Liberty*, and took passage with the company for St. Louis. Running up the river for about a week, I landed with my family in Chester, Illinois, eighty miles below St. Louis. The company continued on to St. Louis."

On account of ice in the river which made it impassable for steamboats, the emigrants were forced to remain in St. Louis until the spring, when the *Maid of Iowa*, Captain Dan Jones, came down from Nauvoo and brought the people up. Under date of April 12th, 1843, the Prophet Joseph writes:

"About five p.m., the steamer *Maid of Iowa*, hauled up at the Nauvoo House landing, and discharged about two hundred Saints, in charge of Elders Parley P. Pratt and Levi Richards. These had been detained at St. Louis, Alton, Chester, and other places through the winter, having left Liverpool last fall. Dan Jones, captain of the *Maid of Iowa*, was baptized a few weeks since; he has been eleven days coming from St. Louis, being detained by ice. I was present at the landing and the first on board the steamer, when I met sister Mary Ann Pratt (who had been in England with Brother Parley,) and her little daughter only three or four days old. I could not refrain from shedding tears; so many of my friends and acquaintances arriving in one day (another company in charge of Lorenzo Snow had arrived the same day) kept me very busy receiving their congratulations and answering their questions. I was rejoiced to meet them in such good health and fine spirits; for they were equal to any that had ever come to Nauvoo."

NINETEENTH COMPANY.—*Swanton*, 212 souls. On Monday, January 16th, 1843, the first British emigrant company of the season sailed from Liverpool, Captain Davenport, with two hundred and twelve Saints on board, bound for Nauvoo, via New Orleans, under the direction of Elder Lorenzo Snow.

During the first four weeks of the voyage, continued head winds prevented the ship from progressing very fast, but on the seventeenth of February the wind became fair, and continued so during the remainder of the voyage. A few days after leaving Liverpool, the company was more fully organized by the appointment of Elders M. Auley and Robert Reed to act as counselors to Lorenzo Snow. The emigrants were also divided into two grand divisions, and twelve officers appointed to attend to the comfort and cleanliness of the Saints. At six o'clock every morning the bell sounded for all to arise; prayer meetings were held every night at seven o'clock; there was preaching every Tuesday and Thursday nights and twice on Sundays. Peace and health prevailed among the people; though some were disposed to murmur a little. Much of the power of God was manifested in the restoration of the sick by anointing with oil, and through the prayer of faith. The following is from the Biography of Lorenzo Snow, written by his sister, Eliza R. Snow, (page 65):

"The commander of the ship *Swanton*, Captain Davenport, and the officers of the crew, were kind and courteous, which contributed much to ameliorate the discomfort incident to life on the ocean. The steward, a German by birth, was a young man, very affable in manner, and gentlemanly in deportment—a general favorite and highly respected by all. During the latter part of the voyage he took sick, and continued growing worse and worse, until death seemed inevitable. All means proved unavailing, and the captain, by whom he was much beloved, gave up all hope of his recovery, and requested the officers and crew to go in one by one, and take a farewell look of their dying friend, which they did silently and solemnly as he lay unconscious and almost breathless on his dying couch."

"Immediately after this sad ceremony closed, one of our sisters by the name of Martin, without my brother's knowledge, went to the captain and requested him to allow my brother to lay hands on the steward, according to our faith and practice under such circumstances, saying that she believed that the steward would be restored. The captain shook his head, and told her that the steward was now breathing his last, and it would be useless to trouble Mr. Snow. But Sister Martin was not to be defeated; she not only importuned, but earnestly declared her faith in the result of the proposed administration, and he finally yielded and gave consent."

"As soon as the foregoing circumstance was communicated to my brother, he started toward the cabin where the steward lay, and in passing through the door met the captain who was in tears. He said: 'Mr. Snow, it is too late; he is expiring; he is breathing his last!' My brother made no reply, but took a seat beside the dying man. After devoting a few moments to secret prayer, he laid his hands on the head of the young man, prayed, and in the name of Jesus Christ, rebuked the disease and commanded him to be made whole. Very soon after, to the joy and astonishment of all, he was seen walking the deck, praising and glorifying God for his restoration. The officers and sailors acknowledged the miraculous power of God, and on landing at New Orleans, several of them were baptized, also the first mate, February 26th, 1843."

At New Orleans the emigrating Saints left the *Swanton*, and, on board the *Amaranth*, wended their way up the Mississippi River to St. Louis, where they arrived Wednesday, March 29th, 1843. There they had to remain a few days, laying in a boat, waiting for the river to open, before they could continue the journey to Nauvoo.

Descriptive of the arrival of the company at Nauvoo, the following occurs in the history of Joseph Smith, under date of April 12th, 1843:

"Before the Elders' Conference closed, the steamer *Amaranth* appeared in sight of the Temple, coming up the river, and about noon, landed her passengers at the wharf opposite the old Post Office Building, consisting of about two hundred and forty Saints from England, under the charge of Elder Lorenzo Snow, who left Liverpool last January, after a mission of nearly three years. I, with a large company of the brethren and sisters, was present to greet the arrival of our friends, and gave notice to the new-comers to meet at the Temple tomorrow morning at ten o'clock to hear instructions. After unloading the Saints, the *Amaranth* proceeded up the river, being the first boat up this season."

In the afternoon of the same day the *Maid of Iowa* arrived in Nauvoo with Parley P. Pratt's company of British Saints.

TWENTIETH COMPANY.—*Yorkshire*, 83 souls. On Wednesday, March 8th, 1843, the ship *Yorkshire*, Captain Bache, sailed from Liverpool with eighty three Saints on board, under the supervision of Elders Thomas Bullock and Richard Rushton. The following is from the history of Joseph Smith, under date of May 2nd, 1843:

"About one o'clock, p.m., the mate of the ship *Yorkshire* opened the Testament at the twenty-seventh chapter of the Acts, and asked the passengers how they would like to be shipwrecked like Paul! Elder Thomas Bullock replied instantly: 'It is very likely we shall be ship-wrecked; but the hull of this old vessel has got to carry us safe into New Orleans.' The mate was then called away to hoist the foretop royal sail."

"Between one and two o'clock next morning, when off Cape St. Antonio, Cuba, there was much vivid lightning, when a white squall caught the foretop royal sail, which careened the vessel, when the foremast, mainmast and mizenmast snapped asunder with an awful crash; the whole of the masts above, with the jib and spanker, and sixteen sails and studding poles, were carried overboard with a tremendous splash and surge, when the vessel righted. At daybreak all on deck was in confusion and a complete wreck. During the day a sail was hoisted from the stump of the main mast to the boy of the vessel, thus leaving nothing but the hull of the vessel to carry the Saints into New Orleans."

From New Orleans the journey was continued up the Mississippi River, and "on Wednesday, May 31st, 1843, the steamer *Amaranth*," writes the Prophet Joseph, " landed in Nauvoo the Saints, who had left Liverpool in the *Yorkshire*, under the care of Elders Thomas Bullock and Richard Rushton, all well; and also some Saints who had left there more recently in another vessel."

TWENTY-FIRST COMPANY—*Claiborne*, 106 souls. March 21st, 1843, the ship *Claiborne*, Captain Burgess, sailed from Liverpool with one hundred and six Saints, bound for Nauvoo, via New Orleans. No account of this voyage is at hand.

TWENTY SECOND COMPANY.—*Metoka*, 280 souls. "The splendid ship *Metoka*, Captain M'Laren, sailed from Liverpool, September 5th, 1843, under very favorable circumstances. The Saints on board gave expression to their feelings in various hymns, which they sang as the vessel was towed into the river. The ship, which is admirably adapted for passengers, together with the respectable appearance of the emigrants, appeared very much to surprise the bystanders, who were compelled to acknowledge that they had not often witnessed the departure of such a people."

The *Metoka* made the trip to New Orleans in seven weeks. The captain M'Laren, together with the other officers of the ship, were kind and attentive to the emigrants during the passage. Three deaths occurred on board, namely one sister and two children. From New Orleans the usual route was taken up the Mississippi River, and a majority of the emigrants landed in Nauvoo November 11th, 1843.

TWENTY THIRD COMPANY.—*Champion*, 91 souls. October 21st, 1843, the ship *Champion* sailed from Liverpool with ninety-one Saints on board, bound for Nauvoo, via New Orleans. The above which is taken from Linforth's "Route from Liverpool to Great Salt Lake Valley," is all the information that I have been able to glean about this company.

TWENTY FOURTH COMPANY.—*Fanny*, 210 souls. The ship *Fanny*, Captain Peterson, sailed from Liverpool, Tuesday, January 23rd, 1844, with two hundred and ten Saints on board, under the direction of Elder William Kay, who in a letter to Reuben Hedlock, dated new Orleans, March 9th, 1844, gives the following account of the voyage:

"We came into New Orleans on the seventh of March, 1844, at seven o'clock in the morning. We should have been in sooner, but for having to stop at the bar for a considerable time to wait for a steamer, and we had also a calm in the bay; but I believe that no people that ever crossed the Atlantic had a more prosperous journey than the Lord has favored us with. The captain and crew declared they never experienced such a passage before; but such a captain and crew for kindness I believe could scarcely be met with; his liberality exceeds all that ever came under our notice. * * * The cabin and its provisions have been at the service of all who stood in need of them, and the captain has with his own hand ministered unto the necessities of all that required it. * * * We have had two deaths on board; the first was the wife of Elder James Jones, of Alfrick; she died on the nineteenth of January, and was buried in the sea on the morning of the twentieth, off the island of Puerto Rico. * * * The other death was the youngest child of Sister Greenhalgh; it died on Monday last. * * * We have had regular meetings o[f] prayer morning and evening, and three times each Lord's day, administering the Sacrament in the afternoon. The Saints generally have shown a willingness to give heed to counsel from myself and Brothers Hall and Cuerden. * * * We have this morning the steamer alongside of us, and intended gathering our baggage on board to-day. I assure you we rejoiced exceedingly at the sight of the steamer, which was the *Maid of Iowa*, and at the thought of going up in a vessel belonging to the Church, and commanded by an Elder of the Church, Brother Dan Jones."

Under date of Saturday, April 13th, 1844, the history of Joseph Smith says: "About five o'clock p.m., the *Maid of Iowa* arrived at the Nauvoo House wharf, filled with passengers from England, let by William Kay. Two hundred and ten souls started from Liverpool and nearly all arrived in good health and spirits. One smaller company had previously arrived."

TWENTY-FIFTH COMPANY.—*Isaac Alerton*, 60 souls. February 6th, 1844, the ship, *Isaac Allerton*, Captain Torney, sailed from Liverpool with sixty Saints on board, bound for Nauvoo, via new Orleans. The company arrived in Nauvoo in the beginning of April, 1844, a few days prior to the company sailing in the ship *Fanny*.

TWENTY-SIXTH COMPANY.—*Swanton*, 81 souls. February 11th, 1844, the ship *Swanton*, Captain Davenport, sailed from Liverpool with eighty-one Saints, bound for Nauvoo, via New Orleans. The history of Joseph Smith says that a company of eighty Saints arrived in Nauvoo, Friday, April 18th, 1844, which undoubtedly was the company that sailed in the *Swanton*.

TWENTY-SEVENTH COMPANY.—*Glasgow*, 150 souls. March 5th, 1844, the ship *Glasgow*, Captain Lambert, sailed from Liverpool with one hundred and fifty Saints on board, under the direction of Hiram Clark, bound for Nauvoo, via New Orleans.

Besides the foregoing, the following from the history of Joseph Smith is all the information I have been able to glean about this company:

"Saturday, April 27th, 1844, Hiram Clark arrived in Nauvoo, accompanied by one hundred and fifty immigrating Saints."

TWENTY-EIGHTH COMPANY.—Norfolk, 143 souls. "The fine ship *Norfolk*, Captain Elliott, sailed from Liverpool, September 19th, 1844, under very favorable circumstances, at a quarter past three o'clock p.m., having on board about one hundred and forty-three souls put on by us. We rejoice to see so practical an illustration of the faith of the Saints being unshaken by the late tragical events in the west, and that the Saints are not living according to the precepts of men, but the word of God."

The above is an editorial published in the *Millennial Star*, Vol. IV., page 80.

This was the first ship load of Saints sent out from England after the martyrdom of the Prophet Joseph Smith.

Proceeding up the river, a number of the emigrants found it necessary, for the lack of means, to settle down temporarily at St. Louis, Missouri, while all who were able continued to Nauvoo.

TWENTY-NINTH COMPANY.—*Palmyra*, about 200 souls. January 17th, 1845, the ship *Palmyra*, Captain Barstow, sailed from Liverpool with a company of Saints under the direction of Amos Fielding, bound for Nauvoo, via New Orleans. According to calculations based on a report made by Reuben Hedlock, stating that he shipped nine hundred and ninety adult passengers between January, 1844, and January, 1846, about two hundred passengers must have sailed on the *Palmyra*. No other information is at hand concerning this company.

THIRTIETH COMPANY.—86 souls. In the *Millennial Star* of January, 1845, (Vol. V., No. 8), the editor says:

"The fine ship *Palmyra*, Captain Barstow, is expected to sail with a numerous party of emigrants on the 16th instant. We would also give further notice *that we shall have a ship sail between the first and tenth of February.*" That such a ship did sail about that time is proven by a letter written by one of the passengers, (James Kay), and dated St. Louis, Missouri, May 20th, 1845. The writer says:

"We landed in New Orleans on the sixteenth of April. On the eighteenth we started up the river on board the *Julia Chateau*, and after a rather miserable passage of nine days, we saw the city of St. Louis. On the twenty-eighth Brother Mackintosh, and as many of the company who would and could go forward, took passage on the *Galena* for Nauvoo.

A number of the Saints remained in St. Louis to seek employment in order to earn means wherewith to continue the journey to Nauvoo. Brother Kay also mentions that a number of the passengers who had crossed the Atlantic on the *Norfolk* and *Palmyra* had taken employment at St. Louis.

THIRTY FIRST COMPANY.—*Oregon*, about 125 souls. Some time in September, 1845, the ship *Oregon*, Captain Borland, sailed from Liverpool with about one hundred and twenty-five Latter-day Saint passengers, bound for Nauvoo, via New Orleans. We have been unable to glean any information about the voyage.

THIRTY-SECOND COMPANY.—*Liverpool*, 45 Saints. January 16th, 1846, the ship *Liverpool*, Captain Davenport, sailed from Liverpool for New Orleans with seventy-seven souls on board, including forty-five Saints, among whom were Hiram Clark and wife, Sister Phebe Woodruff and two children, Elijah F. Sheets and wife, and several families who went to join their friends in their journey across the Rocky Mountains.

This was the last company of British Saints that sailed for America before the emigration was temporarily suspended, because of the exodus of the Saints from Nauvoo.

NOTES TO APPENDIX A

1. Andrew Jenson, "Church Emigration," *The Contributor* 12, no. 12 (October 1891), 441–450.

APPENDIX B

Nauvoo Chronology[1]

1839

April

Thurs. 25.—Joseph Smith, jun., and others visited Iowa for the purpose of finding a location for the Church. Commerce, Hancock Co., Ill., was finally selected as a gathering place for the Saints.

Fri. 26.—Early in the morning a conference was held on the Temple site at Far West, Mo., in fulfilment of the revelation given July 8, 1838. Among those present were Apostles Brigham Young, Heber C. Kimball, Orson Pratt, John E. Page and John Taylor, who ordained Wilford Woodruff and George A. Smith Apostles, "to fill the places of those who had fallen." Alpheus Cutler, the master-workman of the Temple, then commenced laying its foundation, in accordance with revelation, by rolling up a large stone near the southeast corner. Isaac Russell, John Goodson, Luman Gibbs and twenty-eight others were excommunicated from the Church.

May

Wed. 1.—The first purchase of land for the Church at Commerce, Ill., was made by Joseph Smith, jun., and others of the committee. The purchase consisted of two farms bought respectively of Hugh White and Isaac Galland.

Fri. 3.—Six of the Apostles met Joseph the Prophet near Quincy, Ill., for the first time after his liberation from prison.

Sat. 4.—A two days' conference was commenced on the Presbyterian camp ground, near Quincy, Ill. The doings of the Twelve at Far West on April 26th were sanctioned. Elder Oliver Granger was appointed to go to Kirtland, O., to preside, and the Saints in the Eastern States were advised to gather to Kirtland and settle that place as a Stake of Zion. On the 5th it was decided to send Sidney Rigdon as a delegate to Washington, D. C., to lay the grievances of the Saints before the General Government.

Mon. 6.—At a conference, held at Quincy, Ill., Wm. Marks was appointed to preside at Commerce, and John P. Greene over the Saints in New York. A number of Seventies and High Priests were called to accompany the Apostles on their missions to Europe.

Thurs. 9.—Joseph Smith, jun., left Quincy with his family, and arrived the following day at Commerce.

Wed. 22.—Parley P. Pratt, Morris Phelps, Luman Gibbs and King Follett, having obtained a change of venue, left Richmond, Mo., handcuffed, for Columbia, Boone County, where they arrived on the 26th and were thrown into a filthy dungeon.

June—The first house erected by the Saints in Commerce was raised by Theodore Turley.

Mon. 24.—The Church purchased the town of Nashville, in Lee County, Iowa Territory, and twenty thousand acres of land adjoining it. About the same time another tract of land lying west of Montrose, Iowa, opposite Nauvoo, was purchased.

July—Much sickness prevailed among the Saints at Commerce, which at that time was a very unhealthful place, but many of them were miraculously healed by the power of God.

Tues. 2.—Joseph the Prophet advised that a town be built on the Iowa purchase, to be called Zarahemla.

Thurs. 4.—After more than seven months' imprisonment without conviction, Parley P. Pratt and Morris Phelps escaped from the Columbia jail, Boone County, Mo. They arrived in Quincy, Ill., after days of dreadful suffering from hunger and fatigue. King Follett, who also tried to escape, was retaken.

Mon. 22.—Elijah Fordham, Henry G. Sherwood, Benjamin Brown, Joseph B. Noble and many others, at Commerce, Ill., and Montrose, Iowa, were miraculously healed under the powerful administrations of the Prophet Joseph, assisted by other Elders.

August

Thurs. 8.—Apostles John Taylor and Wilford Woodruff left Commerce, Ill., on a mission to England.

Thurs. 29.—Apostles Parley P. Pratt and Orson Pratt and Elder Hiram Clark departed from Commerce on a mission to England.

September

Wed. 18.—Apostles Brigham Young and Heber C. Kimball started from Commerce on a mission to England, leaving their families sick and poverty-stricken.

Sat. 21.—Apostle Geo. A. Smith and Elders Reuben Hedlock and Theodore Turley left Commerce for England on a mission.

October

Sat. 5.—At a general conference, held at Commerce, William Marks was appointed president of that Stake, Edward Partridge, Bishop of the upper Ward, and Vinson Knight, Bishop of the lower Ward. Geo. W. Harris, Samuel Bent, Henry G. Sherwood, David Fullmer, Alpheus Cutler, Wm. Huntington, Thomas Grover, Newel Knight, Chas. C. Rich, David Dort, Seymour Brunson and Lewis D. Wilson were chosen members of the High Council. John Smith was appointed to preside over the Saints on the other side of the Mississippi River, in Iowa Territory, with Alanson Ripley as Bishop. Asahel Smith, John M. Burk, Abraham O. Smoot, Richard Howard, Willard Snow, Erastus Snow, David Pettigrew, Elijah Fordham, Edward Fisher, Elias Smith, John Patten and Stephen Chase were chosen as members of the High Council.

Thurs. 17.—Apostle Heber C. Kimball was poisoned at Terre Haute, Indiana, but his life was saved by the administration of Apostle Brigham Young.

Sat. 19.—The High Council appointed for the Church in Iowa met for the first time, at Nashville, Iowa. Reynolds Cahoon and Lyman Wight were appointed counselors to John Smith.

Tues. 29.—Joseph Smith, jun., accompanied by Sidney Rigdon, Elias Higbee and O. Porter Rockwell left Commerce for Washington,

D. C., to lay the grievances of the Saints before the President and Congress of the United States.

In the latter part of this month King Follett, the last of the Missouri prisoners, was tried and set free.

November—The first number of the *Times and Seasons* was published at Commerce, Ill.

Sun. 3.—James Mulholland, Joseph Smith's clerk, died at Commerce.

Wed. 27.—Brigham Young rebuked the wind and waves on Lake Erie, and he was obeyed.

Thurs. 28.—Joseph Smith, jun., arrived at Washington, D. C.

December

Thurs. 19.—Apostles Wilford Woodruff and John Taylor and Elder Theodore Turley sailed from New York for England; they arrived at Liverpool Jan. 11, 1840.

Sat. 21.—Joseph Smith, jun., arrived at Philadelphia, Pa., (from Washington), where he remained until the 30th, preaching the gospel.

1840

Joseph the Prophet and other Elders visited Washington, D. C., to seek redress for the Saints from the Federal Government, but were unsuccessful. Commerce, Ill., was incorporated as the City of Nauvoo, and Stakes of Zion were organized in different parts of Illinois. The Apostles performed a great missionary work in England, whence also the first missionary was sent to Australia.

January

Sun. 12.—Francis Marion Lyman was born at Macomb, McDonough Co., Ill.

March—Multitudes were baptized into the Church in the United States and England. Apostle Wilford Woodruff built up large branches in Herefordshire, England.

Wed. 4.—Joseph Smith, jun., arrived in Commerce, Ill., from

Washington, D. C., after a fruitless endeavor to obtain redress for the wrongs suffered by the Saints in Missouri. He had presented to Congress claims against Missouri from 491 individuals for about $1,381,000. President Martin Van Buren, in answer to Joseph's appeal, said, "Your cause is just, but I can do nothing for you." The Committee on the Judiciary, to whom was referred the memorial of the Saints, reported adversely to the prayer of the petitioners.

Mon. 9.—Brigham Young, Heber C. Kimball, Parley P. Pratt, George A. Smith and Reuben Hedlock sailed from New York on the ship *Patrick Henry* for Liverpool, where they arrived April 6th.

April
Mon. 6.—A general conference of the Church was commenced at Nauvoo, Ill. It continued three days, On the first day Apostle Orson Hyde was called on a mission to Jerusalem and on the 8th Apostle John E. Page was appointed to accompany him. The conference also adopted a series of resolutions, expressive of sorrow and disappointment at the action of the Committee of the Judiciary at Washington, D. C.

Tues. 14.—At a council of the Apostles held at Preston, England, Willard Richards was ordained one of the Twelve Apostles.

Wed. 15.—Apostle Orson Hyde left Commerce, Ill., on his mission to Jerusalem.

—At a conference held at Preston, England, where 34 branches and 1,686 members were represented, it was decided to publish a monthly periodical in the interest of the Church in England.

Tues. 21.—The Postmaster General at Washington, D. C., changed the name of the postoffice at Commerce, Hancock Co., Ill., to Nauvoo, and appointed George W. Robinson postmaster.

May
Sat. 9.—Elder Theodore Turley, who had been imprisoned in Stafford jail, England, at the instigation of a Methodist preacher, was released.

Wed. 27.—Bishop Edward Partridge died at Nauvoo, 46 years old. He lost his life in consequence of the Missouri persecutions.

—The first number of *The Latter-day Saints' Millennial Star* was published at Manchester, England; Apostle Parley P. Pratt, editor.

June—By this time the Saints had erected about two hundred and fifty houses in Nauvoo.

Sat. 6.—Forty-one Saints sailed from Liverpool, England, on the ship *Britannia*, for the United States, being the first Saints that gathered from a foreign land. John Moon was leader of the company.

Sun. 14.—The Bran Green and Gadfield Elm conference was organized by Apostle Wilford Woodruff in Worcestershire, England, consisting of twelve branches. This was the first conference organized in the British mission.

Sun. 21.—At a meeting held on Stanley Hill, Herefordshire, England, the Froome's Hill conference was organized by Apostle Wilford Woodruff, consisting of twenty branches.

July—The first British edition of the Latter-day Saints' Hymn Book was published in England.

Tues. 7.—James Allred, Noah Rogers, Alanson Brown and Benjamin Boyce were kidnapped from Hancock County, Ill., by Missourians, and taken to Tully, Lewis Co., Mo., where they were imprisoned, whipped and ill-treated until nearly dead. Brown and Allred escaped a few days afterwards.

Sat. 11.—Apostle Geo. A. Smith ordained and set apart Wm. Barratt at Burslem, Staffordshire, England, for a mission to South Australia. He was the first missionary to that country.

Mon. 20.—John Moon's company of British emigrants arrived at New York.

Mon. 27.—Apostle John Taylor sailed from Liverpool for Ireland to open the door of the gospel in that country.

August—Elder Wm. Donaldson, of the British army, sailed from England for the East Indies. He was the first member of the Church to visit that country.

Fri. 21.—Noah Rogers and Benjamin Boyce escaped from their unlawful imprisonment in Missouri, during which they had been put in irons and suffered much.

Mon. 31.—Apostle Heber C. Kimball baptized Henry Conner, a watchmaker, in London, England, as the first fruit of preaching the fulness of the gospel in that city.

September—Apostle John Taylor and others first preached the gospel on the Isle of Man.

Mon. 8.—The ship *North America* sailed from Liverpool, England, with about two hundred Saints, under the presidency of Theodore Turley, bound for Nauvoo, Ill.

Sun. 14.—Joseph Smith, sen., Patriarch to the Church, died at Nauvoo.

Mon. 15.—Gov. Lilburn W. Boggs, of Missouri, made a demand on Gov. Thos. Carlin, of Illinois, for Joseph Smith, jun., Sidney Rigdon, Lyman Wight, Parley P. Pratt, Caleb Baldwin and Alanson Brown as fugitives from justice.

October

Fri. 3.—At the conference held at Nauvoo, Robert B. Thompson was appointed General Church Clerk, instead of Geo. W. Robinson. Almon W. Babbitt was appointed to preside over the Church at Kirtland, O., and a committee was appointed to organize new Stakes for the gathering of the Saints.

Wed. 22.—A Stake was organized by the committee at Lima, Hancock Co., Ill., with Isaac Morley as president and John Murdock and Walter Cox as his counselors.

Sat. 25.—A Stake was organized at Quincy, Adams Co., Ill., with Daniel Stanton, Stephen Jones and Ezra T. Benson as the presidency.

Mon. 27.—A Stake called Mount Hope was organized at the steam mills, Columbus, Adams Co., Ill., with the following brethren as the presidency: Abel Lamb, Sherman Gilbert and John Smith.

November

Sat. 1.—The committee organized a Stake called Geneva, in Morgan Co., Ill., with Wm. Bosley, Howard S. Smith and Samuel Fowler as the presidency.

December

Wed. 16.—The charter for the incorporation of Nauvoo, granted

by the State legislature, was signed by Governor Thomas Carlin, but
not to take effect until the first of February following.

1841

During this year Nauvoo, Ill., began its career as an incorporated city;
the Nauvoo Legion was organized, and the corner stones of the Nauvoo
Temple were laid. The Twelve Apostles returned from their missions to
England, and baptism for the dead was commenced in the Church.

January—The first number of the *Gospel Reflector*, a semi-
monthly periodical published in the interest of the Church, was
issued in Philadelphia, Pa.; Benjamin Winchester, editor.

—The first British edition of the Book of Mormon was published
in Manchester, England.

Tues. 19.—The Saints were commanded by revelation to build a
Temple at Nauvoo, Ill., and also a "boarding house" for the accommodation of strangers, which subsequently became known as the
Nauvoo House. The general authorities of the Church and other officers were named in the revelation, which also contains important
explanations on the order of the Priesthood. (Doc. and Cov., Sec.
124.)

Sun. 24.—Hyrum Smith succeeded his father, Joseph Smith, sen.,
as Patriarch to the Church, and Wm. Law was appointed a Counselor
in the First Presidency, succeeding Hyrum Smith, in that capacity,
according to revelation.

Sat. 30.—At a meeting held at Nauvoo, Ill., Joseph Smith was
elected sole Trustee for the Church, to hold the office during life, his
"successors to be the First Presidency" of the Church.

February

Mon. 1.—The first election took place for members of the city
council of Nauvoo. John C. Bennett was elected mayor; Wm. Marks,
Samuel H. Smith, Daniel H. Wells and Newel K. Whitney, aldermen;
Joseph Smith, Hyrum Smith, Sidney Rigdon, Charles C. Rich, John
F. Barnett, Wilson Law, Don Carlos Smith, John P. Greene and
Vinson Knight, councilors.

Wed. 3.—The city council of Nauvoo elected Henry G. Sherwood, marshal; James Sloan, recorder; Robert B. Thompson, treasurer; James Robinson, assessor; Austin Cowles, supervisor of streets.

Thurs. 4.—The Nauvoo Legion, originally consisting of six companies, was organized with Joseph Smith as lieutenant-general.

Sun. 7.—The ship *Sheffield* sailed from Liverpool, England with 235 Saints, under the leadership of Hiram Clark.

Sat. 13.—Apostle Orson Hyde sailed from New York for Liverpool, on his mission to Jerusalem.

Sun. 14.—The London (England) conference was organized with Lorenzo Snow as president.

Tues. 16.—The ship *Echo* sailed from Liverpool, England, with 109 Saints, under the direction of Daniel Browitt.

March—The Saints were commanded by revelation to build a city in Iowa Territory, opposite Nauvoo, to be called Zarahemla. (Doc. and Cov.. Sec. 125.)

Mon. 1.—The city council divided the city of Nauvoo into four wards. An ordinance was passed, giving free toleration and equal privileges in the city to all religious sects and denominations.

Wed 10.—Governor Thos. Carlin, of Illinois, commissioned Joseph Smith lieutenant-general of the Nauvoo Legion.

Wed. 17.—The ship *Uleste [Alesto]* sailed from Liverpool, England, with 54 Saints, under the direction of Thomas Smith and Wm. Moss, bound for America.

Mon. 29.—Charles C. Rich and Austin Cowles were chosen counselors to Wm. Marks, president of the Nauvoo Stake of Zion.

April

Tues. 6.—A general conference of the Church was commenced at Nauvoo, and the corner stones of the Nauvoo Temple were laid. The conference was continued till the 11th.

Thurs. 8.—Lyman Wight was chosen one of the Twelve Apostles, in place of David W. Patten, martyred in Missouri.

Wed. 21.—Apostles Brigham Young, Heber C. Kimball, Orson Pratt, Wilford Woodruff, John Taylor, Geo. A. Smith and Willard Richards sailed from Liverpool, England, on the ship *Rochester*, accompanied by 130 Saints. They arrived at New York May 20th.

May

Sat. 22.—At a conference held at Kirtland, O., Almon W. Babbitt was chosen president of the Kirtland Stake, with Lester Brooks and Zebedee Coltrin as counselors.

Mon. 24.—The First Presidency at Nauvoo called upon all scattered Saints to gather to Hancock County, Ill., and Lee County, Ia. All neighboring Stakes outside of these two counties were discontinued.

June

Sat. 5.—Joseph Smith was arrested on a requisition from the State of Missouri. He was tried on the 9th and liberated on the 10th on a writ of *habeas corpus*, at Monmouth, Warren Co., Ill.

Tues. 22.—Theodore Curtis, who had been under arrest in Gloucester, England, five days for preaching the gospel, was acquitted.

July

Thurs. 1.—Apostles Brigham Young, Heber C. Kimball and John Taylor arrived at Nauvoo from their missions to England.

Fri. 9.—By revelation, through Joseph the Prophet, Apostle Brigham Young was commanded to send the "word" abroad, and to take special care of his family. (Doc. and Cov., Sec. 126.)

Tues. 13.—Apostle Geo. A. Smith returned to Nauvoo from his mission to England.

Sun. 25.—Wm. Yokum lost his leg by amputation, as the result of a wound received in the massacre at Haun's Mill, Mo.

August

Sat. 7.—Don Carlos Smith, the youngest brother of the Prophet, died at Nauvoo.

Thurs. 12.—Joseph Smith preached to about one hundred Sac and Fox Indians (among whom were the chiefs Keokuk, Kiskuhosh and Appenoose), who had come to visit him at Nauvoo.

Mon. 16.—Apostle Willard Richards arrived at Nauvoo from his mission to England.

Wed. 25.—Oliver Granger died at Kirtland, O.

Fri. 27.—Robert B. Thompson, Joseph Smith's scribe, died at Nauvoo.

September
Tues. 21.—The ship *Tyrean* sailed from Liverpool for New Orleans with 204 Saints, under the direction of Joseph Fielding, bound for Nauvoo.

Wed. 22.—A company of brethren left Nauvoo for the Pineries, Wisconsin, about five hundred miles north, to procure lumber for the Nauvoo Temple.

October
Sat. 2.—An important general conference was commenced in the Grove at Nauvoo. It was continued till the 4th. Joseph Smith declared, as the will of the Lord, that the Church should not hold another general conference until the Saints could meet in the Temple. James Sloan was elected Church clerk, instead of Robert B. Thompson deceased.

Wed. 6.—Apostle Wilford Woodruff arrived at Nauvoo from his mission to England.

Thurs. 7.—In a council of the Twelve, a number of brethren were called on missions, among whom were Joseph Ball to South America and Henry Harrison Sagers to Jamaica, West Indies.

Sun. 24.—Apostle Orson Hyde, who had arrived at Jerusalem, ascended the Mount of Olives and dedicated the land of Palestine by prayer for the gathering of the Jews.

November
Mon. 8.—The temporary baptismal font in the Nauvoo Temple was dedicated.

—The ship *Chaos* sailed from Liverpool with 170 Saints, under the direction of Peter Melling, bound for Nauvoo.

Sun. 21.—Baptisms for the dead were commenced in the font in the basement of the Nauvoo Temple.

Wed. 24.—The *Tyrean* company of British Saints arrived at Warsaw, intending to settle Warren, a new town site, one mile south of Warsaw, which had been selected for a settlement of the Saints, but they soon afterwards removed to Nauvoo, because of oppression on the part of anti-Mormons.

December
Sat. 4.—The Stake organization at Ramus, Hancock County, Ill., was discontinued.

Mon. 13.—Apostle Willard Richards was appointed Joseph Smith's private secretary and general clerk for the Church.

Wed. 22.—John Snider was called by revelation on a special mission to Europe, bearing a message from the Twelve.

1842
A large number of Saints from Great Britain arrived at Nauvoo, Ill. John C. Bennett, who turned traitor against the Church, sought the Prophet Joseph's life. Joseph Smith was arrested on a false charge, tried and acquitted; and when the officers planned to arrest him again, he hid himself and from his places of seclusion wrote important communications to the Saints.

January
Thurs. 6.—A conference was held at Zarahemla, Ia., opposite Nauvoo, when a Stake of Zion, previously organized there, was discontinued, and a branch organized in its stead, with John Smith as president.

Wed. 12.—The ship *Tremont* sailed from Liverpool with 143 Saints bound for Nauvoo *via* New Orleans.

February
Wed. 2.—Moses Thatcher was born in Sangamon County, Ill.

Thurs. 3.—Apostle Wilford Woodruff took the superintendency of the printing office and Apostle John Taylor the editorial department of the *Times and Seasons*, at Nauvoo.

Sat. 5.—The ship *Hope* sailed from Liverpool for New Orleans with 270 Saints.

Sun. 20.—The ship *John Cummins* sailed from Liverpool with about two hundred Saints.

March—The *Millennial Star* office in England was moved from

Manchester (No. 47 Oxford Street) to the Church emigration office in Liverpool (No. 36 Chapel Street).

Sat. 12.—The ship *Hanover* sailed from Liverpool with about two hundred Saints, under the direction of Amos Fielding.

Tues. 15.—Joseph Smith took charge of the editorial department of the *Times and Seasons.*

Thurs. 17.—The organization of the Female Relief Society of Nauvoo was commenced. It was completed on the 24th, with Emma Smith as president; Mrs. Elizabeth Ann Whitney and Mrs. Sarah M. Cleveland, counselors; Miss Elvira Cowles, treasurer; and Eliza R. Snow, secretary.

Sun. 20.—Joseph Smith baptized eighty persons for the dead in the Mississippi river, after which he confirmed about fifty.

Sat. 26.—John Snider left Nauvoo on his special mission to England.

Sun. 27.—Joseph Smith baptized 107 persons for the dead in the Mississippi River.

April
Wed. 6.—A special conference of the Church w[a]s held at Nauvoo; it was continued till the 8th, and during its sessions 275 brethren were ordained Elders.

Wed. 13.—About two hundred Saints arrived at Nauvoo from Great Britain.

Sat. 16.—The *Wasp*, a miscellaneous weekly newspaper, was first published at Nauvoo; Wm. Smith, editor.

Fri. 29.—Joseph Smith wrote: "A conspiracy against the peace of my household was made manifest, and it gave me some trouble to counteract the design of certain base individuals and restore peace. The Lord makes manifest to me many things, which it is not wisdom for me to make public, until others can witness the proof of them."

May
Wed. 4.—Joseph Smith gave James Adams, Hyrum Smith, Newel K. Whitney, George Miller, Brigham Young, Heber C. Kimball and Willard Richards instructions about holy endowments.

Fri. 6.—Ex-Governor Lilburn W. Boggs, of Missouri, was shot, but not killed, at Independence, Mo.

Sat. 7.—The Nauvoo Legion, now numbering 26 companies, or 2,000 men, was reviewed and it fought a sham battle, in which John C. Bennett conspired against the Prophet's life, but failed to carry out his design.

Thurs. 19.—John C. Bennett having resigned the mayorship of Nauvoo, Joseph Smith was elected by the city council to fill the vacancy.

Tues. 24.—Chauncey L. Higbee was excommunicated from the Church by the High Council of Nauvoo, for unchaste and unvirtuous conduct.

Wed. 25.—The authorities of the Church had at this time withdrawn their fellowship from John C. Bennett, who soon afterwards left Nauvoo.

June
Wed. 1.—At a general conference held in Manchester, England, 8,265 officers and members of the Church were represented.

July
Sun. 3.—Joseph Smith spoke to eight thousand people at Nauvoo.

August—Apostle Orson Hyde published a pamphlet of 120 pages in the German language, in Germany, entitled "A Cry in the Wilderness," etc., setting forth the rise, progress and doctrines of the Church.

Sat. 6.—Joseph Smith prophesied that the Saints would be driven to the Rocky Mountains, where they should become a mighty people.

Mon. 8.—Joseph Smith was arrested by a deputy sheriff at Nauvoo, by requisition from Gov. Thos. Reynolds, of Missouri, falsely accused of being accessory to the shooting of ex-Governor Boggs. O. Porter Rockwell was also arrested as principal. A writ of *habeas corpus* was issued by the municipal court of Nauvoo, by which the prisoners were released for the time being.

Wed. 10.—The deputy sheriff returned to Nauvoo to re-arrest Joseph Smith and O. Porter Rockwell, but they could not be found. To escape imprisonment the Prophet had to keep concealed for some time. His first retreat was the house of his uncle John Smith, at Zarahemla, Ia.

Thurs. 11.—Joseph Smith concealed himself in the house of Edward Sayer, in Nauvoo.

Thurs. 18.—Rumors being afloat that the Prophet's hiding place was discovered, he changed his quarters from the house of Edward Sayer to that of Carlos Granger, who lived in the northeast part of Nauvoo. Great excitement prevailed among the people around Nauvoo on account of John C. Bennett's lies.

Fri. 19.—Joseph Smith returned to his own house.

Sat. 20.—Amasa M. Lyman was ordained one of the Twelve Apostles.

Sun. 21.—Sidney Rigdon testified in public meeting, at Nauvoo, that his daughter Eliza, had been raised from the dead by the power of God.

Mon. 29.—After not showing himself in public for three weeks, Joseph Smith spoke to an assembly of Saints at Nauvoo. 380 Elders volunteered to take missions to the various States of the Union for the purpose of refuting John C. Bennett's lies.

September

Thurs. 1.—Joseph Smith wrote an address to the Saints at Nauvoo concerning baptism for the dead. (Doc. and Cov., Sec. 127.)

Sat. 3.—Another effort was made to arrest Joseph Smith without legal process. His house was searched, but he eluded pursuit, and afterwards kept himself hid for some time in the house of Edward Hunter.

Tues. 6.—Joseph Smith wrote another important address to the Saints in relation to baptism for the dead, and the necessity of keeping records. (Doc. and Cov., Sec. 128.)

Sat. 10.—Joseph Smith returned home undiscovered.

Sat. 17.—The ship *Sidney* sailed from Liverpool with 180 Saints; it arrived at New Orleans Nov. 11th.

Sun. 25.—The ship *Medford* sailed from Liverpool with 214 Saints, under the presidency of Apostle Orson Hyde; it arrived at New Orleans Nov. 13th.

Thurs 29.—The ship *Henry* sailed from Liverpool for New Orleans, with 157 Saints, under the direction of John Snider.

October

Sun. 2.—Reports reached Joseph Smith that Gov. Thos. Reynolds, of Missouri, had offered a reward for the arrest of himself and O. Porter Rockwell.

Fri. 7.—Joseph Smith again left home to elude the pursuit of his enemies, leaving his wife Emma sick. He returned on the 20th.

Thurs. 13.—Some of the brethren arrived at Nauvoo from the Pineries, Wisconsin, with 90,000 feet of lumber and 24,000 cubic feet of timber for the Temple and Nauvoo House.

Thurs. 20.—Thomas Ward succeeded Apostle Parley P. Pratt as president of the British Mission, with Lorenzo Snow and Hiram Clark as counselors.

Sat. 29.—The ship *Emerald* sailed from Liverpool with 250 Saints, under the leadership of Apostle Parley P. Pratt. Because of ice in the Mississippi river the company was detained during the winter in St. Louis, Alton, Chester and other places, and did not arrive in Nauvoo until April 12, 1843.

November

Tues. 15.—Apostle John Taylor succeeded Joseph Smith as editor of the *Times and Seasons*.

Thurs. 17.—Alpheus Harmon was frozen to death on the prairie, between Nauvoo and Carthage, Ill., as he was returning home from a mission.

December

Sun. 4.—The city of Nauvoo was divided into ten Bishop's wards.

Wed. 7.—Apostle Orson Hyde returned to Nauvoo from his mission to Jerusalem.

Tues. 20.—Lorenzo D. Barnes died at Bradford, England. His was the first death of an Elder on a foreign mission.

Wed. 21.—Apostle Willard Richards, who had been in the East several months, was appointed Church Historian, etc.

Mon. 26.—Joseph Smith was arrested the third time on a requisition from the State of Missouri.

Tues. 27.—Joseph Smith, accompanied by several brethren, left Nauvoo for Springfield, Ill., where they arrived on the 30th.

1843

During this and the preceding year Joseph the Prophet preached many powerful sermons and uttered a number of important prophecies. While on a visit to Dixon, Ill., he had a narrow escape from being kidnapped under legal pretense and taken to Missouri. The revelation on celestial marriage was given and the first missionaries sent to the Society Islands.

January

Mon. 2.—Joseph Smith prophesied that he should not go to Missouri dead or alive.

Wed. 4.—Joseph Smith was on trial before Judge Pope, of Springfield, on the accusation of being an accessory to the shooting of ex-Governor Boggs of Missouri.

Thurs. 5.—Joseph Smith was proven innocent and acquitted.

Tues. 10.—Joseph Smith and company arrived at Nauvoo from the trip to Springfield.

Mon. 16.—The ship *Swanton* sailed from Liverpool with 212 Saints for New Orleans, led by Lorenzo Snow. The emigrants arrived at Nauvoo April 12th.

Tues. 17.—The Saints being overjoyed because of Joseph Smith's release, meetings of prayer and thanksgiving were held at Nauvoo.

February

Tues. 7.—Apostle Parley P. Pratt arrived at Nauvoo from his mission to England.

Thurs. 9.—Joseph Smith received by revelation three grand keys, by which bad angels, or spirits, may be known. (Doc. and Cov., Sec. 129)

March—A "Young Gentlemen's and Ladies' Relief Society" was organized at Nauvoo, with Wm. Cutler as president.

—Joseph Smith studied the German language.

Fri. 3.—The Illinois legislature passed a bill for repealing the Nauvoo city charter, which, however, was not approved.

Sat. 4.—O. Porter Rockwell was taken prisoner in St. Louis by the Missourians.

Wed. 8.—The ship *Yorkshire* sailed from Liverpool, England, with 82 Saints on board, led by Thomas Bullock; the emigrants arrived at Nauvoo, May 31st, *via* New Orleans.

Wed. 15.—Joseph Smith prophesied that O. Porter Rockwell would get away honorably from the Missourians.

Tues. 21.—The ship *Clayborne* sailed from Liverpool with 106 Saints.

April

Sun. 2.—"Important Items of Instruction" were given by Joseph Smith, at Nauvoo, who also prophesied "that the commencement of the difficulties which will cause much bloodshed previous to the coming of the Son of Man, will be in South Carolina." (Doc. and Cov., Sec. 130.)

Thurs. 6.—At a conference held in the Temple, at Kirtland, O., it was decided that all the Saints residing at that place should remove to Nauvoo, Ill.

—An important conference, which continued its sessions till the 8th, was commenced on the floor of the Temple, at Nauvoo, Ill. Joseph Smith prophesied that Christ would not come until he (Joseph) was eighty-five years of age.

Mon. 10.—About one hundred and fifteen Elders were called on missions to different States, at a special conference held at Nauvoo.

Thurs. 13.—Joseph Smith preached to the British Saints, who had arrived at Nauvoo the day previous.

Sun. 23.—Six brass plates and a skeleton were found by Mr. R. Wiley and others, near Kinderhook, Pike Co., Ill.

May

Wed. 3.—The first number of the *Nauvoo Neighbor,* a newspaper, was issued at Nauvoo, instead of the *Wasp,* suspended.

Tues. 16.—On this and the following day Joseph Smith made some important remarks about the celestial glory, at Ramus, Ill. (Doc. and Cov., Sec. 131.)

Thurs. 18.—Returning to Nauvoo from his visit to Ramus, Joseph Smith dined with Judge Stephen A. Douglas, at Carthage, Hancock Co., Ill. During the conversation which took place Joseph prophesied that Judge Douglas would aspire to the Presidency of the United

States, and added that if he ever turned his hand against the Latter-day Saints, he should feel the hand of the Almighty upon him, etc.

Tues. 23.—Addison Pratt, Noah Rogers, Benjamin F. Grouard and Knowlton F. Hanks were set apart for a mission to the Pacific Islands.

Fri. 26.—Joseph Smith gave endowments, and also instructions on the Priesthood and the new and everlasting covenant, to Hyrum Smith, Brigham Young, Heber C. Kimball and others, at Nauvoo.

June

Thurs. 1.—Addison Pratt, Benjamin F. Grouard, Knowlton F. Hanks and Noah Rogers left Nauvoo on their missions to the Pacific Islands.

Thurs. 8.—Elias Higbee died in Nauvoo.

Sun. 11.—A conference was held at Lima, Ill., and the branch at the place reorganized, with Isaac Morley as president, and Gardiner Snow, Bishop.

Tues. 13.—Joseph Smith left Nauvoo with his wife Emma to visit her sister, living near Dixon, Lee County, Ill.

Fri. 23.—Joseph Smith was arrested and brutally treated by Joseph H. Reynolds, sheriff of Jackson Co., Mo., and Constable Harmon T. Wilson, of Carthage, Ill., without legal process, and only through interference of friends at Dixon saved from being kidnapped and taken to Missouri.

Sat. 24.—The corner stones of the Masonic Temple at Nauvoo were laid.

—Joseph Smith secured a writ of *habeas corpus* and started towards Ottawa to have his case examined by Judge John D. Caton, but, arriving at Pawpaw Grove, the company learned that Judge Caton was not at home, and, therefore, returned to Dixon the following day.

Sun. 25.—News of Joseph Smith being kidnapped reached Nauvoo, and 175 men immediately started on horseback to his rescue.

Mon. 26.—Joseph Smith started under guard towards Quincy, Ill.

Tues. 27.—The company traveling with Joseph Smith was met by the brethren from Nauvoo, when it was decided that instead of going to Quincy to have the writ of *habeas corpus* examined, the prisoner and escort should proceed to Nauvoo.

Fri. 30.—Joseph Smith and company arrived at Nauvoo, nearly the whole city turning out to meet him. In the afternoon he addressed the people, giving the history of his arrest. While he was speaking Officers Reynolds and Wilson started for Carthage and tried to raise a mob; afterwards they petitioned Gov. Thos. Ford for militia to take Joseph out of Nauvoo by force.

July
Sat. 1.—Joseph Smith was tried before the municipal court of Nauvoo on a writ of *habeas corpus* and acquitted.
Sun. 2.—Joseph Smith had a pleasant interview with several Pottawattamie chiefs who had come to visit him, and a very good impression was made upon the Indians.
—The steamboat *Maid of Iowa* returned to Nauvoo, after a very adventurous trip in search of Joseph. The brethren who had participated in that river expedition, numbering about eighty, were blessed by the Prophet.
Mon. 3.—A number of Elders were called to visit the various counties of Illinois, to preach the gospel and disabuse the public mind with regard to Joseph Smith's arrest.
—Charles C. Rich and a company of twenty-five men, who had been out searching for the Prophet, returned to Nauvoo, having traveled about five hundred miles on horseback in seven days.
Tues. 4.—Nauvoo was visited by about one thousand gentlemen and ladies from St. Louis, Quincy and Burlington.
Fri. 7.—Mr. M. Braman arrived at Nauvoo as a messenger from the governor, to learn the particulars of Joseph Smith's late arrest.
Sat. 8.—Bishop George Miller arrived at Nauvoo from the Pineries with 157,000 feet lumber and 70,000 shingles for the Temple.
Wed. 12.—The revelation on celestial marriage was written in the presence of Hyrum Smith and Wm. Clayton. (Doc. and Cov., Sec. 132.)

August
Fri. 11.—General James Adams, of Springfield, and died at Nauvoo.
Thurs. 31.—Joseph Smith moved into the Nauvoo Mansion.

September
Tues. 5.—The ship *Mitoka* sailed from Liverpool with 280 Saints,

bound for Nauvoo.

Wed. 6.—At an anti-Mormon meeting, held at Carthage, Hancock Co., Ill., resolutions were adopted against Joseph Smith and the Saints in Nauvoo.

Fri. 15.—Joseph Smith opened the Nauvoo Mansion as a hotel.

Sat. 30.— Reuben Hedlock and other missionaries from Nauvoo arrived at Liverpool, England.

October

Tues. 3.—Joseph Smith gave a dinner party in the Nauvoo Mansion to about two hundred Saints.

Fri. 6.—A special conference of the Church, which continued its session on the 8th, was commenced at Nauvoo, Ill. Serious complaints were made against Sidney Rigdon.

Sun. 8.—At a meeting of the special conference at Nauvoo, Sidney Rigdon was sustained as a Counselor to Joseph Smith, although the Prophet said, "I have thrown him off my shoulders, and you have again put him on me; you may carry him, but I will not."

Mon. 9.—Addison Pratt, Noah Rogers, Benjamin F. Grouard and Knowlton F. Hanks sailed from New Bedford, Mass., on board the ship *Timoleon*, for the Pacific Islands.

Fri. 20.—John P. Greene returned to Nauvoo, from a mission to the State of New York, with about one hundred emigrants.

Sat. 21.—The ship *Champion* sailed from Liverpool with 91 Saints, bound for Nauvoo.

Sun. 22.—Apostles Brigham Young, Heber C. Kimball and George A. Smith returned to Nauvoo from a mission to the Eastern States.

November

Fri. 3.—Knowlton F. Hanks, one of the missionaries to the Pacific Islands, died. He was the first Latter-day Saint Elder who died and was buried at sea.

Mon. 6.—Erastus Snow returned to Nauvoo with a company of immigrants from Massachusetts.

Sun. 19.—Philander Avery was kidnapped from the neighborhood of Warsaw and carried forcibly across the Mississippi river to Missouri.

December

Sat. 2.—Apostles Orson Hyde, Parley P. Pratt, Wilford Woodruff and George A. Smith and Elder Orson Spencer received their endowments at Nauvoo, Ill.; 35 persons were present.

—Daniel Avery was kidnapped from Bear Creek, Hancock Co., Ill., by a company of Missourians, and imprisoned in Monticello jail, Lewis Co., Mo., where his son Philander was already confined.

Thurs. 7.—The German brethren net at the Assembly Room at Nauvoo, chose Bishop Daniel Garn as their presiding Elder, and organized to have preaching done in their own language.

Mon. 18.—John Ellioth, a schoolmaster, was arrested and brought to Nauvoo, where he was tried and found guilty of having kidnapped Daniel Avery and son.

Tues. 19.—The Nauvoo Legion paraded near the Temple, was inspected by the officers and instructed to prepare for meeting the mob, which was gathering in the neighborhood.

Thurs. 21.—The city council of Nauvoo signed a petition to Congress, praying for redress for the Missouri persecutions.

Fri. 22—David Holman's house, near Ramus, Hancock Co, Ill, was burned by the mob.

Mon. 25—O. Porter Rockwell arrived in Nauvoo from nearly a year's imprisonment in Missouri without conviction, during which time he was subjected to very cruel treatment.

—Daniel Avery was liberated from his imprisonment in Missouri, his son having previously escaped.

Fri. 29.—Forty policeman were sworn into office in the city of Nauvoo.

1844

Joseph Smith the Prophet became a candidate for the Presidency of the United States. Mobs gathered around Nauvoo, and during the ensuing troubles Joseph and his brother Hyrum were martyred in Carthage jail. The Twelve Apostles returned from their missions to the Eastern States and were accepted by the Saints as the presiding Council of the Church. A great number of Seventies were ordained.

January

Tues. 2.—Jonathon Pugmire, sen., and Thos. Cartwright, who had been imprisoned in Chester, England, about six weeks, for the accidental drowning of Mrs. Cartwright during an attempt to baptize her, Nov. 23, 1843, were acquitted.

Wed. 3.—A special session of the city council was held at Nauvoo because of Wm. Law's intimation that his life was in danger.

Fri. 5.—Wm. Marks, president of the Nauvoo Stake of Zion, being alarmed on account of a fire being kindled near his house, made statements before the city council; his fears were unfounded.

Tues. 9.—Elder Horace S. Eldredge, a county constable, was prevented by mob force from performing an official duty at Carthage.

Wed. 10.—John Smith, uncle to Joseph Smith, the Prophet, was ordained a Patriarch.

Tues. 16.—Francis M. Higbee was tried before the municipal court of Nauvoo for slandering Joseph Smith.

Tues. 23.—The ship *Fanny* sailed from Liverpool, England, with 210 Saints under the direction of Wm. Kay, bound for Nauvoo. It arrived New Orleans, March 7th.

Mon. 29.—At a political meeting, held at Nauvoo, Joseph Smith was nominated a candidate for the Presidency of the United States. Soon afterwards a large number of Elders were sent to the various States of the Union to electioneer for him.

February

Tues. 6.—The ship *Isaac Allerton* sailed from Liverpool with 60 Saints, bound for Nauvoo.

Wed. 7.—Joseph Smith completed his address to the people of the United States, entitled: "Views of the Powers and Policy of the government of the United States."

Sun. 11.—The ship *Swanton* sailed from Liverpool with 81 Saints, bound for Nauvoo, where they arrived April 18th.

Sat. 17.—The anti-Mormons held a convention at Carthage, Ill., the object being to devise ways and means for expelling the Saints from the State.

Tues. 20.—Joseph Smith instructed the Twelve Apostles to send a delegation to California and Oregon, to search for a good location, to which the Saints could remove after the completion of the Temple.

Wed. 21.—A meeting of the Apostles was held at Nauvoo for the purpose of selecting "a company to explore Oregon and California and select a site for a new city for the Saints." Jonathan Dunham, Phinehas H. Young, David D. Yearsley and David Fullmer volunteered to go; and Alphonso Young, James Emmett, Geo. D. Watt and Daniel Spencer were requested to go.

Fri. 23—Another meeting was held at Nauvoo, in favor of the California and Oregon expedition. Several of the brethren volunteered to go; among whom were Samuel Bent, John A. Kelting, Samuel Rolfe, Daniel Avery and Samuel W. Richards.

Sun. 25.—Joseph Smith prophesied that in five years the Saints would be out of the power of their old enemies, whether apostates or of the world.

Thurs. 29.—Moses Smith and Rufus Beach volunteered to join the Oregon exploring expedition.

March

Mon. 4.—It was decided in council at Nauvoo to [c]ease work on the Nauvoo House until the Temple was completed.

Tues. 5.—The ship *Glasgow* sailed from Liverpool with 150 Saints, led by Hiram Clark, bound for Nauvoo, where they arrived April 26th.

Mon. 11.—Joseph Smith and the leading authorities of the Church held another council at Nauvoo about the Saints moving to the mountains.

Sun. 24.—Joseph Smith spoke in public meeting against Chauncey L. Higbee, Robert D. Foster, Wm. and Wilson Law and others, as conspirators against his life.

Tues. 26.—Joseph Smith petitioned Congress to protect the citizens of the United States, emigrating west; this he did in view of the Saints going to the mountains in the near future.

April

Fri. 5.—The Masonic Temple, which had been erected at Nauvoo, was dedicated. About five hundred and fifty members of the Masonic fraternity from various parts of the world were present.

Sat. 6.—A conference, which lasted five days, commenced at Nauvoo. The Prophet spoke to 20,000 Saints on the 7th, and on the 8th declared the whole of North and South America to be the land of Zion.

Sat. 13.—Under the leadership of Wm. Kay, 210 British Saints arrived at Nauvoo.

Thurs. 18.—Wm. and Wilson Law, Robert D. Foster and other apostates, formerly prominent in the Church, were excommunicated.

Fri. 26.—Augustine Spencer, Robert D. Foster, Charles Foster and Chauncey L. Higbee were arrested and fined, in Nauvoo, for assault and resisting the officers.

May

Wed. 1.—Elders Addison Pratt, Noah Rogers and Benjamin F. Grouard landed on the island of Tubuai (one of the Austral group), as the first missionaries of the Church to the islands of the Pacific.

Mon. 6.—Joseph Smith was arrested at Nauvoo on complaint of Francis M. Higbee, but took out a writ of *habeas corpus*, and was tried on the 8th before the municipal court of Nauvoo, which resulted in Joseph's acquittal, and Higbee was sentenced to pay the cost of suit.

Tues. 14.—Elders Noah Rogers and Benjamin F. Grouard landed at Papeete, Tahiti, Society Islands, as the first Latter-day Saint missionaries to that group.

Wed. 15.—Anthon H. Lund was born at Aalborg, Denmark.

Fri. 17.—A State convention was held at Nauvoo, Ill., in which Joseph Smith was nominated as a candidate for the Presidency, and Sidney Rigdon for the Vice Presidency, of the United States.

Sat. 18.—The first number of *The Prophet*, a weekly paper devoted to the interests of the Church, was issued in New York City, by a society of Saints.

Tues. 21.—Apostles Brigham Young, Heber C. Kimball and Lyman Wight, and about a hundred other Elders, left Nauvoo, Ill., on political missions to the East. Apostles Wilford Woodruff and Geo. A. Smith and others had left on the 9th.

Thurs. 23.—Joseph Smith had a talk with a number of Sac and Fox Indians at Nauvoo.

Sat. 25.—Joseph Smith learned that the grand jury at Carthage had found two indictments against him, one of them for polygamy.

Mon. 27.—Joseph Smith, accompanied by a number of friends, went to Carthage to have the indictments against him investigated by the circuit court, but, the prosecution not being ready, the case was continued until next term.

June

Fri. 7.—The first and only number of the Nauvoo *Expositor* was published, edited by Sylvester Emmons.

Mon. 10.—The paper and printing material of the Nauvoo *Expositor* were destroyed, according to the proclamation of the city council, declaring it a nuisance.

Wed. 12.—Joseph Smith was arrested on a charge of destroying the *Expositor*, tried before the municipal court of Nauvoo and acquitted. The following day the other members of the city council were tried before the same court, on a similar charge, and honorably acquitted.

Fri. 14.—Joseph Smith communicated the facts connected with the removal of the *Expositor's* printing materials, by letter, to Gov. Thos. Ford.

Sun. 16.—In a public meeting, held at Nauvoo, a number of delegates were called to visit the different precincts in Hancock County, Ill., to lay a truthful statement of the troubles in Nauvoo before the people. Joseph Smith, as mayor of the city, also stated the facts in a proclamation.

—Addison Pratt baptized Ambrose Alexander, a white man, on the island of Tubuai, as the first convert to "Mormonism" on the Pacific Isles.

Mon. 17.—Joseph Smith and a number of others were arrested, on complaint of W. G. Ware, for riot in destroying the *Expositor*, tried before Justice Daniel H. Wells, and, after a long and close examination, acquitted.

—Mobs began to gather in the surrounding country, threatening to drive the Saints from Nauvoo.

Tues. 18.—The Nauvoo Legion was ordered out and the city declared under martial law, by the proclamation of the mayor, Joseph Smith. The Prophet delivered his last public address. An extra of the

Warsaw Signal was read, in which all the "old citizens" were called upon to assist the mob in driving away the Saints.

Wed. 19.—Mobs were gathering at different point to attack Nauvoo.

Thurs. 20.—General Joseph Smith, with other officers of the Legion, examined the approaches to Nauvoo as a preparatory measure for defense. The Prophet also sent for the Twelve Apostles, who were on missions, to come home immediately.

Sat. 22.—Late in the evening Joseph and Hyrum Smith and Willard Richards left Nauvoo and crossed the Mississippi river, with the intention to flee to the West, and thus escape from their enemies.

Sun. 23.—Through the solicitation of Emma Smith, and several supposed friends, Joseph Smith and his companions returned to Nauvoo.

Mon. 24.—Joseph and Hyrum Smith, accompanied by seventeen friends, started for Carthage, to submit to another trial, under pledge of protection from Gov. Thos. Ford. On the way they received a demand from the governor to surrender the State arms in possession of the Nauvoo Legion; Joseph returned and complied with the request, and then proceeded to Carthage.

Tues. 25.—Joseph Smith and his brethren surrendered themselves to a constable at Carthage and submitted to a trial, after which they were, contrary to law, remanded to prison.

Wed. 26.—Gov. Thos. Ford had a long interview with the prisoners in Carthage jail. He renewed his promises of protection and said, if he went to Nauvoo, he would take them with him.

Thurs. 27.—Gov. Thos. Ford went to Nauvoo, leaving the prisoners in jail to be guarded by their most bitter enemies, the "Carthage Greys." About 5:20 p.m. an armed mob with bla[c]kened faces surrounded and entered the jail, and murdered Joseph and Hyrum Smith in cold blood; Apostle John Taylor was severely wounded, while Apostle Willard Richards only received a slight wound on his ear.

Fri. 28.—Apostle Willard Richards and Samuel H. Smith conveyed the bodies of the martyrs to Nauvoo, where they were met by the officers of the Nauvoo Legion, and a very large number of citizens.

Sat. 29.—About ten thousand persons visited and viewed the remains of the martyred Prophet and Patriarch at Nauvoo. The funeral took place in the evening.

July

Tues. 2.—Apostle John Taylor was brought home to Nauvoo from Carthage.

Mon.8.—Apostle Parley P. Pratt arrived at Nauvoo; he was the first of the absent Twelve to return.

Sun. 21.—Addison Pratt baptized four white men and four natives on the island of Tubuai. These natives, whose names were Nabora and his wife Telii, Pauma and Hamoe, were the first of the Polynesian race to embrace the fulness of the gospel.

Thurs. 25.—Erastus Snow and many other Elders arrived at Nauvoo. All seemed weighed down with gloom.

Sun. 28.—Apostle Geo. A. Smith and a party of brethren arrived at Nauvoo.

—A branch of the Church, consisting of eleven members, was organized by Addison Pratt on the island of Tubuai (Society Islands mission). This was the first branch of the Church on the Pacific Islands.

Tues. 30.—Samuel H. Smith, brother of the prophet, died at Nauvoo, as a martyr to persecution.

Wed. 31.—Apostle Amasa M. Lyman arrived at Nauvoo.

August

Fri. 2.—A political meeting of the citizens of Hancock County, Ill., was held near the Temple at Nauvoo. Great excitement prevailed throughout the county. The mob party was determined to elect officers who would screen the murderers of Joseph and Hyrum Smith and exterminate the "Mormons."

Sat. 3.—Sidney Rigdon arrived at Nauvoo from Pittsburgh, Pa.

Sun. 4.—Sidney Rigdon preached to the Saints at Nauvoo, declaring that a guardian should be appointed to build up the Church to Joseph, intimating that he was the man who should lead the Saints.

Tues. 6.—Apostles Brigham Young, Heber C. Kimball, Lyman Wight, Orson Hyde, Orson Pratt and Wilford Woodruff arrived at Nauvoo.

Wed. 7.—The Twelve met in council with Elder Taylor, at his house at Nauvoo; they found him recovering from his wounds. In the afternoon, the Twelve, the High Council and High Priests held a meeting in the Seventies' Hall, where Sidney Rigdon's claim to lead the Church was considered.

Thurs. 8.—A special meeting of the Church was held at Nauvoo, in which Elder Rigdon harangued the Saints about choosing a guardian, etc. In the afternoon meeting the Twelve Apostles, through their President, Brigham Young, asserted their right to lead the Church, which claim was recognized by the unanimous vote of the people.

Mon. 12.—At a council of the Twelve Apostles, Amasa M. Lyman was admitted into their quorum, having been previously ordained to the Apostleship. Elder Wilford Woodruff was appointed to go to England to preside over the British mission.

Thurs. 15.—The Twelve issued an epistle to the Saints in all the world, giving such instructions and words of counsel to the Church as were necessary after the martyrdom of the Prophet.

Wed. 28.—Wilford Woodruff, Dan Jones and Hirum Clark, with their families, left Nauvoo for England.

Sat. 31.—Brigham Young was elected lieutenant-general of the Nauvoo Legion, and Charles C. Rich, major-general.

September

Sun. 8.—At a meeting of the High Council of Nauvoo, Sidney Rigdon was excommunicated from the Church.

Thurs. 19.—The ship *Norfolk* sailed from Liverpool with 143 Saints, bound for Nauvoo.

Tues. 24.—Seventy presidents to preside over the Seventies, and fifty High Priests to preside in different sections of the country, were ordained.

Fri. 27.—Gov. Thos. Ford visited Nauvoo with about five hundred troops and three pieces of artillery, ostensibly for the purpose of bringing the murderers of Joseph and Hyrum Smith to justice.

Sat. 28.—About this time several persons in Hancock County were indicted for the murder of Joseph and Hyrum Smith, among whom was Jacob C. Davis.

October

Mon. 7.—At the general conference held in Nauvoo Wm. Marks was rejected as president of the Stake and John Smith appointed in his stead.

Tues. 8.—A reorganization of the Seventies took place in the general conference at Nauvoo. At the close eleven quorums were filled and properly organized, and about forty Elders organized as a part of the 12th quorum. The senior presidents of these twelve quorums of Seventy were Joseph Young (1st), Edson Barney (2nd), Elias Hutchins (3rd), Jacob Gates (4th), Henry Jacobs (5th), Israel Barlow (6th), Randolph Alexander (7th), John Pack (8th), Phillip Ettleman (9th), Albert P. Rockwood (10th), Jesse P. Harmon (11th), and Hyrum Dayton (12th).

About the same time the 16th quorum of Seventy was organized, with Dana Jacobs as senior president.

November
Sat. 23.—Edward Hunter was ordained a Bishop and set apart to take care of the 5ᵗʰ Ward in Nauvoo.

December
Sun. 1.—Apostle Parley P. Pratt was appointed to go to the city of New York to regulate and counsel the emigration from Europe and preside over all the eastern branches of the Church.

Sun. 22.—The 13th, 14th, and 15th quorums of Seventy were organized in Nauvoo, with Charles Bird, Jonathon Dunham and John Lytle as senior presidents.

1845
Work on the Nauvoo Temple was prosecuted with much vigor; mobs attacked the outlying settlements in Hancock County, Ill., burned a number of houses, and caused much suffering among the Saints.

January—During this month the legislature of Illinois repealed the city charter of Nauvoo.

Fri. 3.—Apostle Wilford Woodruff and accompanying missionaries arrived at Liverpool, England. Wilford Woodruff succeeded Reuben Hedlock as president of the British mission.

Sun. 12.—The 17th quorum of the Seventy was organized at Nauvoo, with Daniel M. Kepsher as senior president.

Fri. 17.—The ship *Palmyra* sailed from Liverpool, England, with a company of Saints, under the direction of Amos Fielding, bound for Nauvoo.

Sun. 26.—The 18th quorum of the Seventy was organized at Nauvoo, with John W. Bell as senior president.

February
Sun. 9.—The 19th quorum of the Seventy was organized at Nauvoo, with Samuel Moore as senior president.

March
Sun. 2.—The 21st quorum of the Seventy was partly organized at Nauvoo with Erastus H. Derby as senior president.

Tues. 18.—The 20th quorum of Seventy was organized at Morley's Settlement, Hancock Co., Ill., with Hirum Blackman, of Bear Creek branch, as senior president.

April
Sun. 6.—The Twelve Apostles issued "A Proclamation to all the kings of the world, to the President of the United States of America, to the governors of the several States, and to the rulers and people of all nations."

—The general conference of the Church was commenced at Nauvoo, Ill. It was continued till the 9th and attended by about twenty-five thousand people. In honor of the Prophet Joseph it was decided by vote to change the name of Nauvoo to "City of Joseph."

Mon. 7.—At a conference held in Manchester, England, Dan. Jones, who had lately arrived from America, was appointed president of the Wrexham conference (Wales), consisting of himself and wife. One year later there were seven hundred members of the Church in Wales, largely through his instrumentality.

Tues. 8.—At a conference held in Manchester, England, the so-called Joint Stock Company was organized, with Thomas Ward as president.

Wed. 9.—The 22nd, 23rd, 24th, 25th and 26th quorums of the Seventy were organized at Nauvoo, with David Clough (22nd), Benjamin Sweatt (23rd), Lewis Eger (24th), Thomas Spiers (25th), and Benjamin Jones (26th) as senior presidents.

Sat. 12.—A U.S. deputy marshal of Illinois arrived at Nauvoo, with writs for Brigham Young and others, but failed to arrest them.

Wed. 16.—As the city charter of Nauvoo had been repealed, a small part of the city was incorporated as the town of Nauvoo.

Thurs. 24.—In a general council held at Nauvoo, it was decided to send a written appeal in behalf of the Saints to the President of the United States, and to the governor of every State in the Union, except the State of Missouri. This resolution was subsequently acted upon, but without any response, except from the governor of Arkansas, who replied in a respectful and sympathetic letter.

May

Mon. 19.—Some of the citizens of Nauvoo went to Carthage, to attend the trial of the murderers of Joseph and Hyrum Smith.

Sat. 24.—President Brigham Young and others who had been secreted for some time, to avoid arrest and persecution by their enemies, appeared at Nauvoo and took part in the laying of the cap stone of the Temple, in the presence of a large number of Saints.

Fri. 30.—The murderers of Joseph and Hyrum Smith were acquitted by the jury at Carthage, although every one who witnessed the trial was satisfied of their guilt.

June—At the close of its fifth volume the *Millennial Star* (England) was changed from a monthly to a semi-monthly periodical.

Sun. 8.—The organization of the 27th quorum of the Seventy was commenced in Nauvoo.

Tues. 10.—The 27th quorum of the Seventy was organized at Nauvoo, with Rufus Beach as senior president.

Mon. 23.—A constable came to Nauvoo with writs for the arrest of Apostles Brigham Young and John Taylor, and others, but he did not succeed in finding them.

Thurs. 26.—The first stone was laid for a new baptismal font in the Nauvoo Temple.

Fri. 27.—This being the first anniversary of the martyrdom of Joseph and Hyrum Smith, the day was spent in prayer and fasting by the Saints in Great Britain.

July

Thurs. 3.—Noah Rogers sailed from Tahiti, Society Islands, per ship *Three Brothers*, on his return to Nauvoo, Ill., where he arrived Dec. 29, 1845. He was the first Latter-day Saint Elder who circum-navigated the globe as a missionary.

Sat. 5.—The first number of the New York *Messenger* was published by Samuel Brannon in New York City, as a continuation of the *Prophet*, suspended.

Sun. 27.—The 28th and 29th quorums of Seventy were orga-nized in Nauvoo, with John Gaylord and Augustus A. Farnham as senior presidents.

August
Sat. 9.—Twenty-eight persons were killed by an explosion in a colliery at Cromstock, near Aberdare, South Wales. Several of the Saints employed in the colliery escaped, having been warned by vision of the catastrophe.

Sat. 23.—The dome of the Nauvoo Temple was raised.

Sun. 31.—The 30th quorum of Seventy was organized in Nauvoo, with Sahiel Savage as senior president.

September—One hundred and thirty-five teams were sent from Nauvoo to bring in the families and grain from the surrounding country.

—The few Saints who still remained at Kirtland, O., were perse-cuted by their enemies, who took possession of the Temple.

—The ship *Oregon* sailed from Liverpool, England, with a company of Saints bound for Nauvoo, Ill.

Wed. 10.—A mob attacked the house of Edmund Durfee, in Morley's Settlement, Hancock Co., Ill., turned the people out of doors, set fire to the buildings and threatened instant death to men, women and children. The mob then burned all the other houses, barns and shops in the settlement and turned the inhabitants into the open air. Also a farming settlement called Green Plains, inhabited by about eighty members of the Church, was burned by the mob.

Mon. 15.—The mob drove Jacob Backenstos, sheriff of Hancock County, from his home at Carthage.

Tues. 16.—The mob made an effort to kill the sheriff. In his defense O. Porter Rockwell killed Frank A. Worrell, one of the leaders of the mob, who was an officer of the guard at Carthage jail when Joseph and Hyrum Smith were killed.

Thurs. 18.—Sherriff Backenstos, with a *posse* consisting of some seven hundred men, surrounded Carthage, Ill., to make arrests, but the house-burners had fled. He also issued a proclamation to the mobbers to disperse, which, however, was not obeyed, as they went to Missouri and other places, preparing for new depredations.

Wed. 24.—As the persecutions in Hancock County continued to rage, the Saints commenced to leave their possessions in the smaller settlements and flee to Nauvoo for protection. The authorities of the Church made a proposition to the mob to have the Saints leave the State of Illinois the following spring.

Tues. 30.—General John J. Hardin arrived at Nauvoo with four hundred troops, pretending to hunt for criminals, but undoubtedly had other motives for his diligent search of the Temple and other public buildings.

October

Wed. 1.—The Apostles at Nauvoo had an important consultation with General John J. Hardin, Senator Sephen A. Douglas, W. B. Warren and J. A. McDougal, comm[i]ssioners from a convention held in Carthage, about the removal of the Saints.

Sun. 5.—The Nauvoo Temple was so far completed that a meeting, attended by five thousand people, was held in it.

Mon. 6.—The first general conference of the Saints for three years was commenced in the Temple, the Prophet Joseph having ordered that they should not hold another general conference until they could meet in that house. They conference continued for three days. Wm. Smith was dropped as an Apostle and Patriarch.

Sun. 12.—Wm. Smith was excommunicated from the Church at Nauvoo.

Sat. 25.—Major Warren came into Nauvoo with a body of troops and threatened to put the place under martial law. After he had left, the authorities of the Church sent E. A. Bedell and Bishop Geo. Miller with a communication to Gov. Thomas Ford. They informed him of Major Warren's threats and implored him to dismiss the troops under his command, as the Saints had more to fear from them than from the mob at large. The governor did not grant their request.

Sun. 26.—The 31st quorum of Seventy was partly organized at Nauvoo, with Edmund M. Webb as senior president.

November—Edmund Durfee was killed by the mob in Green Plains, Hancock Co., Ill. About the same time Joshua A. Smith was poisoned at Carthage.

Sun. 30.—The attic story of the Nauvoo Temple was dedicated.

December

Mon. 15.—After laboring nearly one year and eight months on Tubuai, Elder Addison Pratt left that island to join Elder Benjamin F. Grouard, who had commenced most successful missionary work on Anaa, one of the Tuamotu Islands.

Sun. 21—The 32nd quorum of Seventy was organized at Nauvoo, with Geo. Mayer as senior president.

Tues. 23. The famous "Bogus Brigham" arrest was made, the officers taking Elder Wm. Miller to Carthage, believing that they had captured Apostle Brigham Young.

Sat. 27.—A U. S. Deputy marshal visited Nauvoo, again searching for the Twelve and others, but failed to make any arrest.

During this month many of the Saints received their blessings and endowments in the Nauvoo Temple.

1846

Early in the year the Saints commenced to leave Nauvoo, fleeing from the mob, which later drove the remnants out and took forcible possession of the city. The Nauvoo Temple was dedicated, and many of the Saints received their endowments before going into the wilderness. While traveling through Iowa, the exiled Saints were called upon to raise five hundred men to participate in the war with Mexico. Winter Quarters [w]as established on the Missouri river.

January—The 33rd quorum of Seventy was organized with Albern Allen as senior president.

Tues. 13.—At a council held in the Nauvoo Temple, to take into consideration the means of organizing for the removal of the Saints,

140 horses and 70 wagons were reported ready for immediate service.

Fri. 16.—The ship *Liverpool* sailed from Liverpool, England, with 45 Saints, under the direction of Hiram Clark, bound for Nauvoo *via* New Orleans.

Thurs. 22.—Apostle Wilford Woodruff sailed from Liverpool to return to America, because of the contemplated removal of the Church to the mountains. Reuben Hedlock, with Thomas Ward and John Banks as counselors, succeeded him in the presidency of the British Mission.

Sat. 24.—A general meeting of the official members of the Church was held in the Nauvoo Temple, for the purpose of arranging the affairs of the Church, prior to its removal from Nauvoo.

Fri. 30.—The vane was placed on the Nauvoo Temple.

February

Wed. 4.—The Saints at Nauvoo commenced crossing the Mississippi river for the purpose of moving west. Charles Shumway was the first to cross the river.

—The ship *Brooklyn* sailed from new York with 235 Saints on board. They were well supplied with implements of husbandry, and necessary tools for establishing a new settlement. They also took with them a printing press and materials, which afterwards were used in publishing the first newspaper issued in California.

Thurs. 5.—The 34th quorum of Seventy was organized at Nauvoo, with David W. Rogers as one of the presidents.

About the same time the 35th quorum of Seventy was organized.

Mon. 9—A fire, which broke out in the Nauvoo Temple, was put out before it did much damage.

—John E. Page was disfellowshipped.

Tues. 10.—Joseph Young was appointed to preside over the Saints who remained at Nauvoo.

Sun. 15.—Apostles Brigham Young and Willard Richards, with their families, and Apostle Geo. A. Smith crossed the Mississippi river for the West. They traveled nine miles, and camped on Sugar Creek, where Pres. Young spent the following day organizing the camps of the Saints.

Tues. 17.—Apostle Heber C. Kimball arrived in the camp on Sugar Creek. Willard Richards was appointed camp historian and

Wm. Clayton clerk.

Wed. 18.—President Young and a few others returned to Nauvoo, but rejoined the camp the following day.

Wed. 25.—Bishop George Miller and company were the first to leave the camp ground on Sugar Creek to travel westward.

Sat. 28.—A petition to the governor of Iowa, in which the Saints asked for protection while passing through the Territory, was approved by the Twelve. At this time the camp consisted of four hundred wagons, very heavily loaded. The teams were too weak for rapid journeying. Most of the families had provisions for several months, while some were quite destitute.

March—During the month the camps of the Saints in Iowa traveled about one hundred miles. The roads were almost impassable most of the way, and the Saints suffered much from cold and exposure, the weather being very windy and stormy.

Sun. 1.—The camps of the Saints made a general move from Sugar Creek and traveled five miles in a north-westerly direction.

Fri. 27.—At a council held at Apostle Parley P. Pratt's camp, near the east fork of Shoal Creek, the camps of the Saints were more perfectly organized. Brigham Young was elected president over all the "Camps of Israel."

April—The Saints in England suffered spiritually and financially on account of the Joint Stock Company business, which was urged upon them by speculating Elders.

Fri. 24.—The advance portion of the camps arrived at a place on the east fork of Grand river, 145 miles from Nauvoo, which the Saints called Garden Grove, where a temporary settlement was commenced for the benefit of the companies which should follow after.

Thurs. 30—The Nauvoo Temple was dedicated privately, Elder Joseph Young offering the dedicatory prayer.

May

Fri. 1.—The Nauvoo Temple was publicly dedicated by Apostle Orson Hyde.

Sun. 10—About three thousand Saints met in the Temple at

Nauvoo. Apostle Wilford Woodruff preached.

Mon. 11.—Part of the camps continued the journey from Garden Grove, and on the 18th arrived at the middle fork of Grand river, on the land of the Pottawattamie Indians, where another temporary settlement was established, called Mount Pisgah. This was 172 miles from Nauvoo.

Thurs. 21.—A. General council of the camps at Mount Pisgah had under consideration the subject of sending an exploring company to the Rocky Mountains that year. The subsequent call for the Mormon Battalion, however, made this impossible.

Sun. 31.—Elder Noah Rogers, recently returned from a mission to the Society Islands, died at Mount Pisgah, Iowa. His remains were the first interred in the burying ground at that place.

—A three days' conference convened in Manchester, England, in which the business of the Joint Stock Company was the main topic.

June—Amos Fielding, who returned to Nauvoo this month, counted 902 west-bound wagons in three days. By this some idea may be formed of the number of teams on the road at that time.

Mon. 1.—Elder Jesse C. Little wrote an appeal to James K. Polk, President of the United States, in behalf of the Saints. He afterwards called on the President, Vice-President and several members of the cabinet.

—A conference of the Church was organized on the Isle of Man, with Samuel J. Lees as president.

Tues. 2.—Pres. Brigham Young left Mount Pisgah and continued the journey westward.

Fri. 12.—Elder Jesse C. Little left Philadelphia for the West, accompanied by Col. Thos. L. Kane, who had decided to visit the camps of the Saints.

Sun. 14.—Pres. Brigham Young, Heber C. Kimball, Geo. Miller and Parley P. Pratt arrived on the banks of the Missouri River, with their respective companies. Here a ferry boat was built soon afterwards, when some of the Saints commenced to cross the river.

Tues. 16.—The advance camps of the exiled Saints moved back to the bluffs across Mosquito Creek, and encamped near good water, about nine miles from the trading post. There they remained till the ferry boat was built.

Mon. 22.—At this date about five hundred wagons had arrived on the Missouri river; nine of the Apostles were already there.

Thurs. 25.—The ship *Brooklyn* arrived at Honolulu, Hawaii, on its way to California.

Fri. 26.—Capt. James Allen, of the U.S. army, arrived at Mount Pisgah and had an interview with Apostle Wilford Woodruff and Pres. Wm. Huntington and council. He was the bearer of a circular to the "Mormons," making a requisition on the camps of the Saints for four or five companies of men, to serve as volunteers in the war with Mexico. Capt. Allen was advised to visit the authorities of the Church at Council Bluffs.

Sat. 27.—John E. Page was excommunicated from the Church.

Tues. 30.—Capt. Allen arrived at Council Bluffs, and on the following day he met with the authorities of the Church, showing his authority for raising five hundred volunteers from the camps of the Saints. The same day Pres. Young and Capt. Allen addressed the brethren who had assembled, and the general council voted unanimously to comply with the requisition from the government.

July—The first number of *Prophwyd y Jubili* (The Prophet of Jubilee) was published by Dan Jones, in Wales, as the Church organ in that country.

—The Saints having continued to arrive from the East, there were now fourteen companies encamped on the bluffs near the Missouri river.

Fri. 3.—Pres. Brigham Young and others started for Mount Pisgah, where they arrived on the 6th, after having met eight hundred wagons and carriages.

Tues. 7.—Pres. Brigham Young, Heber C. Kimball and Jesse C. Little addressed a meeting of the brethren at Mount Pisgah on the subject of raising a battalion to march to California. Sixty-six volunteered. Geo. W. Langley was sent to Garden Grove with a letter to the presiding brethren there upon the same subject. A similar communication was sent to Nauvoo.

Thurs. 9.—Pres. Brigham Young and others left Mo[u]nt Pisgah for Council Bluffs, where they arrived on the 12th.

Sat. 11.—John Hill, Archibald N. Hill, Caleb W. Lyons, James

W. Huntsman, Gardiner Curtis, John Richards, Elisha Mallory and J. W. Phillips were severely whipped by mobocrats, while harvesting wheat twelve miles from Nauvoo.

Mon. 13.—In obedience to a call of the authorities of the camps of the Saints the men met at headquarters on Mosquito Creek. Col. Thos. L. Kane, who had arrived in camp, and Capt. Allen were present. Pres. Young, Capt. Allen and others addressed the people in regard to furnishing the battalion. Four companies were raised on that day and the day following. The fifth company was organized a few days later.

At this time severe persecutions were again raging against the few remaining Saints at Nauvoo, and also against the "new citizens" who had bought the property of the members of the Church, who had already left the city for the west.

Thurs. 16.—At a council of the Twelve held at Council Bluffs, Ia., Ezra T. Benson was ordained an Apostle, and took the place of John E. Page, who had apostatized. Apostles Orson Hyde, Parley P. Pratt and John Taylor were appointed to go to England to set the Church in order there; Reuben Hedlock and Thomas Ward, who at that time presided over the British mission, were disfellowshipped for disregard of counsel.

—Four companies of the volunteers were brought together in a hollow square and mustered into service by their respective captains. They were interestingly addressed by several of the Apostles. A few days later (July 20th) they commenced their march towards Fort Leavenworth.

Fri. 17.—A number of men were selected to take care of the families of the volunterrs.

Tues. 21.—A High Council was selected to preside in all temporal and spiritual matters at Council Bluffs.

Wed. 22.—The fifth and last company of the Mormon Battalion left the camps of the Saints and started for Fort Leavenworth.

Thurs. 23.—Samuel Boley, a member of the Mormon Battalion, died on the road to Fort Leavenworth.

Wed. 29.—The Mormon Battalion passed through St. Joseph, Mo.

—The ship *Brooklyn*, with the Saints from the State of New York, arrived at Yerba Buena (now San Francisco), Cal.

August

Sat. 1.—The Mormon Battalion, now numbering 549 souls,

including officers, privates and servants, arrived at Fort Leavenworth.

Fri. 7.—At a council of the Apostles it was decided that the brethren on the west side of the Missouri river should settle together. A municipal High Council, consisting of Alpheus Cutler, Winslow Farr, Ezra Chase, Jedediah M. Grant, Albert P. Rockwood, Benjamin L. Clapp, Samuel Russell, Andrew Cahoon, Cornelius P. Lott, Daniel Russell, Elnathan Eldredge and Thomas Grover, was appointed to superintend the affairs of the Church there.

—A small company of Saints from Mississippi, under the direction of John Brown, arrived at Pueblo, on the Arkansas river, where it wintered, waiting till the following spring for the advance companies of the "Mormon" emigration.

Sun. 9.—The first meeting was held at Cutler's Park, where the exiled Saints at that time intended to spend the winter. The municipal High Council was accepted by the people and the place named Cutler's Park, in honor of Alpheus Cutler. Th[i]s place, which now became the temporary headquarters of the camps, is three miles from the spot where Winter Quarters afterwards was built.

Thurs. 13.—Three companies of the Mormon Battalion began to move west from Ft. Leavenworth, after having received their arms, camp equipage, etc. On the 14th the other two companies took up the line of march.

—About this time the mobbers in Hancock County, Ill., concluded to drive the few remaining "Mormon" families from Nauvoo.

Sun. 23.—Col. James Allen, commander of the Mormon Battalion, died at Ft. Leavenworth. The command then devolved on Capt. Jefferson Hunt, as the ranking officer, but notwithstanding this, Lieut. A. J. Smith shortly after assumed the command.

September

Tues. 8.—Col. Thos. L. Kane left the camps of the Saints for the East.

Thurs. 10.—The few remaining Saints at Nauvoo, of whom only about one hundred and twenty-five were able to bear arms, were attacked by an armed mob, about eighteen hundred strong, who with five pieces of artillery bombarded the city for several days. The brethren organized for self-defense and stopped the mobbers about two miles from the city.

Fri. 11.—The mobbers were prevented from entering Nauvoo by the gallantry of the "Spartan Band," who fired on the enemy with cannons made of steamboat shafts.

—A site for building winter quarters for the Saints was selected on the west bank of the Missouri river. Teams began to return to Nauvoo after the poor.

—The Mormon Battalion reached the Arkansas river.

Sat. 12.—The battle of Nauvoo took place. Wm. Anderson, his son Augustus and Isaac Norris were killed, and others of the defenders were wounded. The mob force, which again was driven back, also sustained considerable loss.

Wed. 16.—The enemy was driven back from Nauvoo the fourth time. Through the negotiations of the one hundred citizens of Quincy, a treaty was completed, by which the Saints should be allowed to move away in peace.

—Some of the families accompanying the Mormon battalion left the main body on the Arkansas river, in care of Capt. Higgins, for Pueblo. About this time Alva Phelps, a member of the Battalion, died.

Thurs. 17.—The mob entered Nauvoo, and, notwithstanding the treaty, immediately drove out the Saints, and treated some of the brethren in a most brutal manner.

Sun. 20.—Norman Sharp, a member of the Mormon Battalion, accidentally shot himself in the arm and died a few days later, from the effect of the wound.

Tues. 22.—A partial reorganization of the Nauvoo Legion took place at Cutler's Park.

Wed. 23.—The Saints began to move to the new location for Winter Quarters.

Thurs. 24.—A conference was held at Putuahara, Anaa, at which 852 members of the Church in the Society Islands mission were represented.

Sun. 27.—The first public meeting at Winter Quarters was held. By this time most of the Saints had removed from Cutler's Park to Winter Quarters.

October—Apostle Orson Hyde succeeded Reuben Hedlock as president of the British Mission, and the Joint Stock Company was dissolved.

—Martin Harris and others, followers of the apostate James J. Strang, preached among the Saints in England, but could get no influence.

Fri. 2.—The Mormon Battalion reached Red river.

Sat. 3.—The Battalion was divided in two divisions, of which the first, containing the strongest and most able-bodied men, arrived at Santa Fe, N. M., on the 9th, and the second containing the sick and the women, on the 12th.

—Apostles Orson Hyde and John Taylor arrived at Liverpool, England, and immediately issued a circular to the British Saints, advising them to "patronize the Joint Stock Company *no more for the present.*"

Wed. 7.—The teams which were sent back to help the poor away from Nauvoo, arrived at the Mississippi river, opposite Nauvoo.

Fri. 9.—The camp of the poor was organized and started for the West. Flocks of quails visited the camp and were easily caught. This was a providential supply of food for the suffering exiles.

Tues. 13.—Capt. P. St. George Cooke assumed command of the Mormon Battalion at Santa Fe, by order of General Kearney.

Wed. 14.—Apostle Parley P. Pratt and Elders Franklin D. Richards, Samuel W. Richards and Moses Martin arrived at Liverpool, England, from the camps of the Saints in the wilderness.

Sat. 17.—On this and the following day a general conference was held in Manchester, England, under the presidency of Apostles Hyde, Pratt and Taylor. Dan Jones reported one thousand Saints in Wales, and a conference was organized in Ireland, with Paul Jones as president.

Sun. 18.—The sick detachment of the Mormon Battalion, consisting of about ninety men, left Santa Fe for Pueblo, under command of Capt. James Brown.

Mon. 19.—The Battalion left Santa Fe for California. One the journey it suffered much from excessive marches, fatigue and short rations.

Tues. 27.—Milton Smith, a member of the Battalion, died on his way with the sick detachment to Pueblo.

November—A memorial to the Queen of England "for the relief, by emigration, of a portion of her poor subjects," was circulated for signatures among the British Saints.

Tues. 3.—James Hampton, member of the Mormon Battalion, died.

Wed. 4.—Milton Kelly, a member of the Battalion, died at Pueblo.

Tues. 10.—A detachment of fifty-five sick men of the Battalion, under the command of Lieutenant W. W. Willis, was separated from the main body and started back to Pueblo. Two days later John Green died.

Tues. 17.—Capt. Brown's sick detachment of the Battalion arrived at Pueblo.

Sat. 21.—John D. Lee and Howard Egan arrived at Winter Quarters, as messengers from the camps of the Mormon battalion beyond Santa Fe.

—Joseph Wm. Richards, a member of the Mormon Battalion, died at Pueblo.

Fri. 27.—Capt. O. M. Allen with the remainder of the sick camp from Nauvoo, arrived at the east bank of the Missouri river.

Sat. 28.—Elijah Freeman and Richard Carter, members of the Battalion (Lieut. Willis' detachment), died, and were buried by their comrades four miles south of Secora, on the Rio Grande.

—The main body of the Battalion reached the summit of the Rocky Mountains.

December—Winter Quarters, afterwards known as Florence, Nebraska, consisted at this time of 538 log houses and 83 sod houses, inhabited by 3,483 souls, of whom 334 were sick and 75 were widows. There were 814 wagons, 145 horses, 29 mules, 388 yoke of oxen and 463 cows. The place was divided in 22 Wards, each presided over by a Bishop. The Ward on the east side of the river contained 210 souls.

—The Saints on the banks of the Missouri river made great exertions to provide themselves with shelter and food for the winter. Notwithstanding this, there was much privation and suffering among them. . . .

NOTES TO APPENDIX B

1. Andrew Jenson, *Church Chronology: A Record of Important Events* (Salt Lake City: Deseret News, 1899), 17–32.

CREDITS

Photographs and Artwork

Valley (Latter-day Saints Book Depot, London, 1855).

p. 76 Lucius N. Scovil, courtesy of Daughters of Utah Pioneers, Springville, Utah.

p. 78 *Vicksburg* by Frederick Piercy, as seen in his *Route from Liverpool to Great Salt Lake Valley* (Latter-day Saints Book Depot, London, 1855).

p. 78 *Memphis* by Frederick Piercy, as seen in his *Route from Liverpool to Great Salt Lake Valley* (Latter-day Saints Book Depot, London, 1855).

p. 79 *St. Louis* by Frederick Piercy, as seen in his *Route from Liverpool to Great Salt Lake Valley* (Latter-day Saints Book Depot, London, 1855).

p. 80 Captain Dan Jones, courtesy of Family and Church History Department, photograph of ambrotype, photographer unknown, 1855.

p. 81 *Natchez* by Frederick Piercy, as seen in his *Route from Liverpool to Great Salt Lake Valley* (Latter-day Saints Book Depot, London, 1855).

p. 82 David Candland, courtesy of Family and Church History Department.

p. 82 *Grand Turk,* courtesy Missouri Historical Society.

p. 83 Parley P. Pratt. Daguerreotype by Marsena Cannon, ca. 1853.

Photograph of daguerreotype courtesy of Family and Church History Department.

p. 84 Joseph Fielding, courtesy of Family and Church History Department. Photographer: Crawshaw.

p. 85 Hiram Clark, courtesy of Family and Church History Department.

p. 86 Joseph Smith Jr., courtesy of Family and Church History Department. Photograph of an oil painting owned by the Reorganized Church of Jesus Christ of Latter-day Saints (Community of Christ).

p. 87 Thomas Steed, courtesy of Family and Church History Department.

p. 87 Christopher Layton, courtesy of Family and Church History Department.

p. 88 Landing near Nauvoo House, courtesy of Family and Church History Department.

p. 94 View of Nauvoo from Bluff Park, courtesy of Family and Church History Department.

p. 96 Widow's Row, courtesy of Family and Church History Department. Photographer: George Edward Anderson.

p. 100 Water Street, courtesy of Family and Church History Department. Photographer: George Edward Anderson.

p. 104   Benjamin F. Johnson, courtesy
of Family and Church
History Department.
Photographer: Edward Martin.

p. 105   Jacob Peart, courtesy of Family
and Church History
Department.

p. 106   Mosiah L. Hancock, courtesy
of Family and Church History
Department.

p. 108   Alexander Neibaur and sons,
courtesy of Thois DeGray.

p. 111   Nauvoo, Illinois, courtesy of
Family and Church History
Department. Daguerreotype
probably by Lucian Foster, ca.
1846. Photograph of daguerreotype by Charles William
Carter.

p. 112   Charles Lambert, courtesy of
Family and Church History
Department.

p. 115   *The Nauvoo Temple* by C.C.A.
Christensen, © Brigham Young
University Museum of Art. All
rights reserved.

p. 117   William Pitt, courtesy of
Family and Church History
Department.

p. 124   President James K. Polk, as
seen in Alfred Pach's *Portraits
of our Presidents*. (Hastings
House, New York, 1943.)

p. 125   *Crossing the Mississippi on the
Ice* by C.C.A. Christensen,
© Brigham Young University
Museum of Art. All rights

reserved.

p. 126   Lorenzo Dow Young, courtesy
of Family and Church History
Department.

p. 127   Anson Call, family photograph.

p. 128   George H. Goddard, courtesy
of Family and Church History
Department.

p. 128   Death Masks of Joseph and
Hyrum Smith, © Don O.
Thorpe.

p. 130   Sidney Rigdon. Photograph
courtesy of Family and Church
History Department. A Fox
and Symons copy of an orig
inal.

p. 131   James J. Strang, family photograph.

p. 132   Brigham Young, courtesy of
Family and Church History
Department. Albumen print,
Marsena Cannon, ca. 1851-51.
Photograph of print possibly
by Charles R. Savage.

p. 134   John C. Fremont, as seen in
*Life Explorations and Public
Services of John Charles
Fremont*. (Ticknor and Fields,
Boston, 1856.)

p. 136   Ezra T. Benson, courtesy of
Family and Church History
Department.

p. 138   Henry Bigler from *Century
Illustrated*, ca. 1887, courtesy
of the Bancroft Library,
Berkeley, California.

p. 138   Hosea Stout, ca. 1852. Used by
         permission. Utah State
         Historical Society. All rights
         reserved.
p. 140   Thomas Bullock, courtesy of
         Family and Church History
         Department.
p. 141   Potter's Slough near Montrose,
         courtesy of Family and Church
         History Department.
         Photographer: George Edward
         Anderson.
p. 142   Helen Mar Whitney Kimball,
         courtesy of Family and Church
         History Department.
p. 143   *Winter Quarters* by C.C.A.
         Christensen, © Brigham Young
         University Museum of Art. All
         rights reserved.
p. 149   *Nauvoo Temple on Fire* by
         C.C.A. Christensen,
         © Brigham Young University
         Museum of Art. All rights
         reserved.
p. 150   Ruins of the Temple at Nauvoo
         by Frederick Piercy, as seen in
         his *Route from Liverpool to
         Great Salt Lake Valley* (Latter-
         day Saints Book Depot,
         London, 1855).
p. 151   Completed Nauvoo Temple,
         © 2002 Arlo E. Sinele, Fly
         Guy Photos.

Selected Bibliography

BOOKS

Allen, James B. and Glen M. Leonard. *The Story of the Latter-day Saints* (Salt Lake City: Deseret Book), 1992.

Allen, James B., Ronald K. Esplin, and David J. Whittaker. *Men with a Mission, 1937-1841: The Quorum of the Twelve Apostles in the British Isles* (Salt Lake City: Deseret Book), 1992.

Backman, Milton V. Jr. *The Heavens Resound: A History of the Latter-day Saints in Ohio* (Salt Lake City: Deseret Book), 1998.

Bagley, Will, ed. *The Pioneer Camp of the Saints: The 1846 and 1847 Mormon Trail Journals of Thomas Bullock* (Spokane: Arthur H. Clark Co.), 1997.

Bennett, Richard E. *We'll Find the Place: The Mormon Exodus, 1846-1848* (Salt Lake City: Deseret Book), 1997.

Black, Susan Easton and Richard F. Bennett, eds. *A City of Refuge: Quincy, Illinois* (Salt Lake City: Millennial Press), 2000.

Bloxham, V. Ben, James R. Moss, and Larry C. Porter. *The Rise of the Church of Jesus Christ of Latter-day Saints in the British Isles, 1837-1987* (Salt Lake City: Deseret Book Co.), 1987.

Brooks, Juanita, ed. *On the Mormon Frontier: The Diary of Hosea Stout, 1844-1861* (Salt Lake City: University of Utah Press), 1964.

Brown, Benjamin. *Testimonies for the Truth: A Record of the Manifestations of God, Miraculous and Providential, Witnessed in the Travels and Experiences of*

Benjamin Brown, High Priest in the Church of Jesus Christ of Latter-day Saints, Pastor of the London Reading, Kent, and Essex Conferences (Liverpool: S. W. Richards), 1853.

Brown, Dee. *Bury My Heart at Wounded Knee* (New York: Bantam Books published by arrangement with Holt, Rhinehart and Winston), 1972.

Cannon, John Q. *George Cannon: The Immigrant: Isle of Man, 1794–St. Louis, U.S.A., 1884* (Salt Lake City: privately printed), 1927.

Carter, Kate B., comp. *Heart Throbs of the West,* 12 vols. (Salt Lake City: Daughters of Utah Pioneers), 1943.

_____. comp. *Our Pioneer Heritage* (Salt Lake City: Daughters of Utah Pioneers), 1973.

Church History in the Fullness of Times (Salt Lake City: The Church of Jesus Christ of Latter-day Saints), 1993.

Coleman, Terry. *Going to America* (New York: Pantheon Books), 1972.

_____. *Passage to America: A History of Emigrants from Great Britain and Ireland to America in the Mid-Nineteenth Century* (London: Hutchinson of London), 1972.

DeVoto, Bernard. *The Year of Decision: 1846* (1942 reprint with a foreword by Arthur Schlesinger, Jr. (New York: Book-of-the-Month Club), 1984.

Evans, Richard L. *A Century of "Mormonism" in Great Britain* (Salt Lake City: Publisher's Press), 1937.

Flanders, Robert Bruce. *Nauvoo: Kingdom on the Mississippi* (Urbana: University of Chicago Press), 1975.

Givens, George W. *In Old Nauvoo: Everyday Life in the City of Joseph* (Salt Lake City: Deseret Book), 1990.

Hartley, William G. *A City of Refuge* (Salt Lake City: Millennial Press), 2000.

Hawthorne, Nathaniel. *The English Notebooks* (New York: Modern Language Association of America), 1941.

Jensen, Richard L. and Malcolm R. Thorpe, eds. *Mormons in Early Victorian Britain* (Salt Lake City: University of Utah Press), 1989.

Jenson, Andrew. *Church Chronology: A Record of Important Events* (Salt Lake City: Deseret News), 1899.

_____. *Latter-day Saint Biographical Encyclopedia: A Compilation of Biographical Sketches of Prominent Men and Women in The Church of Jesus Christ of Latter-day Saints*, 4 vols. (Salt Lake City: Andrew Jenson Memorial Association, 1901–1936).

Kenney, Scott G. ed. *Wilford Woodruff's Journal* (Midvale, Utah: Signature Books), 1983.

Linforth, James, ed. *Route from Liverpool to Great Salt Lake Valley Illustrated with Steel Engravings and Wood Cuts from Sketches Made by Frederick Piercy* (Liverpool: Franklin D. Richards), 1855.

McGavin, E. Cecil. *Nauvoo the Beautiful* (Salt Lake City: Bookcraft), 1972.

McIntyre, Myron W. and Noel R. Barton, eds. *Christopher Layton* (n.p.:Christopher Layton Family), 1966.

Melville, Herman. *Redburn: His First Voyage* (Boston: St. Boltolph Society), 1924.

Miller, David E. and Della S. Miller. *Nauvoo: The City of Joseph* 2d. ed. (Bountiful, Utah: Utah History Atlas), 1996.

Pratt, Parley P. *Autobiography of Parley P. Pratt* (Salt Lake City: Deseret Book), 1985.

_____. *Autobiography of Parley Parker Pratt* (Salt Lake City: Deseret Book), 1980.

FRED E. WOODS

Roberts, B. H. *A Comprehensive History of The Church of Jesus Christ of Latter-day Saints, Century One* (Salt Lake City: Deseret News Press), 1930.

_____. *Ships, Saints, and Mariners: A Maritime Encyclopedia of Mormon Migration, 1830-1890* (Salt Lake City: University of Utah Press), 1987.

Smith, Joseph Jr. *History of the Church of Jesus Christ of Latter-day Saints*, 7 vols., 2d. ed. (Salt Lake City: Deseret Book), 1965.

Smith, Joseph Fielding, comp. *The Teachings of the Prophet Joseph Smith* (Salt Lake City: Deseret Book), 1976.

Sonne, Conway B. *Saints on the Seas: A Maritime History of Mormon Migration, 1830-1890* (Salt Lake City: University of Utah Press), 1983.

Taylor, P. A. M. *Expectations Westward: The Mormons and the Emigration of Their British Converts in the Nineteenth Century* (Ithaca, New York: Cornell University Press), 1966.

Trager, James. *The Peoples' Chronology* (New York: Holt, Rhinehart and Winston), 1976.

Tullidge, Edward W. *The Women of Mormondom* (1877; reprint, Salt Lake City: n.p.), 1975.

Ward, Maurine Carr, ed. *Winter Quarters: The 1846–1848 Life Writings of Mary Haskin Parker Richards* (Logan: Utah State University Press), 1996.

Whitney, Orson F. *Life of Heber C. Kimball: An Apostle—The Father and founder of the British Mission,* 8th ed. (Salt Lake City: Bookcraft), 1978.

_____. Life of Heber C. Kimball: *An Apostle—The Father and Founder of the British Mission,* 9th ed. (Salt Lake City: Bookcraft), 1979.

Williams, Neville. *1776-1900: The Changing World,* vol 3, *Chronology of World History* (Santa Barbara, ABC-CLIO), 1999.

Woodruff, Wilford. n.t. *Official Report of the 68th Annual General Conference of The*

Church of Jesus Christ of Latter-day Saints (Salt Lake: The Church of Jesus Christ of Latter-day Saints) 1898.

Primary Sources

Adams, William. *Autobiography of William Adams, 1822–1894*, typescript, HDA.

Ashby, Benjamin. *Autobiography of Benjamin Ashby*, L. Tom Perry Special Collections, Harold B. Lee Library, Brigham Young University, Provo, Utah.

Ashby, Benjamin. *Autobiography of Benjamin Ashby*, holograph, L. Tom Perry Special Collections Library, Harold B. Lee Library, Brigham Young University, Provo, Utah.

Baker, Jean Rio Griffiths. *Diary of Jean Rio Griffiths Baker*, typescript, HDA.

Boyle, Henry. *Autobiography and Diary of Henry G. Boyle, 1832–1855*, typescript, L. Tom Perry Special Collections, Harold B. Lee Library, Brigham Young University, Provo, Utah.

Brown, Lorenzo. *Journal of Lorenzo Brown, 1823–1900*, vol. 1, 1823–1862, typescript, L. Tom Perry Special Collections Library, Harold B. Lee Library, Brigham Young University, Provo, Utah.

Bullock, Thomas. *Autobiography of Thomas Bullock*, HDA.

Burgess, James. *Journal of James Burgess*, HDA.

Butler, John. *Autobiography of John Lowe Butler, 1808–1861*, typescript, L. Tom Perry Special Collections, Brigham Young University, Provo, Utah.

Candland, David. *Journal of David Candland*, typescript, HDA.

Clayton, William. *Diary of William Clayton*, HDA.

Cluff, Harvey H. *Journal of Harvey H. Cluff, 1836–1868*, typescript, L. Tom Perry

Special Collections Library, Harold B. Lee Library, Brigham Young University, Provo, Utah.

Cordon, Alfred. *Reminiscences and Journal of Alfred Cordon*, HDA.

Cowley, Matthias. *Reminiscences of Matthias Cowley*, typescript, HDA.

Crookston, Robert. *Autobiography of Robert Crookston*, HDA.

Crosby, Jesse. *The History and Journal of Jesse W. Crosby, 1820–1869,* typescript, L. Tom Perry Special Collections Library, Harold B Lee Library, Brigham Young University, Provo, Utah.

Draper, William. *Life of William Draper*, typescript, L. Tom Perry Special Collections Library, Harold B. Lee Library, Brigham Young University, Provo, Utah.

Fielding, Joseph. Journals of Joseph Fielding, HDA.

Hancock, Mosiah. *The Life Story of Mosiah Lyman Hancock*, Americana Collection, L. Tom Perry Special Collections Library, Harold B. Lee Library, Brigham Young University, Provo, Utah.

Maughan, Mary Ann Weston. *Journal and Autobiography of Mary Ann Weston Maughan*, HDA.

Moon, Hugh. *Autobiography of Hugh Moon*, HDA.

Neibaur, Alexander. *Journal of Alexander Neibaur.* L. Tom Perry Special Collections Library, Harold B. Lee Library, Brigham Young University Library, Provo, Utah.

Neibaur, Alexander. *Autobiographical Sketch of Alexander Neibaur, Seventies Record, 5th Quorum*, Biographies, HDA.

Palmer, James. *Reminiscences of James Palmer*, DUP Archives, Salt Lake City.

Peart, Jacob Sr. *Autobiographical Sketch of Jacob Peart Sr.*, typescript, Family History Library, Salt Lake City, Utah.

Pixton, Robert. *Autobiography of Robert Pixton*, HDA.

Rushton, Richard. *Journal of Richard Rushton*, HDA.

Smith, Charles. *Reminiscences and Diary of Charles Smith*, HDA.

Smith, Grace Meldrum, comp. *John Irwin Forsyth*, typescript (story adapted from original typescript, "Life of John Irwin Forsyth," written by Jane Barker Forsyth Snyder.)

The British Mission Manuscript History, 16 January, 1844, HDA.

Thomas Callister Collection, HDA.

Whitaker, George. *Autobiography of George Whitaker*, HDA.

Wright, Alexander. *Journal of Alexander Wright: March 1839–January 1843*, HDA.

ARTICLES

"Advice to Emigrants," *Millennial Star* 2, no. 10 (February 1842), 151.

Allen, James B. "Eight Contemporary Accounts of Joseph Smith's First Vision: What Do We Learn from Them?" *Improvement Era*, April 1970, 6.

Allen, James B., and Malcolm R. Thorp. "The Mission of the Twelve to England, 1840–41: Mormon Apostles and the Working Class," *BYU Studies* 15, no. 4, (Summer 1975), 499–526.

Anderson, Gary A. "Almon W. Babbitt and the Golden Calf," in *Regional Studies in Latter-day Saint Church History: Illinois*, ed. H. Dean Garrett (Provo, Utah: Department of Church History and Doctrine, Brigham Young University, 1995), 35–54.

Andrus, Hyrum L. "Joseph Smith and the West," *BYU Studies* 2, no. 2 (1960), 129.

Backman, Milton V. Jr. "A Warning from Kirtland," *Ensign*, April 1989, 30.

Benson, Ezra Taft. "Ezra Taft Benson, I," *Instructor*, May 1945, 215.

Bitton, Davis. "Kirtland as a Center of Missionary Activity, 1830–1833," *BYU Studies* 11, no. 4 (Summer 1971), 497–516.

Black, Susan Easton. "New Insights Replace Old Traditions: Membership of the Church in Nauvoo, 1839–1846" (paper presented at the Brigham Young University symposium, "Nauvoo, the City of Joseph," Provo, Utah, 21 September 1989), 1–2.

Buice, David. "When the Saints Come Marching In: The Mormon Experience in Antebellum New Orleans, 1840–1855," *Louisiana History* 23, no. 3 (Summer 1982), 221–237.

Cannon, M. Hamblin. "Migration of English Mormons to America," *American Historical Review* 52, (October 1946–July 1947), 436–455.

Cook, Lyndon W. "Isaac Galland—Mormon Benefactor," *BYU Studies* 19, , no. 3, (Spring 1979), 267.

Cowan, Richard O. "The Nauvoo Temple," in *A City of Refuge: Quincy, Illinois*, ed. Susan Easton Black and Richard E. Bennett (Salt Lake City: Millennial Press, 2000), 291.

Ehat, Andrew F. "'They Might Have Known That He Was Not a Fallen Prophet,'— The Nauvoo Journal of Joseph Fielding, *BYU Studies* 19, no. 2 (Winter 1979), 141.

Erekson, Keith A., and Lloyd D. Newell. "'A Gathering Place for the Scandinavian People': Conversion, Retention, and Gathering in Norway, Illinois (1842–1849)," *Mormon Historical Studies* 1, no. 1 (Spring 2000), 28.

"Emigration," *Millennial Star* 1, no. 10 (February 1841), 263.

"Emigration," *Millennial Star* 4, no. 10 (February 1844), 159.

"Emigration," *Millennial Star* 4, no. 4 (August 1843), 63–64.

Enders, Donald L. "The Steamboat Maid of Iowa: Mormon Mistress of the Mississippi," *BYU Studies* 19, no. 3 (Spring 1979), 321–335.

"Epistle of the Twelve," *Millennial Star* 1, no. 12 (April 1841), 311.

"Extract of a Letter from Sister Melling, Who Lately Emigrated from Preston, England, to Nauvoo, United States," *Millennial Star* 2, no. 6 (October 1841), 96.

"Fresh Emigrants," *Quincy Whig* 3, no. 52 (24 April 1841), 1.

Fielding, Joseph. "Joseph Fielding's Letter," *Millennial Star* 3, no. 4 (August 1842), 80.

Freeman, Robert C. "Out of the Ashes: The Story of the Nauvoo Temple," *Religious Studies Newsletter* 14, no. 2 (January 2000), 1–5.

Hansen, Lorin K. "Voyage of the Brooklyn," *Dialogue: A Journal of Mormon Thought* 21, no. 3 (Autumn 1998), 46–72.

Hartley, William G. "How Shall I Gather," *Ensign*, October 1997, 5–17.

Hinckley, Gordon B. "Be a Little Better," *Official Report of the 169th Annual General Conference of The Church of Jesus Christ of Latter-day Saints* (Salt Lake City: The Church of Jesus Christ of Latter-day Saints, 1999), 117.

"History of Joseph Smith," *Deseret News* (20 August 1856).

"Important from America," *Millennial Star* 1, no. 10, (February 1841), 252.

"Information to Emigrants," *Millennial Star* 2, no. 4, (August 1841), 61.

Jensen, Richard L. "Transplanted to Zion: The Impact of British Latter-day Saint

Immigration upon Nauvoo," *BYU Studies* 31, no. 1 (Winter 1991), 84-85.

Jenson, Andrew. "Church Emigration," the *Contributor* 12, no. 12 (October 1891), 441–450.

Kay, William. "Extract of a Letter from Elder William Kay," *Millennial Star* 4, no. 12 (April 1844), 202.

Kimball, Stanley B. "The Saints and St. Louis, 1831–1857: An Oasis of Tolerance and Security," *BYU Studies*, 13, no. 4, (Summer 1973), 489–519.

"Lambert Reminiscences," in *Faith Promoting Series*, book 17, *Gems of Reminiscence* (Salt Lake City: Geo. C. Lambert), 172–173.

"Leaving the City." *Warsaw Signal* 6 (19 June 1844).

"Letter from Nauvoo," *Millennial Star* 4, no. 6 (October 1843), 88.

Little, James Amasa. "Biography of Lorenzo Dow Young," *Utah Historical Quarterly* 14, nos. 1–4 (1946), 46.

Lyon, Edgar T. "Recollections of 'Old Nauvooers' Memories from Oral History," *BYU Studies* 18, no. 2 (Winter 1978), 147–148.

"Modern Representatives of Ancient Families," *Utah Genealogical and Historical Magazine* 25 (1934), 103.

Moon, Francis. "Important form America. Interesting Letter from Elder Moon, Who Lately Emigrated from Preston, England to America," *Millennial Star* 1, no. 10 (February 1841), 253.

"Mormon," *Burlington Hawkeye* 6, no. 16 (12 September 1844).

"Mormon Mutiny," *Liverpool Mercury* 32, no. 1650 (23 December 1842), 2.

"New Mormonite Colony," *Liverpool Mercury* 31, no. 1584 (17 September 1841), 5.

Panek, Tracy E. "Life at Iosepa, Utah's Polynesian Colony," *Utah Historical*

Quarterly 60, no. 1 (Winter 1992), 64–67.

Parrish, Alan K. "Beginnings of the Millennial Star: Journal of the Mission to Great Britain," in *Regional Studies in Latter-day Saint Church History: British Isles*, ed. Donald Q. Cannon (Provo, Utah: Department of Church History and Doctrine, Brigham Young University, 1990), 133.

"Part of a Dispatch form the Governor," *Nauvoo Neighbor* 3, no. 23 (29 October 1845), 1.

Pitchforth, Ann. "To the Saints in the Isle of Man," *Millennial Star* 8, no. 1 (May 1843), 15.

Porter, Larry C. "Brigham Young and the Twelve in Quincy: A Return to the Eye of the Missouri Storm, 26 April 1839," in *A City of Refuge: Quincy, Illinois*, ed. Susan Easton Black and Richard E. Bennett (Salt Lake City: Millennial Press, 2000), 142–148.

Pratt, Parley P. "Narrow Escape," *Millennial Star* 2, no. 2 (June 1841), 23.

Pratt, Parley P. "Prospectus," *Millennial Star* 1, no. 1 (May 1840), 5–6.

Purdy, William E. "They Marched Their Way West: The Nauvoo Brass Band," *Ensign*, July 1980, 22.

Reid, Robert. "Letter from Robert Reid," *Millennial Star* 4, no. 1 (May 1843), 15.

Riley, J. "Poetry, on Emigration," *Millennial Star* 2, no. 10 (February 1842), 160.

Shepperson, Wilbur S. "The Place of the Mormons in the Religious Emigration of Britain, 1840–1860," *Utah Historical Quarterly* 20, no. 3, (July 1952), 213.

Sonne, Conway B. "Liverpool and the Mormon Emigration" (paper presented at the Mormon History Association Conference, Liverpool, England, 10 July 1987), 4–5.

Taylor, Philip A. M. "Mormons and Gentiles on the Atlantic," *Utah Historical*

Quarterly 24, no. 3 (July 1956), 204.

"The Metoka," *Millennial Star* 4, no. 5 (September 1843), 80.
Whitney [Kimball], Helen Mar. "Travels Beyond the Mississippi," *Woman's Exponent* 12 (1 May 1884), 182.

Whitney, Horace A. "The Nauvoo Brass Band," *The Contributor* 1, no. 6 (1880), 135.

Woods, Fred E. "Two Sides of a River: Mormon Transmigration Through Quincy, Illinois, and Hannibal, Missouri," *Mormon Historical Studies* 2, no. 1 (Spring 2001), 139.

UNPUBLISHED WORKS

Berrett, LaMar C. "History of the Southern States Mission, 1831–1861" (master's thesis, Brigham Young University, 1960), 192.

Brown, Viva Skousen, ed and comp. *The Life and Posterity of Alma Platte Spilsbury* (Provo, Utah: privately printed, 1983), 40.

Cannon, M. Hamlin. "The 'Gathering' of British Mormons to Western America: A Study in Religious Migration"(Ph.D. dissertation, American University, 1950), 73–74.

Conway, A. A. "New Orleans as a Port of Immigration, 1820–1860" (master's thesis, University of London, 1949), 79.

Dahl, Paul E. "William Clayton: Missionary, Pioneer, and Public Servant" (master's thesis, Brigham Young University, 1959), 22.

Ellsworth, Samuel George. "A History of Mormon Missions in the United States and Canada, 1830–1860," (Ph.D. dissertation, University of California, 1951), 302.

Genosky, Reverend Landry C. "The Story of Quincy, Illinois, 1819–1860" (master's thesis, Catholic University, 1949), 52.

Journal History of the Church, 25 July 1841, HDA.

Newburn, Issac Butt, comp., 4 vols., *Mormons in Ohio, Illinois, Missouri, etc.* Newspaper clippings, 1831–1848, typescript, Americana Collection, L. Tom Perry Special Collections Library, Harold B. Lee Library, Brigham Young University, Provo, Utah, p. 1:205.

Steed, Thomas. "The Life of Thomas Steed from His Own Diary, 1826–1910," (n.p.: privately printed, 1935), 8.

NEWSPAPERS CITED

Burlington Hawkeye

Daily Picayune (New Orleans)

Keokuk Register

Latter-day Saints' Millennial Star (Liverpool)

Lee County Democrat

Liverpool Mercury

Nauvoo Neighbor

Quincy Whig

Times and Seasons (Nauvoo)

The Times (London)

Warsaw Signal

St. Louis Weekly Reveille

Index

188

Burgess, James, 85, 92 (n. 48)

Burk, John M., 173

Burlington Hawkeye, 130, 139, 145 (nn. 17, 18), 147 (n. 50), 147-48 (n. 51), 148 (n. 52)

Bury My Heart at Wounded Knee, 144-45 (n. 2)

Butler, John, 25, 36 (n. 33), 107, 120 (n. 30)

Bybee, Brother, 115-16

BYU Studies, 11 (n. 8), 12-13 (n. 17), 32 (n. 1), 34 (n. 14), 64 (n. 31), 66 (n. 51), 90 (n. 27), 91 (n. 39), 119 (n. 19), 121-22 (n. 52), 122 (n.57) 145 (n. 6), 147 (n. 38)

Cacique, Chief, 24-25

Cahoon, Andrew, 211

Cahoon, Brent Farrington, 120 (n. 31)

Cahoon, Reynolds, 112, 173

Cahoon, William, 107

California expedition, 193

Call, Anson, 127

Callister, Thomas, 40-41, 62 (n. 4)

"Camps of Israel," 207

Canada, 29

Candland, David, 82, 91 (n. 34)

Cannon, Donald Q., 64 (n. 25)

Cannon, George, 42, 62 (n. 8)

Cannon, John Q., 62 (n. 8), 67 (n. 59)

Cannon, M. Hamblin, 35 (n. 25), 64-65 (nn. 31, 32), 18 (n. 8)

Cannon, Sister (mother of George Q. Cannon), 161

"Capstone March," 116

Carlin, Governor Thomas, 177, 179

Caroline, 64 (n. 29), 65 (n. 33), 153

Carter, Kate B., 62 (nn. 1, 5), 91 (nn. 41, 42), 152 (n. 3)

Carter, Richard, 214

"Carthage Greys," 197

Carthage Jail, 197

Carthage, 186, 190, 191, 193, 195, 196, 197

Cartwright, Mrs., 193

Cartwright, Thomas, 193

Caton, Judge John D., 189

Celestial marriage, revelation on, 187, 190

Century of "Mormonism" in Great Britain, A, 64 (n. 31)

Champion, 154, 167, 191

Chaos, 153, 159, 160, 181

Charity Branch, 30, 37 (n. 46)

Chartered voyages, 51-52, 159

Chase, Ezra, 211

Chase, Stephen, 173

Cheese, John, 157

Chester, Illinois, 83, 163

Chevalier, Michael, 69, 81

Chicago, Illinois, population of Nauvoo vs., 10

Chronology of World History, 34 (n. 16)

Church Chronology: A Record of Important Events, 214

"Church Emigration," 64 (nn. 29, 31), 67 (n. 62), 88 (n. 1), 91 (nn. 33, 35, 38), 146 (n. 31), 170 (n. 1)

Church History in the Fulness of Times, 11 (n. 12), 33 (n. 5), 35 (n. 29), 146 (n. 29), 147 (nn. 42, 43)

Church of Jesus Christ of Latter-Day

Emigration: resulted from call to
gather, 6; revelation, 12 (n. 15), 142-
44; counsel from Church leaders
regarding, 49-51, 89 (n. 13), 142-44;
decrease in, due to exodus, 146 (n. 31).
See also British emigration
"Emigration," 34 (n. 21), 63 (n. 20)
Emmett, James, 194
Emmons, Sylvester, 196
Employment, for incoming emigrants,
97-99
*Encyclopedic History of the Church of
Jesus Christ of Latter-day Saints*, 147
(n. 44)
Enders, Donald L., 90 (n. 27)
Endowment: Prophet gave instructions
on, 183; administered in Nauvoo
Temple, 133, 189, 192, 205
England, missions to, 17-19, 20, 173,
187. *See also* Great Britain
English Notebooks, The, 63 (n. 13, 15)
Enoch, people of, 8
Ensign, 12 (n. 15), 33 (n. 6), 66 (n.
47), 147 (nn. 47, 48)
"Epistle of the Twelve, An," 37 (n. 53),
63 (n. 17), 65 (n. 37)
Erekson, Keith A., 35 (n. 28)
Esplin, Ronald K., 33 (nn. 11, 13), 34
(n. 14)
Ettleman, Phillip, 200
Europe, mission to, 182
Evans, Richard L., 64 (n. 31)
Evil spirits, Heber C. Kimball's experi-
ence with, 19
Excommunication(s), 171, 184, 195,
199, 204, 209
Exodus: persecution hastened, from

Nauvoo, 129-30, 134; beginning of,
135-36; organization of, 136, 143; and
crossing Iowa, 137-39; and deliverance
of poor Saints left behind, 139-140; and
the emigration revelation, 142-44
Expositor, 196
Extermination order, 7, 83, 144
"Extract from Elder Hiram Clark's
Journal, and Address to the Saints in
the British Islands," 91 (n. 40), 92 (n.
46)
"Extract of a Letter from Elder William
Kay," 67 (n. 57)
"Extract of a Letter from Sister
Melling, Who Lately Emigrated from
Preston, England, to Nauvoo, United
States," 118 (n. 17)
"Ezra Taft Benson," 146 (n. 34)

Faith: Satan tried Charles Lambert's,
113-114; deepened by sacrifice, 116;
increased through temple work, 134
Fanny, 41, 53, 60, 86, 112, 154, 167,
193
Far West, Missouri: fleeing to and then
from, 6-7, 9; Temple site at, 171
Fares, for ocean and river passage, 155,
156, 158, 160, 162
Farnham, Augustus A., 2043
Farr, Winslow, 211
Female Relief Society of Nauvoo, 183
Fielding, Amos, 46, 50, 159, 208;
assisted with British emigration, 153-
156, 159, 169, 183, 201
Fielding, Joseph, 33 (n. 9), 91 (nn. 43,
44), 100, 118 (n. 14); and mission to
Great Britain, 17-18; served in British

Mission presidency, 20; on apostasy in
St. Louis, 84; reflections of, at temple
site, 117; assisted with British emigra-
tion, 153, 159, 161, 181
Fielding, Reverend James, 19
Finances. *See* Economics
First Presidency, proclamation(s) by,
97, 107
First Vision, Prophet related, to
Alexander Neibaur, 109-110
Fisher, Edward, 173
Flanders, Robert Bruce, 12 (n. 17), 27,
36 (n. 37)
Florence, Nebraska, 214
Follett, King, 172, 174
Ford, Governor Thomas, 130, 135,
190, 197, 199, 204; pledge of protec-
tion from, 197
Fordham, Elijah, 172, 173
"Foreign Correspondence," 89 (n. 14)
Forsyth family, 65 (n. 35)
Forsyth, John Irwin, 65 (n. 35)
Forsyth, Mary E., 65 (n. 35)
Fort Leavenworth, 210, 211
Foster, Charles, 195
Foster, Robert D., 195
Fowler, Samuel, 177
Fox Indians, 12 (n. 17), 24, 195
Fox, Feramorz Y., 117 (n. 1)
Freeman, Elijah, 214
Freeman, Robert C., 150, 151 (n. 1),
152 (n. 4)
Fremont, John C., 134
"Fresh Emigrants," 90 (n. 26)
Froome's Hill conference, 176
Fullmer, David, 173, 194
"Funds of the Church," 152 (n. 2)

Funeral, general, sermon by Sidney
Rigdon, 106, 120 (n. 28)

Gadfield Elm conference, 176
Galena, 170
Galland, Isaac, 9-10, 12 (n. 17), 118
(n. 9), 171
Garden Grove, 207
Garn, Daniel, 192
Garrett, H. Dean, 36 (n. 38), 106, 120
(n. 27)
Garrick, 18, 33 (n. 10)
Gates, Jacob, 200
Gathering: revelation regarding a
universal, 5-6; concept of, important in
all ages, 6; Joseph Smith on the object
of, 6; temple as a purpose for, 6, 21, 26;
doctrine and keys of the, 15-16; Joseph
Smith broadened concept of authorized,
places, 32; and the Millennium, 48; of
the Jews, 181
"Gathering Place for the Scandinavian
People: Conversion, Retention, and
Gathering in Norway, Illinois (1842-
1849), A," 35 (n. 28)
Gaulter, Louis, 67 (n. 62)
Gaylord, John, 203
Gems of Reminiscence, 121 (nn. 46, 47)
Geneva Stake, 27, 177
Genosky, Reverend Landry C., 11 (n.
13)
*George Cannon: The Immigrant: Isle of
Man*, 62 (n. 8), 67 (n. 59)
George W. Bourne, 90 (n. 23)
German: Alexander Neibaur taught
Prophet, 109; text of New Testament,
120 (n. 36); pamphlet, "A Cry in the

167, 169, 175, 191, 200, 206, 212; mission of, to England, 173; disfellow-shipped, 210

Henry, 71, 88 (n. 3), 153, 162, 185

Herefordshire, England, branches in, 174

Higbee, Chauncey L., 184, 195

Higbee, Elias, 173, 189

Higbee, Francis M., 193, 195

Higgins, Captain, 212

Hill, Archibald N., 209

Hill, John, 209

Hinckley, Gordon B., announced rebuilding of Nauvoo Temple, 150, 152 (n. 6)

Historical Department Archives, The Church of Jesus Christ of Latter-day Saints, 11 (n.13,) 62 (nn. 4, 7, 9), 63 (n. 23), 66 (n. 43), 66 (n. 50), 88 (n. 3), 89 (nn. 5, 6, 9, 10), 90 (nn. 21, 28), 91 (nn. 34, 44), 92 (n. 48), 118 (n. 9), 121 (nn. 38, 42, 45)

History and Journal of Jesse W. Crosby, 1820-1869, The, 36 (n. 44)

History of Joseph Smith, 156, 158, 159, 166, 168, 169

"History of Joseph Smith," 118 (n. 8)

History of Northern Utah, and Southern Idaho, 145 (n. 8)

History of the Church of Jesus Christ of Latter-day Saints, 10 (n. 2), 12 (nn. 14, 15), 13 (n. 18) 33 (n. 7), 33-34 (nn. 9, 15, 17), 36 (nn. 32, 34, 35, 36), 37 (nn. 50, 54), 91 (n. 36), 92 (n. 50), 118 (n. 7), 120 nn. (35-37, 41, 44), 122 (n. 56), 145 (n. 7), 146 (nn. 22, 23)

History of Utah, 90 (nn. 22, 24)

Holman, David, 192

Holzapfel, Richard Neitzel, 121 (n. 52)

Hope, 153, 160, 182

"How Shall I Gather," 12 (n. 15)

Howard, Richard, 173

Hunt, Capt. Jefferson, 211

Hunter, Edward, 185, 200

Huntington, William, 9, 173, 209

Huntsman, James W., 209

Hutchins, Elias, 200

Hyde, Orson, 33 (nn. 9, 13) 153, 162, 198, 210, 213); and mission to England, 17-20; and mission to Jerusalem, 175, 179, 181, 186; published pamphlet in German, 184; led a company of emigrants,185; received endowment, 192; dedicated Nauvoo Temple, 207

Hygiene, on company voyages, 53-54

"I Have a Question," 66 (n. 47)

Illinois, Saints fled to, 7-8; welcomed the Mormons, 9. *See also* specific towns and counties

Immigration: general, of English and Irish, 34 (n. 16), lack of federal legislation regulating, 76

"Important from America," 11 (n. 4), 34 (nn. 19, 20)

"Important from America: Interesting Letter from Elder Moon, Who Lately Emigrated from England to America," 118 (n. 4), 118 (n. 16)

Imprisonment, unlawful, of Church members, 176, 191, 192; unlawful, of Joseph Smith, 197

Improvement Era, The, 121 (n. 39)

176; to Ireland, 176; to Isle of Man, 177; to South America, 181; to Jamaica, 181; to Jerusalem, 181; to Europe, 182; to Society Islands, 187, 198, 202, 212; to Pacific Islands, 189, 191, 195, 196; to New York, 191; to Eastern States, 191, 192

"Mission of the Twelve to England, 1840-41: Mormon Apostles and the Working Class, The," 34 (n. 14)

Missionary work: and doctrine of the gathering, 15-16; events leading up to foreign, 16-18; in Great Britain, 18-20; expansion of foreign, 22, 23; among American Indians, 24-25; more regulated policy on, 32 (n. 2); in Scandinavia, 35 (n. 27); at sea, 62

Mississippi River: sandbar of the 69; and the Balize, 70-71; perils of, travel, 81-84; crossing the, to leave Nauvoo, 135-36; obstacles encountered in, travel, 161-63, 164, 186; baptisms for the dead in, 183. *See also* River travel

Missouri, Saints driven from, 6-7. *See also* specific towns and counties

"Missouri's 1838 Extermination Order and the Mormons' Forced Removal to Illinois," 11 (n. 7)

Mitoka, 190

Mobocracy, 80-81, 134-36, 139, 192, 197, 198, 200, 203, 210, 211, 212. *See also* Persecution

"Modern Representatives of Ancient Families," 66 (n. 48)

Mon, Che-Mo-Ko, 147 (nn. 50, 51), 148 (n. 52)

Montrose, Iowa, 172

Moon, Francis, 21-23, 97, 118 (nn. 4, 16), 156

Moon, Henry (uncle of John Moon), 156

Moon, Henry, 154

Moon, Hugh, 20-21, 34 (n. 18), 99, 118 (n. 9)

Moon, John, 20, 34 (n. 17); led company of British emigrants, 153, 154, 176

Moore, Henry, 154

Moore, Samuel, 201

Moravian, 77, 78

Morgan County, Illinois, 177

Morgan, James, 71

Morley, Isaac, 177, 189

"Mormon," 145 (nn. 17, 18)

Mormon Battalion, 142, 146 (n. 37), 208, 209-14

Mormon Historical Studies, 11 (n. 13), 35 (n. 28)

"Mormon Mutiny," 89 (n. 7)

"Mormonite Colony," 22, 34 (n. 23)

"Mormons, The," 146 (n. 21)

"Mormons and Gentiles on the Atlantic," 63 (n. 23)

Mormons at the Missouri, 1846-1852: And Should We Die. . . , 148 (n. 57)

Mormons in Early Victorian Britain, 66 (n. 44), 90 (n. 19)

Moses: restored keys of gathering, 16; and ancient camp of Israel, 141

Mosquito Creek, 208

Moss, James R., 33 (nn. 9, 10)

Moss, Thomas, 154, 157

Moss, William, 179

Mount Hope Stake, 177

Smith, Emma, 183, 186, 189, 197
Smith, George A., 132, 157-58, 175, 179, 180, 198, 206; ordained an Apostle, 174; missions of, 173, 176, 191; received endowment, 192; political mission of, 195
Smith, Grace Meldrum, 65 (n. 35)
Smith, Howard S., 177
Smith, Hyrum, 118 (n. 5, 6), 120 (n. 29), 126, 178, 183, 189, 190; martyrdom of, 1, 128-29, 150, 197; escaped Nauvoo and then returned, 197; trial of murderers of, 199, 202
Smith, John, 173, 177, 182, 185
Smith, Joseph, 10-11 (n. 2), 11 (n. 6), 120 (nn. 29, 34), 120-121 (n. 36), 121 (n. 37); 13 (nn. 2, 6), 33 (n. 3), 118 (nn. 5, 6), martyrdom of, 1, 128-29, 150, 197; greeted arriving converts, 2, 86-87, 155, 159, 160, 163, 165; on Nauvoo, 5, 10; and destruction of printing press, 5, 10 (n. 1); on the object of gathering, 6; purchased land in Iowa and Illinois, 10; received keys of gathering and sealing, 16; warned Kirtland Saints of apostasy, 16; called Heber C. Kimball on a mission, 17; preached to the Indians, 24, 180, 190, 195; broadened concept of authorized gathering places, 30-31; ran for president, 31, 192, 193, 195; on routes to Nauvoo, 52; was recognized by arriving converts, 86-87; counseled Saints not to expect perfection, 97-98; counseled incoming emigrants, 99, 107; lawsuits against, 99-100; learned languages from Alexander Neibaur, 109; related First

Vision to Neibaur, 109-10; labored to help build temple, 115; on giving to the poor vs. building the temple, 121 (n. 44); worked on Kirtland Temple, 121-22 (n. 52); prophecies of, regarding expansion to Rocky Mountains, 126-28, 184; purchased land at Commerce, 171; efforts of, to seek redress from President and Congress, 171, 173-74; unlawful arrests and attempts to arrest, 177, 180, 182, 184, 185, 186, 189, 193, 196; elected sole Trustee for the Church, 178; was a city councilor, 178; made lieutenant-general of Nauvoo Legion, 179; baptized for the dead, 183; wrote regarding a conspiracy, 183; gave instructions on endowment, 184; was elected mayor of Nauvoo, 184; concealed himself, 184-85; studied German, 187; dined with Stephen A. Douglas, 188-89; gave endowments, 189; moved into Nauvoo Mansion and used it as a hotel, 190-191; escaped Nauvoo and then returned, 197; trial of murderers of, 199, 202
Smith, Joseph F., 35-36 (n. 31)
Smith, Joseph Sr., 177, 178
Smith, Joshua A., 205
Smith, Lieutenant A. J., 211
Smith, Milton, 213
Smith, Moses, 194
Smith, Samuel H., 178, 197, 198
Smith, Thomas, led company of British emigrants, 153, 157, 179
Smith, William, excommunicated, 204
Smoot, Abraham O., 173
Snider, John, led company of British

173, 177, 179, 198; political mission of, 195

Wilbur, Captain, 162

Wilding, David, 157

Wiley, R., 188

Wilford Woodruff's Journal, 66 (n. 49), 67 (nn. 53, 60, 61)

William Clayton's Journal, 147 (n. 47)

Williams, Neville, 34 (n. 16)

Willis, Lieutenant W. W., 214

Wilson, Harmon T., 189

Wilson, Lewis D., 173

Winchester, Benjamin, 180

Windsor Castle, 64 (n. 29), 146 (n. 31), 154

Winter Quarters, 142-43, 207, 212, 214

Winter Quarters: The 1846-1848 Writings of Mary Haskin Parker Richards, 62 (n. 3), 67 (n. 58)

Winthrop John, 95

Wisconsin, 181, 186, 190

Woman's Exponent, 148 (n. 54)

Women of Mormondom, The, 62 (n. 6), 90 (n. 29), 91 (n. 30), 92 (n. 52)

Wood, Captain, 157

Woodhouse, Captain, 158

Woodruff, Phebe, 170

Woodruff, Wilford, 132 (n. 53), 126, 145 (n. 4), 157-58, 174, 176, 179, 181, 182, 199, 206, 209; experiences of, at sea, 57, 61, 157-58; on sacrifices made in building temple, 116; petitioned British Saints for help, 135; missions of, 173, 199, 200; ordained an Apostle, 171; received endowment, 192; political mission of, 195; preached in Nauvoo

Temple, 208

Woods, Fred E., 11-12 (n. 13), 66 (n. 47)

Worcestershire, England, branches in, 176

Workman, John, 30

Worrell, Frank A., 203

"Wreck of the Julia Ann, The," 66 (n. 51)

Wrexham conference, 201

Wright, Alexander, 69, 88 (n. 2), 1575

Wrigley, Thomas, 83-84, 91 (nn. 41, 42)

Year of Decision, The, 144 (n. 1)

Yearsley, David D., 194

Yerba Buena, California, 146 (n. 32), 146-47 (n. 37), 210

Yokum, William, 180

Yorkshire, 88 (n. 3), 153, 166, 188

Young, Alphonso, 194

Young, Brigham, 20, 135, 147 (n. 44), 152 (n. 2), 175, 179, 180, 183, 189, 206, 208; appointed high priests to preside over branches, 31-32; on preference for emigrants' port of entry, 89 (n. 14); on the spirit of gathering, 104; and Alexander Neibaur, 108-09; commented on sacrifice of temple workers, 114; at laying of capstone, 117; was to lead Saints to promised land, 129; tried to end temple work, 133; studied route to Rocky Mountains, 134; generosity of, 137-38; delivered the poor stranded Saints, 142; on burning of Nauvoo Temple, 149; assisted with British emigration, 153,

155, 158, 157-59; at Far West Temple site, 171; missions of, 173, 191; administered to Heber C., Kimball, 173; rebuked wind and waves, 174; political mission of, 195; asserted right of Twelve to lead Church, 199; was appointed lieutenant-general of Nauvoo Legion, 199; attempt to arrest, 201, 202; and exodus to the West, 206-09
"Young Gentlemen's and Ladies' Relief Society," 187
Young, Joseph, 200, 206, 207
Young, Lorenzo Dow, 126
Young, Phineas H., 88 (n. 3), 194

Zarahemla, 172, 179, 185; Stake, 27, 182
Zion, 195